P. V. Smith

History of the English Institutions

Cambridge

P. V. Smith

History of the English Institutions
Cambridge

ISBN/EAN: 9783742817211

Manufactured in Europe, USA, Canada, Australia, Japa

Cover: Foto ©ninafisch / pixelio.de

Manufactured and distributed by brebook publishing software (www.brebook.com)

P. V. Smith

History of the English Institutions

HISTORICAL HANDBOOKS

EDITED BY

OSCAR BROWNING, M.A.

FELLOW OF KING'S COLLEGE, CAMBRIDGE; ASSISTANT-MASTER AT
ETON COLLEGE.

HISTORICAL HANDBOOKS.

HISTORY OF FRENCH LITERATURE.
  Adapted from the French of M. Demogeot. By CHRISTINA BRIDGE.

HISTORY OF THE ENGLISH INSTITUTIONS.
  By PHILIP VERNON SMITH, M.A., *Barrister at Law; Fellow of King's College, Cambridge.*

HISTORY OF MODERN ENGLISH LAW.
  By ROLAND KNYVET WILSON, M.A., *Barrister at Law; late Fellow of King's College, Cambridge.*

THE SUPREMACY OF ATHENS.
  By R. C. JEBB, M.A., *Fellow and Tutor of Trinity College, Cambridge, and Public Orator of the University.*

THE ROMAN REVOLUTION.
  From B.C. 133 to the Battle of Actium.
  By H. F. PELHAM, M.A., *Fellow and Lecturer of Exeter College, Oxford.*

THE ROMAN EMPIRE.
  From A.D. 400 to 800.
  By A. M. CURTEIS, M.A., *late Fellow of Trinity College, Oxford, and Assistant-Master at Sherborne School.*

ENGLISH HISTORY IN THE XIVTH CENTURY.
  By CHARLES H. PEARSON, M.A., *Fellow of Oriel College, Oxford.*

HISTORY OF THE FRENCH REVOLUTION.
  By the Rev. J. FRANCK BRIGHT, M.A., *late Master of the Modern School at Marlborough College.*

THE REIGN OF GEORGE III.
  By W. R. ANSON, M.A., *Fellow of All Souls' College, Oxford.*

THE GREAT REBELLION.
  By OSCAR BROWNING, M.A.

THE REIGN OF LOUIS XI.
  By F. WILLERT, M.A., *Fellow of Exeter College Oxford, and Assistant-Master at Eton College.*

HISTORY

OF THE

ENGLISH INSTITUTIONS

BY

PHILIP VERNON SMITH

BARRISTER-AT-LAW; FELLOW OF KING'S COLLEGE, CAMBRIDGE

RIVINGTONS
London, Oxford, and Cambridge
1873

RIVINGTONS

London . . . . *Waterloo Place*
Oxford . . . . *High Street*
Cambridge . . . . *Trinity Street*

PREFACE

THE various institutions of which the English Constitution, in its present complex form, is made up, are capable of being classified, and must, in order to be profitably studied, be classified under three or four leading divisions. From one point of view they are divisible into local and central; from another, into legislative, judicial, executive or administrative, and fiscal. Then, again, they may be classified as civil and ecclesiastical, or as social and political. And the leading divisions may be subdivided; as, for instance, the local into rural and municipal.

In the present volume the attention of the student will be directed to the origin of our local institutions on the one hand, and of our central government on the other, to the various phases of the development of both, and to the manner in which the latter gradually superseded and suppressed the former in their original shape, and then created a new local machinery to supply the want which their extinction had occasioned. He will also be called upon to observe the gradual limitation and separation into their four great divisions of the at first undefined functions of government, which were originally exercised by the same individual or body of individuals, and still remain theoretically united in the person of the sovereign; but which, at least in our central system, it was found necessary, as the state of society became more complicated, to vest for all practical purposes in different hands. He will see how the judicial element, which was at first the most prominent, became in time subordinated to the legislature; how king, nobles, and commons, have from time to time exercised an exclusive, a preponderating, or a joint control over the latter, and over the executive or the administration of affairs; and how the fiscal department, which hardly existed in a primitive state of things, gradually rose to such importance, that it became the arena of some of the severest struggles for the personal rights and liberties of Englishmen and the due distribution of political power. The close connection which has always existed in this country between the Church and the State will render some notice of ecclesiastical affairs inevitable; but they will be treated of from a political point of view, and only so far as is necessary to illustrate the civil condition of the country.

For the purpose of a review of our institutions, such as that contemplated, it has been found convenient to divide its history into *six great periods:*—

the first extending from the settlement of the Angles and Saxons in this island to the Norman Conquest; the second, from the Conquest to the end of Edward I's reign; the third, terminating with the Reformation; and the fourth with the Revolution; while the fifth will comprise the interval between that event and the Reform Act of 1832; *and the sixth and last will embrace the subsequent forty years. Each chapter is divided into sections numbered so as to correspond with the periods just mentioned.* By this means the student will have the option of either obtaining an independent and continuous view of the particular institutions which form the subjects of those chapters, or of combining the contemporaneous history of all or any of them, in connection with any of the given periods, by reading together the different sections which bear the same number.

The work is further divided into three parts. The first of these treats of the primitive institutions out of which our polity has sprung, and their development in the political and social condition of the people, and in our forms of local government. The second part contains an account of the persons and bodies in whom the central authority has, under our constitution, been from time to time vested; and in the third is traced the mode in which the various branches of government—the legislative, judicial, executive, and fiscal functions—have been distributed among those persons and bodies and have been exercised by them.

The omission of all notice of the law of treason, and of other matters more or less akin to the subject of the work, has been due to a desire to compress the volume within the smallest possible limits.

A glossary or explanation of some of the technical words, the meaning of which does not appear from the text, particularly of those occurring in reference to the pre-Norman period, is given in the Index. Words so explained are for the most part printed in the text in italics. As regards the period just mentioned, I have adopted the modern spelling of the Teutonic proper names, and have avoided the use of the term *Anglo-Saxon*, preferring the name of *English*, which our ancestors in that age themselves employed. Whenever it has been necessary to distinguish the time before the Norman Conquest from the succeeding periods of our history, it has been done by designating the former as the pre-Norman, Teutonic, or early English period.

It has frequently been found convenient to refer to dates by the year of the current reign. In such cases the chronological table at the end of the volume will indicate the corresponding year of the Christian era. When the name of a sovereign has been used to mark a date, it has been in most cases abbreviated. Acts of Parliament are referred

Preface

to in the usual manner by the year of the reign and chapter, but the references to them are accommodated to the Revised Edition of the Statutes now in course of publication by authority.

It is hardly necessary to state that the materials for this volume have been in great part derived from the larger works which treat of the English constitution.[1] The present book will fail of one of its principal objects if it does not lead the student to seek further information for himself from those more ample sources. To assist him in doing so, a list is given of some of the standard books on the different periods of our constitutional history. Should he desire to extend his researches further, he will find in these books references to other authorities from which more detailed information can be obtained.

A list is also given of certain abbreviations in common use, which it has been found convenient to employ in the present volume.

[1] For the statements in chaps. vi. and ix. respecting the king's council and its share in the executive, the author is also much indebted to Mr A. V. Dicey's Essay on the Privy Council, which obtained the Arnold Prize at Oxford in 1860.

4 STONE BUILDINGS, LINCOLN'S INN,
September, 1873.

CONTENTS.

PART I.

Social and Local Development of the Constitution.

CHAPTER I.

ORIGIN OF THE ENGLISH INSTITUTIONS.

Sources of our Institutions—Early Teutonic Institutions—Feudalism 1–4

CHAPTER II.

THE PEOPLE.

1. Classes of the People—Slavery—Defence of the Realm. 2. Feudalism—Villenage—Aliens—Barons or Peers—Purveyance and Pre-emption—Forest Laws—Clergy—Defence of the Realm—Magna Carta—Charter of the Forest. 3. Peers—Decay of Feudalism—Villenage—Liberty of the Subject—Restraint on Religious Opinions—Restriction on Printing—Aliens—Defence of the Realm—Impressment for the Navy. 4. Villenage and Slavery—Extinction of Feudalism—Billeting—Abolition of Feudal Courts—Religious Penalties and Disabilities—Liberty of the Subject—Monopolies and Patents—Restrictions on the Press—Control over the Post—Aliens—Defence of the Realm—Army and Navy. 5. Slavery—Religious Disabilities—Marriage Law—Roman Catholics—Progress of Toleration—Liberty of the Subject—General Warrants—Revenue Laws—Debtors—Political Rights—The Six Acts—Liberty of the Press—Control over the Post—Aliens—Defence of the Realm—Standing Army—Militia. 6. Extension of Freedom—Religious Disabilities—Political Agitation—The Press—Libel—Control over the Post—Aliens—Reserve Forces—Navy . . 4–69

CHAPTER III.

LOCAL GOVERNMENT.

1. Local Institutions—Early Local Divisions—Tithings—Townships—Hundreds—Courts-leet—Shire-moots—Ealdormen—Municipal Government—Encroachments of the Central Authority. 2. Effects of the Conquest—Counties Palatine—Franchises—Control of the Crown—Decline of the old Courts—The Charters—Coroners—Sheriffs—High Constables—Borough Charters—Special Jurisdictions. 3. Sheriffs—Parish Constables—Justices of the Peace—Custos Rotulorum—Power of the Central Authority—Municipal Government. 4. Local Rates—Justices of the Peace—Highways—Poor Law—Decline of old Institutions. 5. County Rates—Lunatic Asylums—Highways—Poor Law—Local Courts—Municipal Government—Vestries—Preservation of the Peace. 6. Local Courts—Constables—Justices of the Peace—Municipal Government—Poor Law—Highways—Public Health—Metropolis—Education . 69–124

PART II.

Constituents of the Central Authority.

CHAPTER IV.

THE KING.

1. Origin of Royalty—Pre-Norman Kings. 2. Early Norman Kings. 3. Growth of the Hereditary Principle—Disposition of the Crown by Parliament. 4. Successors of Henry VIII—The Stuart Monarchs. 5. Acts of Settlement. 6. Present Succession . 125–135

CHAPTER V.

PARLIAMENT.

1. THE WITENAGEMOT, GREAT COUNCIL AND PARLIAMENT.

1. Witenagemot. 2. Great Council—Representation—The Clergy. 3. Parliament—Meeting of Parliament—Privilege—Freedom of Debate. 4. Meeting of Parliament—Irregular Assemblies—Privilege—Punishment of Members—Publication of Debates. 5. Meeting of Parliament—Privilege—Privilege of Debate. 6. Presence of Strangers—Publication of Proceedings—Privilege 136–153

II. THE HOUSE OF LORDS.

3. Members—Number of Peers—Chancellor. 4. Status of Peers—Protests and Proxies. 5. Increase of Peerage—Creation of Peers. 6. Spiritual Peers—Life Peerages—Proxies—Number of Peers 153–159

III. THE HOUSE OF COMMONS.

3. Early Composition—Imperfect Representation. 4. Members—New Boroughs. 5. Members—Exclusion—Elections—Acts of Union—Representation. 6. Members—Exclusion—Representation 159–175

CHAPTER VI.
THE KING'S COUNCIL.

1. Pre-Norman Period. 2. Concilium Ordinarium. 3. Origin of Privy Council. 4. The Council under the Tudors and Stuarts. 5. The Council since the Revolution. 6. Committees of the Council 175–180

PART III
Central Government.
CHAPTER VII.
LEGISLATION.

1. Pre-Norman Legislation. 2. Early Norman Legislation—Early Parliamentary Legislation. 3. Growth of Power of Parliament—Bills—Legislation by King in Council—Suspending and Dispensing Powers of the King—Ecclesiastical Legislation. 4. Limitation of the King's Powers—Passing of Bills—Ecclesiastical Legislation. 5. Bill of Rights—Abuse of Power by House of Commons—Royal Assent—Classification of Acts. 6. Power of House of Commons—Delegation of Legislative Functions — Simplified Form of Legislation 181–197

CHAPTER VIII.
JUDICATURE.

1. Judicial power of King—Procedure. 2. Jurisdiction of King—Severance of Common Law Courts—Jurisdiction of Chancellor, &c.—Justices in Eyre—Ecclesiastical Courts—Pro-

cedure – Hue and Cry—English Common Law. 3. Jurisdiction of Courts—Trial by Jury. 4. Ecclesiastical Courts—Star Chamber—Courts of Law and Equity—Parliament—House of Lords—Judges—Juries. 5. Bill of Rights—Judges—Juries—Parliament—Impeachment. 6. Privy Council—Central Criminal Court—Probate and Divorce Court—Parliament—Contempt—Supreme Court of Judicature . . 197-232

CHAPTER IX.
THE EXECUTIVE.

1. Power of the King—Control of the Witan. 2. Power of the King—Officers of State—Advice of the Great Council—Magna Carta. 3. Regencies—Control of Parliament— Power of Council — Privy Council — Growing Power of Commoners. 4. Ecclesiastical Supremacy—Power of the Crown in Civil Matters—Control of Parliament—Cabinet Council—Political Parties. 5. The Ministry—Control of Parliament—Increased Power of Executive—Personal Influence of the Sovereign—Regencies—Substitution for Royal Sign-Manual. 6. Personal Influence of the Sovereign—Ministers—Growth of Executive Power—Military Forces 232-264

CHAPTER X.
TAXATION.

1. Early English Finance. 2. Feudal Sources of Revenue—Crown Lands—Imposition and Collection of Taxes—Magna Charta—Control of the Great Council. 3. Control of Parliament—Taxation of the Clergy—Relative Power of the two Houses—Subsidies—Increase of Taxation—Loans and Benevolences. 4. Reigns of Elizabeth and James I.—Post-Office—Reign of Charles I.—Reign of Charles II.—Control of the Commons—Taxation of the Clergy—National Debt—Reign of James II. 5. Control of Commons—Public Revenue—Civil List—Crown Lands—Duties—Direct Taxation—Legacy Duty—Income Tax—Penal Taxation—Lotteries—National Debt. 6. House of Lords—Civil List—Public Expenditure—Sources of Revenue . . . 264-293

CHRONOLOGICAL TABLE 295
INDEX AND GLOSSARY 296

LIST OF AUTHORITIES.

The following, among others, may be mentioned as leading works on the English Institutions, during the different periods into which their history is divided in the present volume:

First Period.—Hallam's Middle Ages (vol. 2), ch. viii. pt. 1.—Freeman's Norman Conquest (vol. 1), ch. iii.—Stubbs' Illustrations of English Constitutional History.

Second Period.—Hallam's Middle Ages (vols. 2, 3), ch. viii. pts. 2, 3.—Stubbs' Illustrations of English Constitutional History.

Third Period.—Hallam's Middle Ages (vol. 3), ch. viii. pt. 3.—Hallam's Constitutional History of England (vol. 1), ch. i. ii.

Fourth Period.—Hallam's Constitutional History of England (vols. 1-3), ch. iii.-xiv.

Fifth Period.—Hallam's Constitutional History of England (vol. 3), ch. xv. xvi.—May's Constitutional History of England, 3 vols.

Sixth Period.—May's Constitutional History of England, 3 vols.

Our political Institutions also form the subject of various chapters in Blackstone's Commentaries on the Laws of England, and the more recent Commentaries by Stephen, and by Broom and Hadley. Some useful statistics as to the present condition of the country are furnished in the Statesman's Year Book, by Fred. Martin (published annually).

LIST OF ABBREVIATIONS.

ACTS of Parliament are thus referred to :—

St. 32 Hen. 8, c. 16, s. 13, or simply, 32 Hen. 8, c. 16, s. 13 = the statute of the 32nd year of Henry VIII.'s reign, chapter 16, section 13.

2 Ric. 2, st. 1, c. 4 = the 1st statute of the 2nd year of Richard II's reign, chapter 4.

1 Will. & Mar. sess. 2, c. 2 = chapter 2 of the second session of the reign of William and Mary.

Art. sup. cart = Articuli super Cartas.

8 B & S = Best & Smith's (Queen's Bench) Reports, vol. viii.

4 Burr. = Burrow's Reports (King's Bench), vol. iv.

11 Cl. & F. = Clark and Finnelly's House of Lords Reports, vol. xi.

J., following a name, = Judge; thus "Powell J." = Judge Powell. [So C. J. = Chief Justice].

10 Q. B. = Queen's Bench Reports (by Adolphus & Ellis) vol. x.

Stat. Wynton. = Statute of Winchester.

1 W. Blackst. = Sir Wm. Blackstone's Reports, vol. i.

2. Wils. = Wilson's Reports, Part ii. (Common Pleas).

PART I.

Social and Local Development of the Constitution.

CHAPTER I.

ORIGIN OF THE ENGLISH INSTITUTIONS.

Sources of our Institutions.—The political and social institutions of the people of England, which together make up what is called the Constitution, derive their origin mainly from two sources—(1) The laws and customs of the Teutonic tribes, who in the time of the old Roman Empire occupied the central parts of Europe; and (2) The feudal system, which grew out of those laws and customs at a period subsequent to the settlement of the Angles and Saxons in Britain, and which was imported into this country at the Norman Conquest. In Continental Europe the Teutonic tribes, when they overran and subjugated the countries previously under the sway of Rome, adopted in great part the institutions, civil and ecclesiastical, of the population among whom they settled as conquerors,—institutions which were established by the authority of Rome, and were based on her civil law. Hence we find that Roman law remains to this day the groundwork of all the legal systems of Western Europe, except the English. The Angles and Saxons, on the contrary, when they invaded Britain, swept away all traces of Roman civilisation and institutions from the districts which they occupied. The constitution, therefore, which first developed itself as that of Wessex, Mercia, and the other kingdoms of the so-called Heptarchy,[1] and which, when the West-Saxon kingdom absorbed its rivals, became, with various local modifications, the constitution of all England, was almost entirely Teutonic in its origin and growth.

Early Teutonic Institutions.—The early political and social condition of the German tribes is described by Tacitus in his *Germania*.[2] Among its essential features, we notice the natural freedom of every individual of the community, coupled with the possibility, under certain circumstances, of being reduced to slavery; and the right of every man to take part in the deliberations on all important affairs of state, in the trials of offenders who were accused before the general council, and in the choice of magistrates, who were appointed to administer justice throughout the districts and villages, with the assistance of a hundred of the common people as assessors. This democratic state of things was, however, tempered by the existence, first, of kings possessed of a limited authority, and chosen on account of their high birth; and, secondly, of *principes* who were dignified with that rank, either for the same reason, or as the reward of personal merit, and who transacted the details of public business without consulting the mass of the people. Another counterpoise to the democratic element in the Teutonic institutions, was furnished by the practice which Tacitus mentions of each *princeps* attaching to himself a large body of his fellow-tribesmen as

---

[1] The number and dimensions of these kingdoms were perpetually varying. The name Heptarchy is derived from the fact that seven attained to a greater prominence in size and importance than the others.
[2] See Tac. Germ. cc. 7, 11-14, 24, 25.

followers (*comites*), who attended him devotedly in war, and looked to his bounty for remuneration. This practice was destined to play a most important part in the political history of the future nations of Western Europe, being the groundwork on which the system of feudalism was eventually erected. In succeeding chapters, the characteristics of German polity, thus described by Tacitus, will be traced in the early English constitution and its subsequent development; though partially concealed beneath various modifications and additions, arising out of the changing circumstances of the people and the progress of events.

Feudalism.—A sketch of the principal features of feudalism will be given in chap. ii. § 2 (see p. 7), when attention will be drawn to the effect of its introduction at the Norman Conquest upon the condition of the English people. It will be sufficient to observe here that, while in the early Teutonic polity the relations of the people to their rulers and among themselves were purely personal in their nature, these relations under the feudal system were almost as exclusively territorial. It is true that our pre-Norman ancestors had already begun to blend the territorial with the personal principle in their institutions; but nearly all the changes effected in the constitution of the country at the Norman Conquest were connected with the predominance then given, by the introduction of continental feudalism, to the territorial relationship which had previously existed in the country in a comparatively imperfect and subordinate form. But though dominant for a time, it did not stamp out or even permanently override the incidents of personal relationship. Whatever excellence our institutions possess over those of other nations, is due in great measure to the fact that the personal element was left in our constitution sufficiently strong to contend with and eventually overmaster the territorial element, receiving, however, in the course of the struggle some moderating and tempering influences from the opponent principle.

CHAPTER II.

THE PEOPLE.

1.[1] **Classes of the People.**—The English settlers in Britain were from the first divided into the two great hereditary classes of Eorls (the *principes* of Tacitus) and Ceorls,[2] both free, but the former of noble, the latter of ignoble birth. The oath of an eorl availed against that of six ceorls, and there was a corresponding difference in the amount of the weregild or compensation-money to be paid for the murder of a member of the two classes; which in the case of a ceorl was only 200 shillings (whence he was called a *twyhyndman*), but in that of an eorl 1200 shillings. Besides these distinctions between the two classes, another was introduced, which had not existed when the people dwelt in the forests of Germany. Their private wealth had then consisted of household furniture, armour, and cattle, while their land was regarded as the common property of the tribe. But after settling upon the conquered soil of Britain, they made continually increasing encroachments on the folc-land, or land common to the whole people, by converting portion after portion of it into boc-land—land held by private individuals, by book or charter. Landed wealth was at first the accompaniment of noble birth or personal merit, and when it became dissociated from these, it was gradually looked

[1] For the periods of our history to which the sections marked 1-6 in the different chapters correspond, see the Preface.
[2] The words have now, under the modernised forms of *earl* and *churl*, acquired totally different meanings.

upon as in itself constituting a claim to peculiar political privileges. If an eorl was always presumed to have a considerably larger amount of landed wealth than a ceorl, the supposition was no doubt at first invariably in accordance with the fact. But when the presumption came to be notoriously violated, as in process of time it was inevitable that in particular cases it should be, it led to a division of the eorls into *twelfhyndmen*, or those who held a due amount of land, and whose weregild was therefore retained at 1200 shillings; and *sithcundmen*, men of gentle blood, but of small means, who were subsequently denominated *syxhyndmen*, from the fact that their weregild was reduced to 600 shillings. At the same time, the purely hereditary basis of the English nobility was modified and ultimately supplanted by the practice which has been mentioned (p. 2) of personal attachment to a chieftain. The chieftain was called the *hlaford*[a] or *loafgiver*, as the dispenser to his followers of rewards for their services; and they were denominated his *thegns* (in its Latin form *thanes*) or *servants*, with occasionally a prefix denoting their special branch of service; as in the case of the king's *dish-thegn*, *bower-thegn*, and *horse-thegn*, who, notwithstanding their menial titles, held high rank in the state. The twelfhyndmen, the highest grade of eorls, became converted into the king's thegns, who owned him as their immediate *hlaford*. The syxhyndmen, who had not property or position enough to serve the king directly, became the *thegns* of some caldorman or bishop. It was at length established as a fixed principle, that a man must be *commended*, as the phrase was, to some lord, or he would be treated as an outlaw. As regards the ceorls, the lord to whom they were commended was determined

[a] Hence the modern word *lord*, as *lady* is from the feminine *hlæfdige*.

by their place of residence; all the ceorls living within a certain district, called on that account a lordship (see ch. iii.), being commended to the thegn who was lord of that district. This relation constituted no small restraint upon the personal liberty of the ceorl; for he could not change his place of residence, which involved a change of lord, without the leave of the former lord. Although the ceorls thus had all of them their hlaford, they were not dignified, in relation to him, with the title of *thegns*, a title which now carried with it a definite political and social rank. But a ceorl was admitted to the rank of thegn who had crossed the sea three times in commercial enterprise at his own risk, or whose family had held five hydes (600 acres) of land, with a church and mansion, for three generations. A ready way to the privileges of thegnhood also existed through the ranks of the clergy. For, on the one hand, the Church admitted into the ministry men of every degree alike; and, on the other, all presbyters were placed civilly on a level with the thegns, and in some respects stood higher. Thus their oaths were taken as an equivalent to those of twenty ceorls. And bishops and abbots were regarded as among the highest nobility of the land. But while many roads were thus opened for individuals among the ceorls to rise, the class as a whole became gradually depressed. The mere fact that the leading men were being perpetually taken out of it, created of itself a natural tendency in that direction.

Slavery.—The institution of slavery, which had existed among the Teutonic tribes on the Continent, was perpetuated among those who settled in Britain. The class of *theows* or *thralls* was originally composed only of *Welshmen* or foreigners, being Britons who survived the general extermination in the districts occupied by the Teutonic invaders, or who were subsequently taken prisoners in war. But an Englishman might be reduced to this class by failing to pay a weregild incurred by him, or by the commission of certain offences. The class was like the others hereditary, but escape from it might be obtained by manumission on the part of the owner of the thrall. The thralls were not considered part of the body politic; and they were the absolute property of their owner, to whom was paid the compensation money in case one of his thralls was killed.

Defence of the Realm.—Under the early English system all freemen, or at any rate all who held land, were soldiers; and those of each shire were led to the field in time of war, as each tribe had formerly been, by the ealdorman. As the principle of lordships gained ground, the various lords would hold subordinate commands over their own vassals. The *huscarls* or body-guard, which Cnut kept about his person, were the earliest germ of a standing army, not only in England, but probably in all modern Western Europe.

2. **Feudalism.**—We have seen that before the Conquest the classification of the people was becoming gradually more and more territorial in its character. The existence of this tendency no doubt rendered the introduction of continental feudalism, by which the tendency was converted into an absolute fact, more natural and easy; but the complete establishment of the feudal institutions in this country was mainly owing to the revolts of the English in the first few years after the Conquest, and the consequent extensive confiscations of land, which created a void in the political and social organisation of the country, and thus afforded room for a new system. Under the feudal *régime*, the old orders of thegns, ceorls, and thralls gave place to the new division

of the rural population into barons, freemen, and villeins. The clergy became separated into an isolated class of their own, and the burgesses in the privileged towns occupied a distinct and independent position; but the political and social status of the three former classes was associated with the terms of their ownership or occupation of land.

According to feudal principles, all the land of a country belonged to the king, not as representing the community, but as sovereign feudal lord. Out of this land the king granted portions to his subjects, on condition of their paying him *homage* and *fealty*, and rendering him active military service for forty days in every year. The portions granted to his more immediate and distinguished followers, who were called his barons, were termed *baronies*, and were of large extent; and the barons in their turn made subinfeudations or under-grants of parts of them to their own retainers, on similar conditions to those imposed upon themselves. The grantor of the land was called the lord, and the person to whom the grant was made the tenant in chivalry—tenant by knight's service, or military tenant. The immediate tenants of the king were called tenants *in capite* or in chief, in order to distinguish them from the subtenants.

The military tenants, or at any rate those who held of the king *in capite*, were liable to be required to receive the honour of knighthood, and undertake the incident services and burdens. About the end of Edw. 1's reign those whose lands yielded less than £20 a-year were exempted from the requirement; and exemption of it could be purchased by the others on payment of a composition or fine. In addition to homage and fealty, and assistance in the field, the lord was entitled to receive from his military tenants certain *aids* or contributions in money on special occasions; namely, towards making his eldest son a knight, providing once a suitable marriage for his eldest daughter, and ransoming him if he was taken prisoner in war. Besides these legal contributions, a tyrannical lord not unfrequently extorted aids from his tenants on other occasions.

The relation between landlord and tenant, though at first merely life-long, soon came to be regarded as hereditary, the heir becoming entitled on the death of the tenant to occupy his land upon the same terms. But if the heir was under age (full age for this purpose being considered twenty-one in case of males, and sixteen in case of females) the lord became the guardian in chivalry, with a right to receive the profits of the land for his own benefit; and, moreover, with power to arrange a marriage for the ward, a refusal of which subjected the latter to the forfeiture of the estimated value of it to the lord. On attaining full age, the ward obtained *livery* or *ouster-le-main* from the lord on paying a fine of half a year's profits of the land, and entered upon the full privileges and liabilities of the former tenant. If, on the other hand, the heir was of age at the time of the tenant's death, the lord received a *relief* or pecuniary fine upon his succeeding to the property; and the king was further entitled from the heirs of his tenants to *primer seisin*, or the first year's profits of the estate. And if a tenant died without heirs the land was liable to *escheat* or return to the lord. This might occur in two ways: first, if the kindred or blood of the tenant altogether failed; and, secondly, if the tenant committed one of a certain class of crimes called felonies, and was either tried, convicted, and sentenced for it, or fled the country, and was outlawed for it, for in both cases he was said to be attainted—that is, his blood was corrupted, and his heirs and kindred cut off, so that he could not transmit the inheritance to them. If the crime committed was treason, the land was forfeited not to the lord, but to the king. As the interest of the lord in the land thus by no means ceased when he granted it to a tenant, and as it made a considerable difference to him what were the personal capabilities and character of his tenant, it evidently could not be allowed to the latter to sell and part with his land, or leave it away by his will whenever and to whomsoever he pleased without the consent of the lord. Accordingly we find that it was long before this freedom of alienation was obtained. In the mean time the lord's consent was frequently purchased by the payment of a fine; or recourse was had to the other and readier mode of alienation by way of subinfeudation, which has been already noticed as practised from the first by the great barons. The tenant retained his relationship towards his lord, but granted parts of his land to others to hold as tenants of himself upon the usual feudal conditions. Thus a new *lordship*, or, as it was also termed, *manor* was created within the old one, and this process was capable of multiplication to any extent.

Such was the character of tenancy *by knight's service* which prevailed over the greater part of the lands of the kingdom. Some lands, however, were held in *socage* tenancy, involving the payment of a certain yearly rent, and a liability to the feudal aids and to escheat, and also in a mitigated form to relief and primer seisin, but free (except in the case of socage tenants *in capite*) from the burdensome incidents of wardship and marriage, and also from the duty of rendering personal military service. The existence of these exemptions, and particularly of the last, rendered it a matter of less importance to the lord who his socage tenants were. We consequently find that the right of free alienation of socage lands was acquired at a comparatively early period.

Villenage.—All the land which either the king, as sovereign lord, or an inferior lord retained in his own hands, instead of granting to a vassal, was called his *dominica terra* or *demesne land*, the land of the lord. This land was cultivated by the lord's villeins—peasants who, holding no land by feudal tenure, resided on the lord's land on sufferance as his serfs. The origin of villenage and of the villein class is not very clear. It was, in some respects, a continuation of the old English slavery or thraldom, but it embraced a far larger proportion of the population than the older institution had ever included. In fact, after the Conquest, the majority of the old ceorl class were reduced into a state of villenage; a degradation which was in part made easy by the previous existence of restrictions on the ceorls, such as inability to leave their lord without leave, similar to those to which the villeins were afterwards subjected. The depression of the villein class appears to have reached its lowest point in the reign of Hen. 2. A villein was then destitute of any property of his own, and was absolutely dependent upon the will of his lord, to whom he was compelled to perform unlimited services. A writ *de nativitate probanda* was issued for his recovery if he fled from his lord's service. The class was divided into villeins *regardant*, who had from time immemorial been attached to a certain manor, and villeins *in gross*, where such prescription had never existed, or had been broken through the sale of the villein by his lord or in some other way. From the time of Hen. 2 onwards the condition of the villeins in England was continually improving, and their number constantly decreasing. This was not owing to any legislation in their favour, but was the indirect effect of various causes, among which may be reckoned the subinfeudation and transfers and leases of land, which severed the connection between the villein and his original lord; the gradual substitution of a fixed though onerous tenure of land called *copyhold* tenure, instead of the villein tenure, which it had rested absolutely with the will of the lord to continue or terminate at any time without previous notice; the difficulty of recovering absconded villeins owing to the imperfect means of communication, and the legal technicalities attending the process; the regulation that a villein who resided unmolested for a year and a day in a walled city or borough, or who took holy orders, became free; and the practice, which was sometimes employed, of voluntary manumission, or of manumission on purchase of his liberty by the villein out of money which, contrary to the theory of the law, he had been allowed to appropriate to himself.

Aliens.—The inability of an alien not only to hold public offices and to exercise any civil rights, but also to acquire landed property in this country, was not peculiar to feudalism, though of course in accord with its principles. The disqualification could be removed by *denization*, the king having the prerogative by letters patent to make an alien a denizen, which gave him thenceforward the status of a subject. It was also more effectually removed by *naturalisation* by Act of Parliament, which had a retrospective effect, enabling the previously-born as well as after-born children of the naturalised alien to inherit land from him, and enabling the man himself to inherit from others. One class of aliens, namely, the Jews, were subjected to special legislation. Their utility as money-lenders led to their being given certain privileges, but these were more than counterbalanced by the restrictions to which they were subjected; and in Edw. I's reign the feeling against them was so strong, that they were banished from the kingdom.

Barons or Peers.—To return to the barons. Their feudal relation to the king gave them the right of attending his feudal court or council, and assisting him by their counsel in the transaction of its business. This right was sometimes recognised as extending to the inferior tenants *in capite*, but belonged in a special degree to the barons, who were all deemed *pares*, peers or equals, one of another. With the exception of a few distinguished individuals, to whom the Conqueror assigned the government of shires, with the old English or Danish title of *Earl* (see ch. iii. § 1), or its Norman equivalent *Count*, they were all originally alike styled *barons*. About the reign of Hen. 2, the practice was begun of giving the title of earl as a mere mark of distinction, and in order to confer precedence, without attaching to it any administrative duties. The other ranks were not created till later. The bishops, and those abbots and priors who held from the king sufficient lands to constitute a barony, were reckoned among the barons as spiritual lords. Besides the political privileges enjoyed by the peers of attending the king's great council, and subsequently the upper house of Parliament, they likewise possessed certain peculiar privileges in case of being subjected to judicial proceedings; as, for instance, that they were entitled to be tried by members of their own order, and were exempt from arrest in civil cases. Moreover, the use of language derogatory to them was deemed a special offence, and designated as *scandalum magnatum*. With one exception noticed later, there is no instance of a peer having lost his dignity except by death or attainder. The hereditary nature of the peerage was doubtless in its origin connected with the hereditary descent and inalienability of the lands which formed the barony; and our nobility appears from the first to have differed from the continental nobility in the fact, that it descended to the eldest male representative, or in default of male representatives, the eldest female representative of the line alone, while the other members of the family passed into the ranks of the commons. It is impossible to overestimate the advantages of this regulation, not only to the peerage itself, but also to the whole English nation. Under it, even the king's children (except his eldest son, who, since Edw. 3's reign, is, by birth, Duke of Cornwall) are in the eye of the law, until specially raised to the peerage, simply commoners. For the title of prince is as much a title of mere courtesy as that of lord or lady applied to the younger children of some peers, or to the eldest before succeeding to the peerage.

Purveyance and Pre-emption.—Besides the onerous accompaniments of feudal tenure, the whole of the free rural population was, through the king's prerogative of purveyance and pre-emption, subjected after the Conquest to a burden which had previously fallen only upon the occupiers of folcland (see ch. x.) When the king journeyed from one part of the kingdom to another, his purveyors had the right of forcibly buying at an arbitrary value provisions and necessaries for the use of the court on the route; and the crown had also the power of impressing horses and carriages, and cutting down wood for royal or national purposes.

Forest Laws.—The tyranny arising from an oppressive exercise of these powers was, however, far exceeded by that resulting from the forest laws imposed at the Conquest throughout the old forests, and extended to the districts *afforested*, or depopulated and turned into hunting-grounds by the Conqueror and his successors. Proceeding upon the principle that animals of the chase and game were, like the land, the exclusive property of the king and the persons to whom he granted rights over them, these laws inflicted the penalty of death on a person who killed deer without authority, and visited with various punishments of more or less severity any minor damage done to the king's *vert* or *venison*, to the sward and feeding-grounds of the animals, or to the animals themselves.

Clergy.—The clergy after the Conquest held, from a civil point of view, a less honourable but more privileged position than before. With the exception of the higher ecclesiastics, who held baronies, they were thenceforth excluded from the right of participating in the judicial and administrative business of the whole kingdom, and of the separate shires and hundreds. On the other hand, this very exclusion exempted them from the performance of many onerous duties, and the lands held by them were free from the ordinary feudal burdens; and they possessed the right of taxing themselves independently of the rest of the community. Further, offences committed by them, and matters affecting them were tried, not in the civil courts and by the law of the land, but in the ecclesiastical courts and according to the foreign canon law. The abuses arising from this state of things led in Hen. 2's reign to the enactment of the constitutions of Clarendon (A.D. 1164), which restricted gifts of land to the Church, from a regard to the loss of feudal service which the king suffered from the practice; and regulated the proceedings of the ecclesiastical courts, considerably limiting their jurisdiction, and transferring to the civil courts the cognizance of many matters which they had assumed the right to decide. By forbidding the clergy to leave the kingdom without royal license, it was sought to check the increasing tendency to carry ecclesiastical appeals to Rome, which was yearly giving the Papal See more and more power over the English Church. The exercise of the power of excommunication was controlled, and the right of the king to a voice in the election of bishops, abbots, and priors asserted. Lastly, it was declared that villeins should not be ordained without the consent of the lord on whose lands they were born. Most of the provisions of the constitutions of Clarendon were speedily disregarded, and the liberties of the Church were solemnly guaranteed by the Great Charter, and reasserted in all the confirmations of it. But many statutes, called Statutes of Mortmain, were directed, in Edw. 1's reign, and subsequent reigns, against the dedication of land to the Church, and its consequent withdrawal from liability to contribute to national purposes,—a practice which naturally became common when alienation of land was permitted, and the hope was set before profligate landowners of atoning on their deathbed for the sins of their past life, by bestowing their possessions on the Church.

Defence of the Realm.—The old English national force was dissolved during the confusion which followed the Conquest, and no substitute for it was immediately provided. For so late as 1085, we find that feudal tenures, with their military and other incidents, had been by no means universally established. But the alarm excited in that year by the prospect of a fresh Danish invasion, caused attention to be directed to the defenceless state of the country, and no doubt gave a considerable impetus to the completion of the feudal partition of land in the country. This partition was ultimately so far developed by William I. as to secure for him an army of 60,000 men, in a constant state of preparation and equipment, and bound to perform annually forty days' service whenever he required it. In later reigns, however, when the ranks of the feudal army were thinned by the prevalence of commutation for personal service, it became necessary to revive the old pre-Norman organisa-

tion, which a levy under William Rufus, and a muster to
repel the Scottish invasion in 1173, had proved to be not
wholly extinct. Accordingly, Henry 2's Assize of Arms
(A.D. 1181), and afterwards the Statute of Winchester
(13 Edw. 1. c. 6), required every free man to provide
himself with arms suitable to his condition.

Magna Carta.—The oppressions to which all classes
of the people were subjected under the feudal system,
during the reigns of Hen. 2 and his sons, led at length
to the powerful combination of barons, which extorted
from John in 1215 the first grant of the Great Charter.
This instrument, of which repeated confirmations were
obtained from the two succeeding kings, has justly been
regarded as the great bulwark of English freedom. While
it erected safeguards for our liberties on almost every
conceivable point, a large portion of it was naturally
directed against feudal abuses. After the general confirmation of the liberties of the Church, and of all freemen, provisions were inserted which limited the amount
of relief to be paid by the heir of a deceased count, baron,
or military tenant on succeeding to the inheritance, and
the extent of the profits to be taken by a guardian in
chivalry from his ward's lands; and required the guardian
to maintain the ward's property in good repair and condition, and to provide a suitable marriage for the ward,
giving previous notice of the match to the ward's rela-
tives. The dower of widows was also secured to them,
and they were not to be obliged to remarry, if they preferred to remain in widowhood; though if they did remarry, it must be with the consent of their immediate
lord. The mode of recovering crown debts was rendered
less oppressive. No lord, except the king, was to take
any aid from his free tenants, except for the purpose of
ransoming himself, making his eldest son a knight, and

providing a marriage once for his eldest daughter, and the contributions for these objects were not to be excessive. No tenant was to be required to render more than the due amount of military or other service. If a manor escheated to the crown the tenants were not therefore to be liable to any greater reliefs or services than under the former lord. With regard to the lands of those who were convicted of felony, the king was not to hold them for more than a year and a day, and then they were to relapse to the immediate lord. Some of these provisions had been inserted in the Charter of Liberties published by Henry I. at his coronation, but had not been subsequently observed. A prohibition was added against the royal constables or bailiffs taking a man's crops or effects without his consent, or without at once paying their value; and against the king or any sheriff, or any king's bailiff, or other person using the horses or vehicles, or cutting down the wood of a free man, for fortifications or other royal or public purposes, without his leave. And a knight was not to be required to pay towards the garrisoning of a castle, if he was willing to garrison it himself, or was summoned away on military service.

But, as has been already said, the Great Charter was not confined to the alleviation of feudal burdens. It contained an explicit stipulation on the far more important subject of personal liberty. "Let no free man," so runs c. 39, "be taken or imprisoned, or *disseised*, or outlawed, or banished, or be in any way destroyed; nor will we pass upon him, nor will we send upon him, except by the lawful judgment of his equals, or by the law of the land."[4]

[4] "Nullus liber homo capiatur, vel imprisonetur, aut dissaisiatur aut utlagetur, aut exuletur, aut aliquo modo destruatur, nec super eum ibimus, nec super eum mittemus, nisi per legale judicium parium suorum, vel per legem terræ."

International relations were also regulated. A free ingress, egress, and right of sojourning in England, without the liability to any unjust imposts, was conceded to all merchants for purposes of trade, except to subjects of a hostile state in time of war; a provision being inserted that any of the latter, who chanced to be in the country at the breaking out of the war, should be detained until it appeared what treatment was accorded to English merchants happening at the time to be in the enemy's country, and should be treated in like manner. The next clause granted a general liberty of leaving the country, and returning to it, except temporarily in time of war, when the public interests required a restraint.

Charter of the Forest.—The Great Charter had prohibited for the future the erection of weirs for private fisheries in rivers; and as to the forests had declared that all which had been afforested during the reign of King John, should be at once disafforested, and all bad customs respecting forests and warrens should be inquired into by 12 chosen knights of the shire, and be irrevocably abolished. The forestal abuses, however, required to be met by a distinct charter, called the *Carta de foresta*, which was first granted in 1217 in the reign of Hen. 3, and was afterwards confirmed at intervals, together with the Great Charter. It removed or alleviated many of the severe restrictions of the forest laws; and with regard to the most heinous offences against those laws, enacted that no man from henceforth should lose either life or limb for killing the king's deer; but should pay a heavy fine, or, if unable to do so, should be imprisoned for a year and a day; and after the expiration of that time, if he could find sufficient sureties he should be discharged, but if not he should abjure the realm of England.

3. **Peers.**—During the period between Edw. I's reign and the Reformation the number of the barons was enormously reduced, first by the Scottish and French wars, but above all by the internecine wars of the Roses. During the same period distinctions were introduced among them by the introduction of three new titles. Edward III. (who was also the institutor of the order of the Garter), when on assuming the style of King of France he gave up that of Duke of Normandy, introduced the degree of *duke* into the English nobility by creating Edward the Black Prince Duke of Cornwall, and gave it the highest place in the peerage. His successor, Richard II., created a new rank of *marquess*, with precedence next in order to that of duke. In Hen. 6's reign the title *viscount*, originally the Norman-French designation of the sheriff, was first given, with a rank next to an earl, as an honorary distinction, independently of the office which had been up to that time attached to it. In Edw. 4's reign a noble, holding one of these new titles, George Neville, Duke of Bedford, was degraded from the peerage by Act of Parliament on account of his poverty, which rendered him unable to support his dignity. This proceeding has no parallel in our history either before or since.

Decay of Feudalism.—The details of the feudal land laws became, as time went on, more and more difficult to work, owing, among other causes, to the increased facilities for the alienation and transfer of land. In Hen. 6's reign the power of alienating land from the legal heir by will was at last conceded, though with some qualifications; but it had before that time been practised in an underhand way, through the device of alienation during life to a stranger, who agreed to hold the land upon the trusts and for the purposes directed by the will, the performance of these trusts being in such cases compelled by the Court of Chancery. The continued enforcement of the feudal obligations is, however, evidenced by the establishment, in the same reign, of a court of wards and liveries, for the decision of questions as to the rights of the king against his tenants in these particulars.

Villenage.—The gradual extinction of villenage, which was at this time in progress, by the blending of the villeins with the labouring class of free men, is evidenced by the Statute of Labourers, as it is called, passed in 1349, after the great plague of that year, to remedy the refusal to work except for excessive wages, to which labourers were tempted by the depopulation of the country and consequent scarcity of labour. That statute, on the one hand, imposed compulsory labour on both free and bond alike; but, on the other hand, it recognised the right of the latter as well as the former to receive moderate wages. An Act of 1388, on the same subject, extended to labourers and servants generally the restrictions on change of residence to which villeins had been always subject; obliged persons who had been engaged in husbandry to continue in it through life; and forbad agricultural labourers to wear arms. And in Hen. 4's reign we find the practice of labourers putting out their children as apprentices in towns, and so occasioning a dearth of farm labour, complained of and forbidden, and the labourers dwelling in every *leet* are required to be sworn every year to serve according to the labour statutes of the two preceding reigns. At the same time, any one, whatever his condition, is permitted to put his children to school wherever he pleases. These various restrictions, while they had the immediate effect of depressing the poorer free men to the level of villeins, probably assisted eventually in abolishing the latter as a distinct class; for when they fell into disuse,—as it was inevitable that they very soon should,—the villeins and freemen, who had become intermixed in degradation, emerged from it indistinguishably together.

Liberty of the Subject.—Many statutes were passed about the time of Edw. 3, for the protection of the liberty of the subject, some of which were nothing more than detailed provisions for the due observance of the stipulations of the Great Charter. The right of purveyance was regulated so as to press as lightly as possible upon the persons still subject to it. It was repeatedly laid down that none should be imprisoned nor put out of his freehold but by the law of the land. And with regard to the military service required from all freemen, it was enacted that no man should be compelled to go out of his own shire, except in case of necessity or of sudden invasion, nor be liable to provide soldiers, unless bound to do so by his feudal tenure, or required by special authority of Parliament.

Restraint on Religious Opinions.—The first distinct instance of State intervention to repress the teaching and spread of opinions at variance with the doctrines which the Church of England at that time held in common with the rest of Christendom, occurs in Hen. 4's reign. The writ *de hæretico comburendo* appears to have existed in our common law from a much earlier period; but the introduction into this country and the growth of the sect of the Lollards in the 14th century, led at the beginning of the following century to the passing of st. 2 Hen. 4, c. 15,[5] which regulated the mode of enforcing in the ecclesiastical courts the penalty of the flames against a teacher of heretical opinions who refused to abjure them, or relapsed into them after abjuration, and inflicted imprisonment on persons favouring such teachers or keeping

[5] As to this statute see below, ch. vii. § 3.

heretical books in their possession. By an Act of Hen.
5's reign heretics were made amenable to the civil courts.
And during the struggles of the Reformation, in the reigns
of Hen. 8 and Mary, the rigour of the laws against heresy,
and the severity with which they were enforced, rose to
the highest point.

Restriction on Printing.—With one exception, a
special notice of the restrictions which have from time to
time been placed upon the exercise of various trades and
manufactures in this country does not fall within the
scope of constitutional history. The one case which
requires notice is that of printing, which, since its inven-
tion in the 15th century, has inevitably exercised a most
important influence upon the politics as well as the other
affairs of all civilised nations. No sooner was the destined
extent of this influence perceived than the press was
throughout Europe subjected to a rigorous censorship.
No writings were permitted to be published without
license, and the printing of unlicensed works was visited
with the severest punishments. Until the Reformation
the censorship of the press was looked upon as an ecclesiastical affair, and Henry VIII. assumed an absolute control
over it by virtue of his ecclesiastical supremacy.

Aliens.—Notwithstanding the privileges granted to
foreign merchants by the Great Charter, the residence of
aliens in England continued subject to many restrictions.
Not only were aliens liable to pay a higher proportion of
duties and taxes than subjects, but many statutes were
from time to time passed, forbidding them to engage in
manufactures or in retail trade on their own account,
restricting their commerce and their employment of servants and apprentices, and placing them under strict
supervision. St. 32 Hen. 8, c. 16, extended their inability to hold land by prohibiting them from taking any

dwelling-house or shop on lease, and declared all previous leases to them void.

Defence of the Realm.—In times of public danger it became usual to issue commissions of array into the different counties for the purpose of ascertaining that the inhabitants were in a due state of military equipment. In 1485, Henry VII. followed the example of Cnut (see p. 7), and established as a royal bodyguard the yeomen of the guard, whose number, commencing with 50, ultimately reached 200. And in the following reign was founded the London Artillery Company, a voluntary association for the practice of archery.

Impressment for the Navy—In the reign of Ric. 2 occurs the first statutory notice of the power of the Crown to impress seamen for the royal navy, a power of which it is not easy to discover the origin. Its exercise, however, was at any rate at that period recognised as undoubtedly lawful, for 2 Ric. 2, st. 1, c. 4, inflicted penalties in case of the desertion of the seamen impressed; and the power is sanctioned and regulated by subsequent statutes.

4. **Villenage and Slavery.**—The causes before alluded to as tending to the extinction of villenage had before the Reformation operated so powerfully in that direction, that in Edw. 6's reign no instance of a villein in gross was known throughout the country, and the few remaining villeins regardant were attached to the lands of the Church, or to those which had been confiscated from her in the preceding reign; the clergy and monastic orders having been careful to inculcate on the laity the peril of keeping fellow-Christians in bondage, but having refrained from carrying their precepts into practice themselves from a regard to the duty, in their eyes paramount, of main-

taining intact the possessions of the Church. That reign witnessed the first and only attempt since the Norman Conquest to create a new kind of slavery by statute. In 1547 it was enacted that a runaway servant, or idle vagabond, brought up by any person before two justices, should be adjudged slave to that person for two years, and be fed on bread and water, and compelled, by beating, chaining, or otherwise, to do any kind of work, and might have an iron ring put round his neck, arm, or leg. If he absented himself from his master for 14 days during the two years, his slavery was to become perpetual. Runaway apprentices were condemned to be the slaves of their master for the rest of their term of service. And slavery for a limited period was also imposed on convict clerks. But this Act was repealed two years afterwards.

Extinction of Feudalism.—All feudal distinctions and divisions of the community were at the time of the Reformation, together with villenage, fast disappearing. This was due in part to the abolition of the jurisdiction of the local feudal courts which accompanied the subjection of the whole country to the central judicature, and in part to the increased facilities for the alienation and transfer of land, which loosened the ties between lords and tenants. Further, the increase of commerce and of moveable property created a wealthy and influential class within the kingdom, who were wholly without the pale of feudal institutions, and the existence of this class could not fail to weaken the hold of those institutions upon that part of the community which was subject to them. The last occasion on which feudal tenants were summoned to render personal service was in the expedition against the Scotch in 1640. Their liability to this service was recognised by an Act of that year (16 Cha. 1, c. 28), which after laying down in the preamble that "by the laws of this realm none of his Majesty's subjects ought to be impressed or compelled to go out of his country to serve as a soldier in the wars, except in case of necessity of the sudden coming in of strange enemies into the kingdom, or except they be otherwise bound by tenure of their lands and possessions," empowered justices of the peace and the mayors of municipal towns to impress soldiers to serve against the rebels in Ireland. In the same year one of the most onerous of the feudal incidents was abolished. James I., who for the purpose of raising money, sold peerages and instituted a new order of hereditary knights called baronets, to which he granted admission on payment of a stated sum of money, had also revived the practice, which, with the exception of having been once resorted to by Elizabeth, had for some time become obsolete, of requiring military tenants to receive knighthood or pay the composition instead. This practice was renewed by Charles I., who carried it out with excessive rigour. But in the first session of the Long Parliament it was enacted (16 Cha. 1, c. 20) that no one should thenceforth be compelled to receive knighthood, or to pay any fine for not doing so. Another Act of that session restrained the attempts of the king to revive the obsolete tyranny of the forest laws, and to extend them to districts which had practically long since ceased to be treated as parts of the royal forests.

Billeting.—There was another burden to which the people were subjected in Cha. 1's reign, not exactly feudal, but connected with the defence of the realm. This was the practice of forcibly billeting soldiers and sailors in private houses. The Petition of Right (3 Cha. 1, c. 1), after reciting its prevalence and its illegality, prayed that the king would be pleased to remove the billeted soldiers and marines, and that the people might not be so burdened in time to come. The assent of the king to the petition did-not, however, put a stop to the practice. Fifty years later the continued practice of billeting rendered it necessary to pass an express enactment that no officer, military or civil, or any other person whatever, should thenceforth presume to quarter or billet any soldier upon any subject or inhabitant of the realm of any degree, quality, or profession, without his consent, and that any such subject or inhabitant might lawfully refuse to admit such soldier, notwithstanding any command to the contrary (31 Cha. 2, c. 1, s. 32).

Abolition of Feudal Courts.—After the Restoration, a decisive blow was dealt at feudalism by st. 12 Cha. 2, c. 24. That Act put an end to the Court of Wards and Liveries, and to all wardships, liveries, primer seisins, and ouster-le-mains, values of marriages, wardships, fines for alienation, escuages and aids, and other incidents of tenure by knight's service or socage tenure *in capite*, and converted all such tenures into free and common socage tenure. Copyhold tenure was however retained. The king's right to purveyance and pre-emption was by the same Act finally abolished. Thus was completely swept away all that was burdensome in the remnants of feudalism; for we cannot regard as such the surviving traces of it, some of which even now exist in many of our institutions, and especially in our law of landed property.

Religious Penalties and Disabilities.—But while the feudal distinctions were dying out, events were leading to the introduction and growth in importance of a totally different kind of distinction among the people of England. The repression of heresy as such by the civil power in preceding reigns has been already noticed. This, though really incompatible with the principles of Protestantism, was not wholly abandoned at the time of the Reformation.

Heretics were burnt on five occasions in the reign of Elizabeth, and twice in the following reign. But the popular compassion exhibited on the last of those occasions was so great that it was thought expedient not to carry into effect the sentence which had been passed on a third offender. And in 1667 the writ *de haeretico comburendo* was at length abolished by statute. Religious opinions were, however, now taken notice of by the State in another mode. Before the Reformation, with a few inconsiderable exceptions, all the individuals of the community had professed one religious belief and belonged to one religious body, the Church of England, which was then like the Continental churches, though not to the same extent, subject to the paramount authority of the Papal See; and sectaries were liable to the penalties attaching to heresy, so that there was no occasion to impose upon them any civil disabilities in addition. But when the Church of England became reformed and reconstituted in the reigns of Hen. 8 and his son and younger daughter, and when the sovereign and the mass of the nation cast off the yoke of Rome, a certain portion of the people remained attached to the old order of things, while another portion were for making still more radical alterations in religious matters than were in fact accomplished. In those times the practice of resorting to political means in order to produce religious changes in a nation was considered both proper and efficacious; and no doubt in some cases it proved to be successful. The general adoption of this practice rendered it necessary for a government, like our own, which was then looked upon as one of the mainstays of Protestantism, to protect itself against the political intrigues of its own Roman Catholic subjects, by debarring them from civil offices, the holding of which might give them an opportunity of endangering or at least harassing the existing form of government. It is important, therefore, to bear in mind that the restrictions which were at this time placed upon Roman Catholics and afterwards upon Protestant Nonconformists, whatever may be thought of their expediency, were imposed on political grounds, and were upon those grounds perfectly justifiable. We find, in fact, that their severity was increased or diminished in proportion to the activity or otherwise of the agents of the Papacy, and notably of the Jesuits, in intriguing against the government of the country. In the first place, the stas. 1 Eliz. c. 1, and 5 Eliz. c. 1, required the oath of supremacy, to the effect that the queen was supreme both in ecclesiastical and in temporal matters (to the former part of which a Roman Catholic was of course unable to assent), to be taken by every lay as well as ecclesiastical officer, and every person in receipt of a salary from the crown; also by graduates of the universities and all persons in any way connected with the law. Only temporal peers were exempt, the queen being "otherwise sufficiently assured of the faith and loyalty of the temporal lords of her high court of parliament." The many acts of the same reign inflicting penalties on non-attendance at the services of the Church of England, were directed alike against Protestant and Popish Nonconformists; but it is not surprising that in the following reign the discovery of the Gunpowder Plot should have led to measures of special severity against the latter. They were made liable to forfeit all their goods and two-thirds of their lands to the king; were debarred from certain trades and professions, and from being executors, administrators, or guardians; and were forbidden to possess arms or ammunition. Their marriage or burial, and the baptism of their children, except in the parish church, was strictly prohibited. And the fear of Popish tendencies being imbibed on the continent, led to a general prohibition of any children being sent abroad without special license. One reasonable enactment made at this time is still law, namely, that which, in the case of a Roman Catholic having the patronage of a benefice, forbids him to exercise it, and gives the appointment to one of the two universities (3 Ja. 1, c. 5). During the Commonwealth Cromwell professed to allow freedom of worship to all except Papists and Prelatists, declaring "that none be compelled to conform to the public religion, by penalties or otherwise." He extended toleration even to the Jews, who were permitted to return to the kingdom after having been banished since Edw. 1's reign. But he was sometimes led, by political considerations, into severe measures against Episcopalians whether of the Church of England or of that of Rome. After the Restoration the predominant church party indulged in stern retaliation for the treatment they had received during the Commonwealth. The Corporation Act (13 Cha. 2, st. 2, c. 1) imposed the reception of the sacrament as a condition for holding any municipal office. At the same time a new Act of Uniformity (14 Cha. 2, c. 4) was passed, which prohibited all deviations from the prescribed forms of prayer in churches, and obliged all persons in orders, and all schoolmasters and others engaged in tuition, to make a declaration that it was not lawful on any pretence to take up arms against the king; that they abjured the Solemn League and Covenant; and that they would conform to the liturgy of the Church of England. This was followed by Acts for suppressing seditious conventicles, which inflicted imprisonment, and upon a third conviction, seven years' transportation, on persons above the age of 16 who should be present at any religious meeting held otherwise than in accordance with the regulations of the Church of England (16 Cha. 2, c. 4; 22

Cha. 2, c. 1). The Five Mile Act (17 Cha. 2, c. 2) went
further, and required all Nonconforming ministers or
preachers to take an oath devised four years previously, to
the effect that it was not lawful on any pretence to take
up arms against the king, and that they would never
attempt any alteration of the government in Church or
State. Those who did not take this oath were forbidden
to come within 5 miles of any parliamentary borough.
And all Nonconformists alike were declared incapable of
being schoolmasters, or of teaching in schools. Finally,
the Test Act (25 Cha. 2, c. 2) though, as its title stated,
it was primarily designed "for preventing dangers which
might happen from Popish recusants," and though it was
with that view actually promoted by the Protestant Dissenters, yet, by imposing the reception of the sacrament as a
requisite for holding any office civil or military, or receiving
any pay from the Crown, excluded these latter as well as
Roman Catholics from all public posts. And a few years
later members of both houses of Parliament, as well as the
royal servants, were required to subscribe a declaration
against transubstantiation and the invocation of saints
(30 Cha. 2, st. 2), and thus Roman Catholic peers were
disabled from sitting in the House of Lords and excluded
from the king's presence. The arbitrary assumption of
prerogative by James II. in dispensing with these laws
against Roman Catholics and Dissenters in individual instances, and in suspending some of their provisions altogether by the Declaration of Indulgence, constituted one of
his chief violations of the fundamental laws of the kingdom
which were formally condemned at the Revolution.

Liberty of the Subject.—In other respects, great
advances were made during the 17th century towards
securing the personal liberty of the subject against
stretches of the royal prerogative or of the power of the

government. The Petition of Right (3 Cha. 1, c. 1) recited that, contrary to the Great Charter and to an Act of Edw. 3, divers of the king's subjects had of late been imprisoned without any cause shown; and that when for their deliverance they were brought before the king's justices by writ of *habeas corpus*, and their keepers commanded to certify the causes of their detainer, no cause was shown but that they were detained by the king's special command signified by the lords of the privy council, and yet they were returned back to prison without being charged with anything to which they might make answer according to the law; and it prayed that no freeman, in any such manner as was before mentioned, should be imprisoned or detained. And in 1640 it was enacted that, if any person was thereafter committed or imprisoned by order of any Court pretending to have the jurisdiction of the Star Chamber, or by command and warrant of the sovereign in person, or of the privy council or any of its members, he should at once on application to the judges of the King's Bench or Common Pleas have a writ of *habeas corpus*, directed to the person in whose custody he was, to bring him into court, and certify the cause of his imprisonment; and the judges should liberate, bail, or remand the prisoner according to the circumstances (16 Cha. 1, c. 10, s. 6). The method of vindicating liberty by means of a writ of *habeas corpus* was rendered more efficacious in 1679 by st. 31 Cha. 2, c. 2, which is commonly known as the Habeas Corpus Act. This Act required that the sheriff or other officer to whose custody any person was committed should, upon receiving a writ of *habeas corpus*, bring up the person before the court or judge specified in the writ, within a limited period, varying from three to twenty days according to the distance to be traversed. It directed the Lord

Chancellor, Lord Keeper, or any of the judges of the
Courts of King's Bench, Common Pleas, or Exchequer,
in vacation as well as in term-time, to grant a *habeas
corpus* in all cases of detention on a criminal charge,
except where the charge amounted to treason or felony, or
to being accessory to a felony; and to liberate the prisoner, after binding him, upon his own bail and that of
sureties, to appear at his trial in due course. The Act
further declared that no person set at liberty upon a
habeas corpus should be again imprisoned for the same
offence, except by order of the court in which he was
bound to appear for trial. If the trial of a person committed on a charge of treason or felony was unduly postponed, he too might be discharged upon bail. And
persons committed to one prison were not to be removed
into a different custody except by a formal writ. Writs
of *habeas corpus* were to run and take effect in the counties palatine, cinque ports, and other privileged places,
and in the Channel Islands. No English subject was to
be sent as a prisoner to Scotland, Ireland, or the Channel
Islands, or beyond the seas, except in cases of transportation after conviction for felony.

Monopolies and Patents.—The absolute right of
the king to impose regulations on trade and commerce
at his own discretion was a prerogative which had been
early asserted and exercised. In Eliz.'s reign it took the
form of granting to favoured individuals exclusive monopolies of manufacturing or trading in certain articles, and
became so intolerable that in 1601 the Commons obtained
from Elizabeth a promise that it, as well as the practice
of offenders purchasing from the sovereign dispensations
from the penalties imposed on them by law, should be
discontinued. This promise was renewed by James I. in
1610, but as it was not strictly observed, an Act (21 Ja.

1. c. 3) was passed in 1623, declaring all such monopolies and dispensations void. In the case of the former, however, an important exception was made, which has proved the foundation of our present law as to patents. It was declared that the abolition should not extend to letters patent, granting to the first inventor of *new manufactures* the privilege of sole working or making of them for a period not exceeding 14 years. Notwithstanding the statute against monopolies, Charles I. attempted to revive them by establishing chartered companies with exclusive privileges of exercising certain manufactures, as, for instance, making soap and starch. The odium excited by these new monopolies was, however, so great that he judged it prudent in 1639 to revoke them all by proclamation. Since then the only similar privileges granted have been confined to places beyond the sea, as, for instance, in the cases of the East India Company and Hudson's Bay Company.

Restrictions on the Press. — The protracted struggles for liberty between the time of the Reformation and the Revolution effected positively nothing towards the emancipation of the press. The privilege of printing was in the first instance limited to members of the Stationers Company under regulations established by the Star Chamber in Mary's reign, which restricted the number of presses, and appointed a licenser of new publications; and Queen Elizabeth interdicted any printing except in London, Oxford, and Cambridge. While the Star Chamber existed, political discussion in print was repressed by all the punishments which that Court was capable of inflicting, and which included the dungeon, the pillory, mutilation, and branding. Even under its *régime*, however, the news-letter or newspaper sprang into existence, the earliest example of it being the *Weekly*

News, first published on May 23d, 1622. After the fall of the Star Chamber in 1640, tracts and newspapers were prodigiously multiplied, and entered hotly into the contest between the Crown and Parliament. Thus more than 30,000 political pamphlets and newspapers were issued from the press between 1640 and 1660. The Long Parliament did not, however, affect toleration in the matter. It passed severe orders and ordinances in restraint of printing, and would have silenced all royalist and prelatical writers. In fact, John Milton stood well-nigh alone in that age in denouncing the suppression of books by the licenser, which he affirmed to be the slaying of "an immortality rather than a life."[6] After the Restoration the Licensing Act of 1662, a temporary statute which was subsequently from time to time renewed, placed the entire control of printing in the Government, confining it to London, York, and the universities, and limiting the number of master printers to 20. The Act also revived, and vested in the Secretary of State, the power of issuing general search warrants to the Government messenger of the press for the purpose of discovering and seizing alleged libels against the Government. Authors and printers of obnoxious works were, under this Act, hung, quartered, and mutilated, or exposed in the pillory and flogged, or fined and imprisoned, according to the temper of the judges; and their productions were burnt by the common hangman. The Licensing Act was severely enforced under James II.; but the restraint on printing was not due to its existence alone. For when in Cha. 2's reign it had been suffered to expire for a time, Chief Justice Scroggs, and the other eleven common law judges, declared it criminal, at common law, to publish any public

[6] *See* Milton's Areopagitica: a speech for the liberty of unlicensed printing.

news, true or false, without the king's license. This opinion was not judicially condemned till the time of Lord Camden, Chief Justice of the Common Pleas. A monopoly of news being thus created, the public were left to seek intelligence in the official summary of the *London Gazette*.

Control over the Post.—Concurrently with this power over the press, the Crown exercised the right of opening and examining letters confided to its care for transmission through the Post Office. Foreign letters were in early times constantly searched to detect correspondence with Rome and other Continental powers, and during the Long Parliament foreign mails were searched by orders of both Houses; and Cromwell's Postage Act expressly authorised the opening of letters in order "to discover and prevent dangerous and wicked designs against the peace and welfare of the commonwealth." Charles II. interdicted by proclamation the opening of any letters except by warrant from the Secretary of State.

Aliens.—Notwithstanding the protection to foreigners afforded by Magna Charta, the Crown continued to claim the right of ordering them to withdraw from the realm, when it seemed expedient to do so. This right was acted upon in Eliz'a. reign in 1571, 1574, and 1575, but has never been exercised since. The naturalisation of aliens was restricted in Ja. 1's reign by the requirement as a preliminary condition that they should take the oaths of allegiance and supremacy, and partake of the Lord's supper (7 Ja. 1, c. 2).

Defence of the Realm.—About the time of the Reformation the old office of ealdorman, or military head of the shire, was revived in the lord-lieutenants, then first appointed by the crown with the same powers as had been previously given to the commissions of array (see p. 24). St. 4 & 5 Ph. & Mar. c. 2, reclassified the freemen for military purposes, and altered the kind of arms to be borne by each class; but this Act, and the enactments of the Statute of Winchester on the subject (see p. 17), were abrogated at the beginning of the following century. In 1638 an unconstitutional order in council was issued, charging the equipment of cavalry on holders of land of a certain value. The final rupture between Charles I. and the Parliament was caused by the latter passing an ordinance conferring on themselves the command of the militia, and the nomination of governors of fortresses and lord-lieutenants of counties. This illegal proceeding was expressly condemned after the Restoration, when it was laid down that the sole supreme command of the militia, and of all the forces by sea and land, and of all forts and places of strength, was and ever had been, by the laws of England, the undoubted right of the Crown, and that neither House of Parliament could pretend to it, nor could lawfully levy any war, offensive or defensive, against the king (13 Cha. 2, st. 1, c. 6; 14 Cha. 2, c. 3). Provision was at the same time made for raising an adequate militia in the different counties, by requiring persons possessed of landed estates to furnish a number of men proportionate to the value of their property.

Army and Navy.—On the disbanding of the army of the Commonwealth in 1660, General Monk's foot regiment, called the Coldstream, and one horse regiment were retained by the king, and a third regiment was formed out of troops brought by him from Dunkirk. Thus was commenced, under the name of Guards, our present regular army. They amounted in 1662 to 5000 men, but were increased by James II. to 30,000. The regular discipline of the navy also was, shortly after the Restoration, made the subject of legislation; the first Articles of War for its regulation being established by an Act of 1661.

5. Slavery.—No form of slavery had existed in England since the extinction of villenage about the close of Eliz.'s reign; but nearly two centuries more elapsed before it was declared absolutely illegal in the country. It was, on the other hand, distinctly legalised in the colonies by acts passed in the reigns of Will. 3 and Geo. 2; and though in Queen Anne's reign we find an opinion expressed by Lord Chief Justice Holt, that "as soon as a negro comes into England he becomes free," and by Powell J., that "the law takes no notice of a negro," the first positive decision to that effect was the judgment of Lord Mansfield in the case of the negro Somerset, in 1772. In 1799 the freedom of the colliers and salters in Scotland, who had previously been in a state of serfdom, was finally established; and, seven years later, the Slave Trade was abolished.

Religious Disabilities.—The dissenters having largely assisted in bringing about the Revolution, it was natural that their political condition should be benefited by it. Accordingly, by the Toleration Act of 1688 (1 Will. & Mar. c. 18) a concession was made to Dissenting ministers who took the oath of allegiance to the sovereign, and an oath in repudiation of the doctrine that princes excommunicated by the Pope might be deposed or murdered, together with a declaration that no foreign prince, prelate, or potentate had or ought to have any ecclesiastical or spiritual jurisdiction within the realm. The taking of these oaths was long a necessary qualification for various offices and professions in this country; an additional oath, in abjuration of the Stuart dynasty, and stigmatising them as pretenders, being added after the close of Will.

3's reign. But by the Act just mentioned, dissenting ministers who took these oaths (or who, if Quakers, made a declaration to the like effect) and subscribed the declaration required by 30 Cha. 2, st. 2 (see p. 31), and the 39 Articles (with certain stated exceptions, and with a reservation, in the case of Baptists, as to the clause on infant baptism in Art. 27), were allowed to officiate in meeting-houses with doors unlocked, and were exempted from serving on juries or in parochial or county offices; and disturbers of their worship were to be punished. Unitarians as well as Papists were, however, expressly excluded from the benefit of the Toleration Act, and the former were further disabled by st. 9 Will. 3, c. 35, from holding any ecclesiastical, civil, or military office. The toleration granted by st. 1 Will. & Mar. c. 18, was somewhat restricted in the last four years of Anne's reign; but it was again conceded in Geo. 1's reign. And in the following reign began the series of annual indemnity Acts, by which persons who had exercised the office or followed the professions, for which oaths or tests were required, without taking them, were exempted from the penalties incurred by so doing. These Acts, though nominally dealing only with accidental omissions, became a means of shielding deliberate evasions of the law.

Marriage Law.—On the other hand, a new and oppressive restriction was, in 1753, imposed on Dissenters by Lord Hardwicke's Marriage Act, which was designed for preventing clandestine marriages. They had previously been allowed to be married in their own places of worship; but under that Act the marriages of all persons except Jews and Quakers were required to be solemnised in a parish church, by ministers of the Establishment, and according to its ritual.

Roman Catholics.—As might have been expected

after the conduct of James II. and his advisers, the laws against Roman Catholics were at the Revolution made more severe. The Act 30 Cha. 2, st. 2, which had been intended to be only temporary, was continued in force against them; they were declared incapable of purchasing or inheriting lands; with a few specified exceptions, they were to be banished from London and Westminster; and within ten miles of those cities were to keep no horses above the value of £5, nor arms. Moreover, a Popish priest was to be punished for exercising his functions by perpetual imprisonment. These severe laws were never thoroughly carried out, notwithstanding that the vigorous execution of them was enforced by royal proclamation in Queen Anne's reign, by Act of Parliament after the rebellion of 1715, and again by royal proclamation after that of 1745.

Progress of Toleration.—In proportion as the apprehensions of political danger from those who were disaffected towards the Established Church passed away, measures for the relief of their disabilities were introduced. Thus in 1779 Protestants who declared their belief in the Scriptures were relieved from the necessity of subscribing the 39 Articles in order to have the benefit of the Toleration Act, and were enabled to keep schools and teach. Nor was the relaxation of the law entirely confined to Protestant Dissenters. An Act was passed, in 1778, and another in 1791, by which various penalties on Roman Catholics were remitted in the case of those who took the oath of allegiance and acknowledged the king's temporal supremacy—peers who did so being relieved from the banishment from the king's presence inflicted by 30 Cha. 2, st. 2,—and their worship was permitted under certain restrictions. These measures, however, did not become law without considerable difficulty, and the passing

of the Act of 1778 led to an agitation for its repeal, which
in 1780 caused the disturbances in London known as the
Lord George Gordon Riots. Meanwhile the political disabilities of the Roman Catholics remained, though, in 1801,
an increasing difficulty was thrown in the way of their continuance by the union of Great Britain with Ireland, where
the Romish religion prevailed. After that event Mr Pitt
and his colleagues were of opinion that Roman Catholics
might be safely admitted to office, and to the privilege of
sitting in Parliament; and that Dissenters should at the
same time be relieved from civil disabilities. Mr Pitt
also projected the idea of attaching the Roman Catholic
clergy to the State, by making them dependent upon the
public funds for a part of their provision and subject to
State superintendence, for which purpose the Irish Roman
Catholic bishops had consented to allow the crown a veto
on their nomination. But George III., was irrecon-
cilably opposed to any concessions of the kind, and the
difference of opinion between him and his prime minister
on the subject led to the resignation of the latter. The
question, however, continued to be agitated, and occasioned
the fall of another ministry, that of Lord Grenville, in
1807. Four years later the king became permanently in-
disposed, and during the regency considerable advances
were made in the removal of religious restrictions. In
1811, freedom of worship was practically, though not by
any legislative enactment, conceded to Roman Catholic
soldiers. It was agreed among the members of Lord
Liverpool's administration, on taking office in 1812, that
Roman Catholic emancipation should be an open question. In that year an Act was passed which rendered
it unnecessary for persons officiating in certified meeting-houses to take the oaths and make the declaration,
unless required to do so by a justice of the peace; and in

the following session the disabilities under which Unitarians laboured were removed. In 1817, the Military and Naval Officers' Oath Act virtually opened all ranks in the army and navy to Roman Catholics and Dissenters. At length, towards the close of Geo. 4's reign, throughout the whole of which the question had been annually contested in Parliament, an Act repealing the Test and Corporation Acts and the Roman Catholic Relief Act, were carried,—the one in 1828 and the other in 1829. The former (9 Geo. 4, c. 17) abolished the taking of the Lord's supper as a test for any of the offices or situations for which it had previously been required. The latter (10 Geo. 4, c. 7), while it continued the incapacity of Roman Catholics to act as regent, or to be Lord Chancellor or Lord Keeper, or to hold certain positions in Scotland and Ireland, abolished in all other cases the necessity of making the declaration against transubstantiation and the invocation of saints, and permitted Roman Catholics to vote at parliamentary elections and sit in either House of Parliament, and to hold civil and military offices, on taking the oath of allegiance, with a repudiation of the doctrine that princes excommunicated by the Pope might be deposed or murdered. The Act contained stringent provisions for regulating the residence of Jesuits and members of other male religious orders of the Church of Rome then within the kingdom, and forbad, with certain exceptions, under penalty of banishment, the future ingress of any such persons or the admission of any person within the kingdom into those orders. These restrictive provisions have, however, not been enforced, and are practically a dead letter. In 1832 an Act was passed placing Roman Catholics, in respect of their schools, charities, and places of worship, and the persons employed about them, on the same footing as Protestant Dissenters.

Liberty of the Subject.—The passing of the Habeas Corpus Act did not secure for the personal liberty of Englishmen complete protection from irregular interference on the part of the Government. In the first place, the Act itself was frequently suspended during the first few years after the Revolution. Nor can we wonder that it should have been so during the rebellions of 1715 and 1745. At the time of the American war of independence, the king was empowered to secure persons suspected of high treason committed in America or on the high seas, or of piracy; and in 1794 the political excitement occasioned by the French Revolution and the troubles on the continent was considered sufficient to warrant another temporary suspension of the Act. This suspension was continued by periodical renewals till 1801, when the termination of the suspension was accompanied by an Act of Indemnity to all persons who since 1793 had been concerned in the apprehension of persons suspected of high treason. The last occasion of the suspension of the Habeas Corpus Act in Great Britain was in 1817; but it has since been more than once suspended in Ireland.

General Warrants.—Besides, however, the suspension of the Habeas Corpus Act, another mode of interference with the liberty of the subject was practised by the Government in the early part of the 18th century. When an offence had been committed against the Government, *general warrants* were issued for the apprehension, not of individuals specified by name, but of any persons whom the public officers might, on investigating the matter, suspect of having been concerned in it. The last case in which the practice was resorted to was upon the publication of No. 45 of the *North Briton*, written by the celebrated John Wilkes, and containing a bitter attack upon the Government. A general warrant was issued for the apprehension of all persons concerned in the authorship, printing, and publication of it, under which 49 persons, including Wilkes himself, were arrested on suspicion and committed. Wilkes, being a member of the House of Commons, was released by a writ of habeas corpus, and actions were immediately brought by him against the Under-Secretary of State, and also, under his directions, by the committed printers against the messengers who had arrested them. In the course of these latter actions, Lord Mansfield and the other judges of the King's Bench pronounced the warrant illegal, declaring that no degree of antiquity could give sanction to a usage bad in itself (*Money* v. *Leach*, 1 W. Blackst. 555). This decision gave a death-blow to general warrants, notwithstanding the refusal of the Lords in the following year (A.D. 1766) to concur in a declaratory bill in condemnation of them, which had been passed in the Commons.

Revenue Laws.—But while liberty was thus vindicated in one direction, considerable infringements were inflicted upon it in another, by the increasing severity of the revenue laws; especially in the department of excise, not only through the powers given to the excise officers, for the purpose of preventing frauds, of entering and searching, in many cases by night as well as by day, the houses of dealers in exciseable goods, but also through the summary method of procedure against alleged offenders before commissioners of excise or justices of the peace, without a jury. And persons punished by fines were, like others who owed debts to the crown, subject to life-long imprisonment in case of failure to pay.

Debtors.—The liability just mentioned was in truth only in keeping with the hardships of the general law of debtor and creditor which prevailed at this time. A debtor, at any time after proceedings had been com-

menced against him by a creditor, real or pretended, and
before the debt was legally proved, was liable to be
arrested on *mesne process*,[7] as it was called, and thrown
into prison, where he remained until the cause was tried,
unless he could find sufficient bail. By Acts of Geo. 1
and Geo. 3 arrest on mesne process was restricted to the
case of debts exceeding £10, and this limit was afterwards raised to £15, and ultimately to £20. But after
a debt, however small, was proved against a person, he
was liable to imprisonment in the Fleet or Marshalsea
prison until payment. The horrors of these prisons were
so great as to lead in 1772 to the establishment of a
charitable society, called the Thatched House Society, for
purchasing the liberty of poor debtors detained there, by
payment of their debts. So trifling were the amounts for
which the majority were suffering incarceration, that the
Society, in twenty years, were able to release 12,590 by
an average payment of 45s. per head. Temporary Acts
for the relief of Insolvent Debtors were passed from time
to time in Queen Anne's reign, and again in the early
part of Geo. 3's reign; but it was not till 1813 that in-
solvents were placed under the jurisdiction of a special
Court, and became entitled to seek discharge on rendering a true account of all their debts and property—a measure which led to the liberation of 50,000 debtors within
the succeeding 13 years. A tremendous power of imprisonment was still wielded by the Court of Chancery, as a
punishment for *contempt* or failure to perform its decrees,
the result in some cases of obstinacy, but in others
of mere poverty and inability. In the early part of the
present century several cases occurred of persons who,
failing to purge their contempt, died in prison after a
confinement of upwards of 30 years.

[7] *See* Index and Glossary.

Political Rights.—The Declaration of Rights at the time of the Revolution (ratified by the Bill of Rights, 1 Will. & Mar., sess. 2, c. 2), went beyond a mere establishment of personal liberty. The right of Protestant subjects to have arms for their defence, suitable to their conditions and as allowed by law, was asserted, by way of condemnation of the conduct of James II. in having caused several good subjects to be disarmed, while Papists were both armed and employed contrary to the law. Again, inasmuch as that monarch had committed and prosecuted the seven bishops for petitioning him that they might be excused from concurring in the dispensing and suspending powers assumed by him, the Declaration asserted that subjects had a right to petition the king, and that all commitments and prosecutions for such petitioning were illegal. The practice of putting a pressure upon the executive otherwise than through the medium of Parliament, and of endeavouring to influence Parliament itself on particular subjects by means of petitions, public meetings, and political agitation, may almost be said to date from the 18th century. It is true that the right of petitioning Parliament for the redress of personal and local grievances had existed from the earliest time, and political petitions had been presented to the Long Parliament, which had encouraged or punished the petitioners according as their sentiments agreed or were at variance with its own opinions. But an Act of 1661 had prohibited petitions to the king or Parliament for alterations of matters established by law in Church or State, and it was not till after the Revolution that the practice of petitioning Parliament on matters of general political interest became usual. In 1701 the Commons voted the Kentish petition scandalous, insolent, and seditious, tending to destroy the constitution of Parliament, and to subvert the established government of the realm; and they committed five of the petitioners to prison till the end of the session. This petition had implored them to tender bills of supply to the king, and enable him to assist his allies before it should be too late. Several petitions were presented in 1716 against the septennial bill; and in 1721, praying for justice on the directors of the South Sea Company, after the bursting of the bubble. And in 1753 the city of London presented a petition against the bill for the naturalisation of the Jews, which however met with some animadversion in the House. The petitions in 1779 for reform in Parliament, and the petitions for the abolition of the slave trade in 1787, attained a number far in excess of what had ever been previously known; and those against the slave trade exercised a considerable influence upon Parliament. The practice which prevailed in the House of Commons at that time, and down to a recent date, of allowing discussions on any petitions which might be presented to have precedence over the matters set down for consideration, however important, proved exceedingly inconvenient when towards the end of Geo. 3's reign petitions became enormously multiplied. With regard to petitions against bills imposing duties or taxes, it had early become a settled rule that they should not be received. But even on this subject public meetings and agitations might be brought to bear; and an extensive resort to these methods forced Sir R. Walpole to withdraw his excise scheme in 1733. The repeal of the Act for the naturalisation of the Jews was produced in a similar way in 1754, and the riots of the Spitalfields silk weavers in 1765 led to an Act prohibiting the importation of foreign silks. In no long time political agitation became reduced to a system, by the establishment of societies, such as the Protestant Association under the presidency of Lord George

Gordon, and the Association for the abolition of the slave trade in 1787. Upon the outbreak of the French Revolution, several democratic and revolutionary associations, called corresponding societies, were formed in England. Although the acquittal of Horne Tooke and other leading members of these societies in 1794 proved that their proceedings did not go to the length of treason, their existence was deemed incompatible with the public safety. Accordingly in December 1795 an Act was passed for the prevention of seditious meetings, which prohibited under severe penalties the holding of meetings of more than 50 persons (except county meetings and other meetings recognised by the law), for deliberating on any public grievance, or on any matter or thing relating to any trade, manufacture, business or profession, or upon any matter in Church or State, except under certain stringent conditions. The same Act declared lecture and debating rooms to be disorderly places, unless held under a license for one year from the justices at quarter sessions, which they were empowered at any time to revoke. These provisions as to lecture rooms, were repeated in 1799, when all the corresponding societies were absolutely suppressed (39 Geo. 3, c. 79). Meanwhile voluntary associations were, on the other hand, established to assist the government in repressing sedition. The outrages of the Luddites in the manufacturing districts (A.D. 1811-1814) arose from the prevailing distress, and had no political significance; but in 1817 it was deemed necessary to renew the measure of 1795 against seditious meetings. The Act then passed (57 Geo. 3, c. 19), the material parts of which, like those of the Act of 1799, are still law, contains a clause prohibiting the meeting of more than 50 persons, or the convening of such a meeting, in any square or street in Westminster within one mile of

Westminster Hall for the purpose of considering or preparing an address or petition to the king or regent, or to both or either of the Houses of Parliament, for the alteration of matters in Church or State, during the sitting of Parliament or of any of the Courts at Westminster Hall.

The Six Acts.—In addition to the measures just noticed, the state of the country towards the end of 1819 occasioned the passing of what were known as the Six Acts. The first of these (60 Geo. 3 & 1 Geo. 4, c. 1), which is still law, prohibited the training of persons to the use of arms, and the exercise of them in military evolutions under the penalty of transportation or imprisonment on the persons training, and of fine and imprisonment on those trained. The second (c. 2), which was only a temporary Act, and has expired, authorised justices of the peace, in certain disturbed northern and midland counties, and any others which should thereafter be declared by proclamation in council to be in a disturbed state, to seize and detain any arms collected or kept for purposes dangerous to the public peace. The object of the third (c. 4) was the prevention of delay in the administration of justice in cases of misdemeanour. The fourth (c. 6, "for more effectually preventing seditious meetings and assemblies") which was to continue in force for five years, contained provisions very similar to those of the Act of 1795. The remaining two will be noticed hereafter (see pp. 50, 53). Owing partly to these measures, and partly to an improved spirit among the people, the reign of Geo. 4 was not disquieted, at least in England, by the holding of seditious meetings. But the power of political agitation made itself triumphantly felt in procuring the passing of the Reform Act at the commencement of the next reign.

Liberty of the Press.—After the Revolution the

Commons refused to renew the Licensing Act, which accordingly expired in 1695. But two distinct methods were employed by the Government for restraining the free expression of opinion through the press: first, the stamp duty on newspapers; and secondly, the law of libel. Newspapers assumed their present form, combining intelligence with political discussion, in the reign of Anne; and the *Daily Courant*, the first daily paper, was started in 1709. When during that reign the press became an instrument of party, the dominant party exerted itself to repress the publications which took the side of the opposition. Proposals were even made for reviving the Licensing Act; but the stamp duty on newspapers and advertisements was devised instead, avowedly for the purpose of repressing libels. This policy being found effectual in limiting the circulation of cheap papers, was carried further in subsequent reigns. The newspaper stamp was gradually raised to fourpence, and was eventually extended, by st. 60 Geo. 3 & 1 Geo. 4, c. 9 (the last of the Six Acts), to cheap political tracts published periodically. The advertisement duty was also increased during the reign of Geo. 3. But a far more important engine in the hands of the Government for restraining political discussion existed in the law of *libel*. This law was rigorously enforced in the first two reigns after the Revolution. Under Geo. 1 and Geo. 2 the press generally enjoyed a greater amount of toleration, owing, not to a diminution of its influence, which on the contrary was yearly increasing, but in great part to the fact that Sir Robert Walpole was personally indifferent to its attacks, and avowed his contempt for political writers of all parties. At the commencement of the reign of Geo. 3, a sudden advance in the freedom of discussion occasioned a renewal of the conflict between it and the Government. The king's unpopular minister, Lord Bute, was the subject of furious attack, the lead in which was taken by the *North Briton*, conducted by Wilkes. Contrary to the practice which had previously been followed, even by the *Annual Register*, of avoiding the use of names and giving merely the initials of ministers and others in treating of domestic events, this paper assailed the foremost statesmen by name, whilst its insinuations touched even the king himself. On the appearance, in April 1763, of No. 45 of the *North Briton*, commenting upon the king's speech at the prorogation, and upon the unpopular peace recently concluded, a general warrant was issued for the discovery and arrest of the authors and printers; and an information for libel was filed against Wilkes in the King's Bench, in which a verdict was obtained (*Rex* v. *Wilkes*, 4 Burr. 2527, 2574). The illegality of this general warrant for the apprehension of individuals has been already noticed. About the same time (A.D. 1765), Lord Camden, as Chief Justice of the Common Pleas, decided in the case of *Entick* v. *Carrington* (2 Wils. 275), that a Secretary of State had no power to issue a *general search warrant* for the discovery and seizure of a person's books and papers. It was true that many such warrants had been issued since the Revolution, but he wholly denied their legality. The practice had originated in the proceedings of the Star Chamber. After the abolition of that court, it had been revived and authorised by the Licensing Act of Cha. 2, in the person of the Secretary of State; but its continuance, after the expiration of that Act, was altogether unjustifiable. The further inequitable measures taken by the Government against Wilkes raised a burst of public feeling in his favour, and blinded the people to the justice of the verdict and sentence in the King's Bench against him. The mode of procedure in cases of State libel was also calculated to render the Government prosecutions unpopular. On an information by the Attorney General, the accused was at once arraigned without any previous finding of a grand jury, such as preceded ordinary criminal trials. Moreover, contrary to the presumption which prevailed in other criminal cases, a publisher was held criminally answerable for the actions of his servants, unless it was proved that he was neither privy nor assenting to the publication of the libel. And the judges decided that exculpatory evidence on behalf of the publisher was inadmissible, holding the publication of a libel by a publisher's servant to be proof of his criminality. Lord Mansfield further laid down that it was the province of the judge alone to decide as to the criminality of the libel, thereby removing this question from the province of the jury, who were merely called upon to determine as to the fact of its publication. The frequency of Government prosecutions for libel, and the tendency of the judges to adopt an unfavourable construction of the language complained of, induced Mr Fox, in 1791, to bring in a bill, similar in terms to one for the introduction of which leave had been refused twenty years previously. This bill provided that on a trial or information for libel the jury might give a general verdict on the whole matter, and should not be directed to find the defendant guilty merely on proof of the publication of the alleged libel by him, and of the sense ascribed to it in the indictment or information. The bill passed the Commons, but was lost in the Lords. It however became law in the following session (32 Geo. 3, c. 60). In the course of 1792 a royal proclamation was issued, warning the people against wicked and seditious writings, and commanding magistrates to discover the authors, printers, and promulgators of such writings. Similar proclamations had been issued in the reigns of Anne and Geo. 1; and on this occasion, though denounced by Fox and the opposition, it met with the approval of both Houses of Parliament, and was followed by numerous prosecutions of publishers. On the other hand, the Government refused to accede to the demands of Napoleon, who, as First Consul, in 1802, after the peace of Amiens, irritated by the strictures of English newspapers on French affairs, required that certain unconstitutional restraints should be placed upon them. One libeller of the French government was however tried and convicted under the existing law, and only escaped punishment through the renewal of hostilities. Meanwhile the repression of libels against the home Government continued. In 1808 power was given to the judges of the King's Bench to commit or hold to bail persons charged with publishing libels, as well as with other offences, before indictment or information. In 1817 Lord Sidmouth sent a circular letter to the lord-lieutenants of counties, requesting them to communicate to the justices at quarter sessions the opinion of the law officers of the crown, that a justice might issue a warrant to apprehend any person charged on oath with the publication of a blasphemous or seditious libel, and compel him to give bail to answer the charge; and directing that sellers of pamphlets or tracts should be considered as subject to the Pedlars' Act, and accordingly liable to punishment if they sold without a license. Two years later, the fifth of the Six Acts (60 Geo. 3 & 1 Geo. 4, c. 8, "for the more effectual prevention and punishment of blasphemous and seditious libels"), provided that on verdict or judgment by default for composing, printing, or publishing any blasphemous or seditious libel, the seizure and detention might be ordered of all copies of the libel found in the possession of the convicted person or any other person specified in the order; and on a second conviction, the person might either be condemned to suffer the punishment for high misdemeanours, or be banished from the British dominions for such term of years as the Court should order. This punishment of banishment was, however, repealed eleven years later.

Control over the Post.—The power already noticed of opening letters sent through the post was confirmed by the Post-office Act of 1710, which permitted a Secretary of State to issue warrants for their detention and inspection. This power was continued by later statutes; and in 1783, the Lord-Lieutenant of Ireland was entrusted with a similar authority. During the rebellion of 1745, and at other periods of public danger, letters were extensively opened. The object of the warrants was not restricted to the detection of crimes or practices dangerous to the State; they were constantly issued for discovery of forgery and other offences, on the application of persons concerned in the apprehension of offenders.

Aliens.—Jealousy of the foreigners whom William III. had brought over with him and exalted to high positions in the State, and the fear that kings of the House of Brunswick, if they mounted our throne, would follow his example, led to the insertion in the Act of Settlement (12 & 13 Will. 3, c. 2), of a clause enacting that after the accession of the House of Brunswick to the throne, no person born out of the British dominions, although naturalised or made a denizen (unless born of English parents), should be capable of being a privy councillor or member of either House of Parliament, or of holding any civil or military office, or receiving any grant of land from the Crown. And by way of insuring the observance of these provisions, it was enacted, in 1 Geo. 1, that no Bill for the naturalisation of any person should thereafter be received in either House of Parliament, unless it contained a clause expressly disabling him from occupying the prohibited posts. The object of this enactment was however in special cases occasionally superseded by a somewhat circuitous process. When it was desired that an individual should, upon his naturalisation, receive the prohibited rights, an Act was first passed permitting the introduction into Parliament of a Naturalisation Bill without the disabling clause, and the Bill was then introduced, which on becoming law gave the desired rights. In 1708 an Act was passed naturalising all foreigners who took the oaths of allegiance and abjuration, made the declaration against transubstantiation and invocation of saints, and received the Lord's supper in some Protestant congregation in England. This measure was, however, repealed three years later. But in the reigns of Geo. 2 and Geo. 3 many Acts were passed conferring naturalisation as a reward for services rendered to the State; service, for instance, as sailor in an English ship in time of war or in the whale fishery, and military service, or residence in America. In 1753 an Act was passed permitting the naturalisation of Jews without taking the sacrament as required by st. 7 Ja. 1, c. 2. It was, however, repealed by the very first Act of the following session, on the ground that occasion had been taken from it "to raise discontents, and to disgust the minds of many of his Majesty's subjects;" and it was not until 1825 that the requirement of st. 7 Ja. 1, c. 2, was finally abrogated, and the reception of the Lord's supper was declared unnecessary as a condition for naturalisation. Other disabilities on foreigners were imposed in the latter half of the 18th century. In 1774, it was enacted that no bill for the naturalisation of any person should be received by either House of Parliament, unless it contained a clause disabling the person from having any of the immunities or indulgences in trade belonging to natural born subjects by treaty or otherwise, until after seven years' subsequent continuous residence in the kingdom. And the number of foreigners, who came here for refuge at the time of the French Revolution, led to the passing, in 1793, of an Alien Act, placing restrictions for one year on their arrival and residence in this country. At the same time it was made treason for any resident in Great Britain, not only to supply material aid to the enemy, but also during the war to invest money in land in the French dominions; and any subjects going there without royal license, and any residents in Great Britain, whether subjects or foreigners, who insured French ships or goods, were made liable to imprisonment. The Alien Act was renewed from time to time during the war; but its provisions were temporarily relaxed on the establishment of peace in 1802. England then resumed her character of an asylum for refugees, and our Government, except in the solitary case of M. Georges, who had been concerned in circulating papers hostile to the French authorities, refused the demand of the First Consul, that we should remove out of British dominions all the French princes and their adherents, together with the bishops and men of political notoriety. The provisions of the Alien Act were again relaxed after the peace of 1814, and were finally abandoned in 1826, when a simple registration of aliens was adopted in their place.

Defence of the Realm.—The practice of impressment for compulsory military service, which had arisen out of the original duty of all feudal tenants to serve in the army, was, as we have seen (p. 26), condemned by an Act of the first session of the Long Parliament. It was, however, occasionally resorted to even after the Revolution, but only under the authority of Parliament, instead of, as previously, under that of the royal prerogative. Thus, in 1779, during the American War, the Legislature permitted the impressment of all idle and disorderly persons who were not either following a lawful trade, or in possession of substance sufficient for their maintenance. Since that time, however, voluntary enlistment, encouraged by the offer of bounties, has proved sufficient for the recruiting of our land forces.

Impressment for the navy, on the other hand, was practised down to a much later period. It was, properly speaking, restricted to seamen, but landsmen were often seized under the pretext of being sailors in disguise. And in great emergencies the customary exemptions from liability to it were temporarily withdrawn: as for instance, in 1779; and again in 1795, when the impressment into the navy of able-bodied rogues and vagabonds and persons following no lawful calling was expressly authorised.

Standing Army.—By one of the clauses of the Declaration of Rights, it was laid down that the raising and keeping of a standing army within the kingdom in time of peace, except with consent of Parliament, is against law. This assertion has since been annually repeated in the preamble to the Mutiny Act, which also declares that "no man can be forejudged of life or limb, or subjected in time of peace to any kind of punishment within the kingdom by martial law, or in any other manner than by judgment of his peers, and according to the known and established laws of the realm." Yet, since (as the Act affirms) it is adjudged necessary by the Sovereign and by Parliament that a body of forces should be maintained for the safety of the kingdom and defence of the possessions of the crown, and since it is requisite for retaining the forces in their duty, that an exact discipline should be observed, and that soldiers who mutiny or stir up sedition, or desert, or are guilty of breaches of discipline, should be brought to a more exemplary and speedy punishment than the usual forms of the law will allow, the Act proceeds to authorise the sovereign to make Articles of War for the government of the army, and to empower courts-martial to inflict death and other punishments on soldiers for offences against the Act or the Articles made under its authority. Moreover, after reciting the provisions of the Petition of Right, and of st. 31 Cha. 2, c. 1, against the quartering and billeting of soldiers, the Act suspends those provisions, and expressly permits billeting in inns and victualling houses. The first Mutiny Act was passed in 1688. It was to continue in force for one year only—a precedent which has ever since been followed as to the British Isles; though for the more distant parts of the Empire the operation of the Act is extended to a somewhat longer period. The maintenance of the army is thus absolutely dependent upon the will of Parliament; for if in any year Parliament were not to be summoned, or were to refuse to pass a new Mutiny Act, the means of maintaining its discipline would cease. But notwithstanding this, so great at the time of the Revolution was the jealousy with which any standing army was regarded, that in 1697, after the Peace of Ryswick, the Commons voted that all the troops raised since 1680 should be disbanded, thus reducing the army to 7000 men, a number which they were with difficulty persuaded to increase to 10,000. From the reign of Geo. 1 till the close of the century the ordinary peace establishment, including the garrisons of Minorca and Gibraltar, but exclusive of the troops in Ireland, and, of course, of the East India Company's army, was about 17,000 men. The Irish force was fixed in Will. 3's reign at 12,000, and in Geo. 3's reign at 16,000 men. The same jealousy of a standing army led in 1735 to the passing of an Act which directed that no troops should come within 2 miles of any place except the capital or a garrison town during a parliamentary election; and in 1741, the military having been called in to quell a disturbance at a Westminster election, it was resolved by the Commons "that the presence of a regular body of armed soldiers at an election of members to serve in Parliament is a high infringement of the liberties of the subject, a manifest violation of the freedom of elections, and an open defiance of the laws and constitution of this kingdom;" and the persons concerned in the matter having been ordered to attend the House, received on their knees a very severe reprimand from the Speaker.

Militia.—The militia was remodelled in 1757, when a certain number of men was fixed to be raised in each county. They were to be chosen by ballot to serve for a limited number of years, and during that time were subjected for a certain portion of the year to military training; and when called out, were to be under martial law. They were to be officered by the lord-lieutenant, deputy lieutenants, and other landholders of the county, and were not to be compelled to march out of their county, except in case of invasion or rebellion. In 1802 the Militia Laws were consolidated by st. 42 Geo. 3, c. 90, but the system remained substantially the same as that established in 1757. In addition to the regular militia, bodies of volunteer cavalry called yeomanry, and of volunteer infantry, were raised during Geo. 3's reign, to repel the threatened invasion of this country by the French; and when embodied were subjected to certain statutory regulations. And these troops being considered insufficient for the defence of the realm, a supplementary force called Fencibles was established in 1803, and another under the

name of the Local Militia in 1808. The number of the
latter in each county, together with its volunteers and
yeomanry, was not to exceed 6 times the number of the
regular militia for the county, to which the force bore a
strong resemblance in respect of its regulations. Upon
the conclusion of the peace the volunteer infantry were
disbanded, but the yeomanry were still kept on foot. In
1816 an Act was passed empowering the king, by order in
council, to suspend the balloting for an enrolment of the
local militia, which was forthwith done; and in 1829
the practice was commenced of passing annual acts for
suspending the ballot for the regular militia.

6. Extension of Freedom.—Since the Reform Act
of 1832 there has been an increasing tendency to abolish
all political distinctions between different sections of the
community, as well as all needless restrictions on individual
freedom and on the expression of opinion whether
by word of mouth or in print. On the 1st of Aug.
1834 slavery was abolished by law throughout the British
dominions. And the law of imprisonment for debt,
which, notwithstanding the mitigations of it already
noticed, still remained in an unsatisfactory state, underwent
further modifications, the necessity for which is
shown by the fact that in 1861 they resulted in the liberation
from the Queen's Bench Prison of a debtor who had
been there since 1814. Moreover the Bankruptcy Laws
were subjected to considerable alterations, particularly in
1849 and 1861. Those made on the last occasion were
found by experience to have rendered the law unduly
favourable for the debtor, allowing him to rid himself of
his past debts on too easy terms. A new Bankruptcy Act
(32 & 33 Vict. c. 71) was therefore passed in 1869,
which simplified the proceedings in cases of bankruptcy,

and diminished the facility with which a bankrupt could obtain a complete discharge from all his obligations. In the same year all arrest and imprisonment for debt, or default in payment of money, were expressly abolished except in a few specified cases; but as a counterpoise to this indulgence to debtors, it was enacted that persons who combined fraud with their indebtedness, should, in certain cases, be deemed guilty of a misdemeanour and be punishable with imprisonment for one or two years with or without hard labour.

Religious Disabilities.—The principal religious disabilities had already been swept away, but some of less importance still remained, to form the subject of legislation during the late and present reigns. In 1833, Mr Pease, the first Quaker who had been elected to the House of Commons for 140 years, was allowed to take his seat on making an affirmation in lieu of an oath. In the same year two acts were passed, allowing Quakers, Moravians, and Separatists to make affirmations instead of taking oaths in all cases where an oath was required by law. In 1836, st. 6 & 7 Will. 4. c. 85, removed the grievance of Dissenters as to marriage, by permitting under certain restrictions the solemnisation of marriages in their places of worship, and also before the superintendent district registrar of births, deaths, and marriages at his office. It also allowed in certain cases churches and chapels of the Church of England, not being parish churches, to be licensed for the celebration of marriages. And the establishment in the present reign of cemeteries, with a chapel for Dissenters, and with part of the ground left unconsecrated for their use, has given them facilities for conducting their burials according to their own form. In the years 1844-1846, the Penal Laws against Roman Catholics, Dissenters, and Jews were expressly repealed; and Jews

were exempted from making the declaration imposed by
9 Geo. 4. c. 17 (which was to be made "on the true faith
of a Christian"), and were thus again enabled to hold
municipal offices, to which before the passing of that
Act they had, together with Dissenters, been admitted
under cover of the annual Indemnity Acts. Twelve
years later, after a considerable struggle, the barrier
against the admission of Jews to Parliament was removed
by st. 21 & 22 Vict. c. 49, which authorised either
House of Parliament, in the case of a Jew otherwise
entitled to sit and vote, to allow the words "upon the
true faith of a Christian" to be omitted from the oath.[1]
The uniform current of legislation in the direction of
removing the religious restrictions on Roman Catholics
suffered in one respect a temporary check. A Papal
brief in 1850, dividing England (in which the Roman
Catholics had previously been under the spiritual supervision of eight vicars apostolic) into one metropolitan and
twelve episcopal sees, led to the passing in the following
year of the Ecclesiastical Titles Act (14 & 15 Vict. c. 60),
which prohibited, under a penalty of £100, the procuring
or publishing of any brief conferring episcopal jurisdiction or title in the kingdom, and the assumption of the
title of bishop or dean of any town or place in the kingdom, by any person not being a bishop or dean of the
Established Church or of the Scottish Episcopal Church.
But the penalty, as years passed on, was not enforced, and
in 1871 was expressly repealed; with a declaration, however, on the part of the legislature, that no ecclesiastical
title, or see, or deanery, can be validly created in the
kingdom, otherwise than by the sovereign, and according
to the laws of the realm, and that the repeal of the
penalty was not to be taken as implying or sanctioning

[1] See further st. 23 & 24 Vict. c. 63.

the contrary. In the years 1867-1868 the oaths and declarations to be taken before admission to civil offices and rights were considerably simplified, and the number of offices and privileges for which anything of the kind is required, was very much diminished; and since 1867 the practice of passing an annual Indemnity Act, to relieve persons who had omitted to take the necessary oaths on assuming office, has been discontinued as unnecessary.

The Lord Chancellorship of Ireland has been expressly thrown open to all persons, whatever their religious opinions; and the same office in England, which was kept specially closed against Roman Catholics in 1829, seems to be now equally open, though the mode in which the law as to oaths and declarations has been tinkered by the various acts on the subject has left this somewhat uncertain. Lastly, in 1871, the Universities Tests Act opened all offices and emoluments in the Universities of Oxford and Cambridge and their colleges to persons of any religious belief; so that at present there appears to be no public position in England, not directly ecclesiastical, for the tenure of which adhesion to a particular religious body or belief is required, except the throne itself, and the office of head or governor of the colleges of Westminster, Winchester, and Eton (see 14 Cha. 2, c. 4, s. 13).

Political Agitation.—With the improved representation of the people in Parliament consequent upon the Reform Act of 1832, and still more on that of 1867, the same reasons have not existed as before for political agitation outside Parliament, by petitions and meetings. Yet the practice has not been altogether abandoned, and its exercise has more than once since 1832 influenced the course of politics and legislation. As examples of this may be mentioned the Anti-Corn-Law League (A.D. 1838-1846), the Reform League previously to the Reform Act of 1867, and the National Education League and National Education Union, with respect to the Education Act of 1870. On the other hand, the Chartist organisation (A.D. 1835-1848), which at one time assumed a threatening attitude, fell to pieces without the attainment of any one of the five points on which its members had insisted. The multiplication of petitions attained its greatest proportions between 1835 and 1850, and has since somewhat diminished. In 1839 the House of Commons was obliged, by the increased pressure of business, to prohibit all debate upon the presentation of petitions; and since that time a record of the petitions has been kept instead.

The Press.—Criticism of the Government and public men, together with invective against their conduct and measures, has been freely permitted since 1832, without fear of State prosecution under the Libel Laws. The dissemination of this criticism and of general news has been greatly facilitated by the reduction and ultimate abolition of the newspaper and paper duties. The advertisement duty was lowered in 1833, and abandoned altogether in 1853. In 1836 concurrently with a remission of a portion of the paper duty, the stamp on newspapers was reduced to 1d., after which the evasions of the duty which had previously been frequent, and had led to numerous prosecutions, wholly ceased; and in 1855, the stamp and the duty were entirely abolished. The paper duty met with the same fate in 1861.

Libel.—The latest alterations in the law of libel have been effected by Lord Campbell's Libel Act (6 & 7 Vict. c. 96). Sect. 6 of that Act allows, on an indictment or information for a defamatory libel, a plea that it was true and that its publication was for the public benefit; and sect. 7 alters the rule noticed above (p. 52), as to the conviction of a publisher for the acts of his servants, by enacting that a defendant may, in all cases, prove that the publication was made without his authority, consent, or knowledge, and did not arise from any want of due care or caution on his part. In 1846, a short Act was passed prohibiting proceedings under stats. 39 Geo. 3, c. 79, and 57 Geo. 3, c. 19, except in the names of the law officers of the crown. In 1869 the restrictive enactments on newspapers and printers were repealed; but the latter are still required to keep copies of papers printed by them, and to print their name and address on every such paper; and are liable to punishment for omission to do so.

Control over the Post.—The practice of opening letters, which has been noticed as prevalent in the 18th century, was expressly sanctioned by the Post Office Act of 1837. In 1844 the exercise of the power, by the detention and opening of the letters of one individual, led to a complaint in Parliament on the subject, and the appointment of committees of both Houses to consider it. These committees recommended that there should be no change in the law, and the Secretary of State consequently retains his authority in the matter.

Aliens.—Fresh provisions for the registration of aliens were made in 1836 by st. 6 & 7 Will 4, c. 11; but they gradually fell into neglect, and in 1844 a considerable improvement in the status of aliens resident in this country was made by Mr Hutt's Act (7 & 8 Vict. c. 66). This Act enabled children of British mothers to hold property of all kinds in the kingdom, and gave to aliens, subjects of a friendly state, full power to acquire and hold all kinds of personal property, except British ships and leasehold property, of which they might not take a lease for more than 21 years. It also facilitated their naturalisation, by confining the formalities of the process to the obtaining of a certificate from the Home Secretary, and taking the oath of allegiance. This naturalisation was to give them all the rights and privileges of British subjects, except the power of becoming a member of either House of Parliament, or of the Privy Council, or any other rights expressly excepted in the certificate. Four years afterwards the disturbed state of Europe, and the apprehension of troubles in connection with the Chartist movement in this country, led to the passing of an Act authorising for one year the Home Secretary in England, and the Lord-Lieutenant in Ireland, to order out of the kingdom any aliens who had been resident within it for less than three years, and the departure of whom he might have reason to think desirable. The power thus conferred was however never exercised, and it was not deemed necessary to renew the Act.

On the other hand, in 1858 we refused to surrender to France for punishment certain persons who had been concerned in Orsini's plot to assassinate the French Emperor, which was concocted in England, and who were shielded by the fact that our law at that time treated conspiracy to murder as only a misdemeanour and not a felony. The strong indignation which this excited in France gave rise to an equally strong feeling in opposition in this country. Lord Palmerston attempted to pass a bill making the offence a felony—a change in the law which was reasonable in itself, and was actually made three years later, when our criminal law was consolidated. But he was now defeated, and his ministry resigned. And when Simon Bernard was indicted for complicity in the murder of two persons who had been the victims of the shells directed against the Emperor's life, the feeling that the proceeding was in reality a political one, and that the right of foreigners to find an asylum in this country was in danger of being compromised, led to the trial being regarded with extraordinary interest, and to the verdict of acquittal being received with tumultuous applause.

The present law as to aliens rests on an Act of 1870 (33 & 34 Vict. c. 14), which enables them to acquire, hold, and dispose of property in the kingdom of every description, except British ships, as fully as natural-born subjects, but without a right to any office or franchise. It further provides simple methods for aliens to obtain naturalisation (which will now entitle them to all political and other rights and privileges, and subject them to all the obligations of natural-born subjects); and also for natural-born subjects to expatriate themselves (a proceeding which in the eye of our law was previously impossible), and afterwards obtain readmission into British nationality. In the same year an improvement was made in the law respecting the extradition or surrender to a foreign state of criminals, who, after committing an offence against its laws, should escape for refuge to this country.

Reserve Forces.—The first germs of a military reserve force were formed by two Acts of 1843 and 1846, which provided for the enrolment of a certain number of out-pensioners of Chelsea Hospital,—men who had served their time in the regular army,—as a local force to aid the civil power in the preservation of the peace; with liberty to volunteer in certain cases for home garrison duty. But in 1859 a real reserve force was created, into which men who had served in the Royal or East Indian army might enlist. It might be called out when occasion required, to aid the civil power, and was also liable to serve for the defence of the realm in case of war or of apprehended invasion; and, when under training or on duty, was to be subject to the Mutiny Act and the Articles of War. In 1867 the Reserve force was

augmented and reorganised (30 & 31 Vict. c. 110); and a
militia reserve was formed, consisting of a certain number
of militiamen voluntarily enrolling themselves, who were
not thereby to cease to be militiamen, but merely became
liable on the outbreak of a war to be immediately drafted
into the army; and when this took place, but not before,
their places in the militia would be filled up. The supply
of men for the Militia has during the late and present
reigns been met by voluntary enlistment, and the provisions for enrolment of militiamen by ballot have been
annually suspended, but they still remain the law of the
land, and would immediately come into force, should
Parliament in any year refrain from renewing the suspending Act. Moreover in this very Act power is reserved
for the Queen in council at any moment to order a ballot,
if a necessity for it should arise. In the winter of 1859
and spring of 1860 the apprehension of a French war
and invasion caused the formation of a volunteer force,
which speedily swelled to considerable dimensions. An
Act for the regulation of the force was passed in 1863
(26 & 27 Vict. c. 65) which placed them, as to the com-
missioning of their officers and for other purposes, under
the direction of the lord-lieutenants of counties, though
the Crown retained a direct control over them in certain
matters. They might be called out for active military
service in case of actual or apprehended invasion of the
United Kingdom. In 1871, st. 34 & 35 Vict. c. 86, s. 6,
provided for the resumption by the Crown of all the
jurisdiction and command over the militia, yeomanry,
and volunteers which had previously been vested in or
exercisable by the lord-lieutenants of counties. These
forces were thus put under the immediate command of
the War Office; and the commissions of the officers in
them were to be granted in the same way as those of

officers in the army. By the same Act (s. 8) volunteers, when training with the militia or regular forces, were subjected to the Mutiny Act and the Articles of War, to which they had by the Act of 1863 been subjected only when on actual military service.

Navy.—The power of manning the navy in time of war by means of impressment has not yet been formally renounced. It was indeed distinctly recognised by st. 5 & 6 Will. 4, c. 24, which limited the time of compulsory service in the navy to 5 years. But the practice is contrary to the spirit of the times, and it can scarcely be doubted that (to use the words of the report of the Commission on the subject in 1859) "the system, as practised in former wars, could not now be successfully enforced." In 1866 the Naval Articles of War were re-enacted with amendments by st. 29 & 30 Vict. c. 109; which also regulated the courts-martial and punishments, and other matters connected with the service. In the same year as the army reserve was established (A.D. 1859), a naval reserve was set on foot; to be composed of volunteer merchant seamen, who on entering the force were to become liable to twenty-eight days' training during the year, and might be called upon to serve for three years, and afterwards for an additional two, if the safety of the country required it.

CHAPTER III.

LOCAL GOVERNMENT.

1. Local Institutions.—The history of our local government presents less continuity than that of any other part of our constitution. In its early form our local system exactly displayed the features which Tacitus describes as presented by the old Teutonic institutions. But the paramount central government, which was established upon the amalgamation of the old independent districts or communities into one kingdom, gradually absorbed all authority into itself; and for the most part our present local institutions are the result of a reaction towards decentralisation, and are emanations from the central government rather than relics of past local self-government.

Early Local Divisions.—The Angles, Jutes, and Saxons came over into Britain in several distinct tribes, each led by a chieftain, who in war, as military commander, bore the title of *heretoga*, and in time of peace performed the duties of *ealdorman* or chief civil magistrate. The territory occupied by each tribe was called a *scira* or shire (and in Latin *comitatus* or county).[1] It was divided into districts called *mægths*, each of which was occupied by settlers united by ties of kindred, who, having fought and conquered together, took up their abode together on the land they had won. Among the old Teutonic tribes, while the executive or administration of affairs was devolved upon the nobles, the whole mass of the people was entrusted with judicial and legislative powers. For the exercise of these powers every defined community, whether large or small, had its *gemot*, or assembly of its freemen; and its chief executive officer, its *gerefa* or *reeve*, was periodically elected by this assembly from among the nobler portion of the community. The existence, therefore, of the *mægth* involved the meeting of a *mægth-gemot* and the appointment of a *mægth-gerefa*. The shire, too, had its *scirgemot;* and subseqently, when the shires became only divisions of a larger state, its *scir-*

---

[1] Although the application of a Latin nomenclature to these old Teutonic institutions is of a later date, it is convenient to notice it when mention of them is first made.

gerefa—shire-reeve or sheriff. For an amalgamation of a greater or less number of shires into one kingdom soon took place; and when this occurred, or when fresh divisions of a kingdom were made, on the model of the old units of territory, and like them called shires, a *scir-gerefa* or *vicecomes* was appoined in each, as the deputy of the king and representative of the central authority, to act side by side with the *ealdorman* or *comes*, whose office perpetuated the memory of the old county independence. It was from the times of this independence, and from the fact that the shire originally consisted of a distinct tribe or community, as well as from the popular character of the assembly, that the scir-gemot derived its name of *folc-gemot* or folkmoot, a name by which it was long known. When the land became permanently settled and portioned out among individuals, and when members of the original families of a district migrated, and strangers came and took their place, it was inevitable that the tie of kindred should give place to that of neighbourhood as the bond of the community. Hence the mægth early disappeared as a recognised institution, and in its place there arose, side by side, four small divisions of the community and territory, owing their origin to different causes:—(i.) The *mark*, *township*, or *vill*, a purely territorial division, which seems to have been the immediate successor of the mægth, and had its *tun-gemot*, and *tun-gerefa*—town-reeve or head-borough. (ii.) The *lordship*, subsequently called the *manor*, consisting of the land of a *hlaford* or *lord*, to whom all the resident freemen were commended (see pp. 5, 6). (iii.) The *parish*, the ecclesiastical division, having as its officers the incumbent, and two church-reeves, or, as they were afterwards called, church-wardens—laymen who were appointed annually either by the incumbent or the parishioners, or one by the incumbent and the other by the parishioners. (iv.) The *tithing*, to the explanation of which it will be necessary to devote a few words.

Tithings.—The main functions of government in a primitive community are not so much legislative as judicial,—the decision of disputes between individuals, and above all the maintenance of the peace and protection of the persons and property of the people by the suppression of outrages and crimes. In order to enlist the active assistance of all in furtherance of this latter object, as well as to secure compensation to the injured parties, our ancestors adopted the principle of making a community responsible for the preservation of the peace within its district, and for the good conduct of all the individuals belonging to it. If any individual was accused of a crime, the community was bound to present him to justice, under penalty of themselves paying the fine to which his crime had rendered him liable. The community, in respect of this joint suretyship for the good behaviour of its members, was called a *frith-borga*. The mægth, as composed of the kindred of the criminal, was naturally, while it existed, the responsible community. Afterwards the responsibility devolved on voluntary associations called *gilds;* and eventually the *tithings* or *decenniæ*, consisting originally, as the name implies, of ten men, were instituted for the express purpose of the mutual liability. One of the ten was chosen head, with the title of *tithing-man, tyenth-heved, frithborge-heved*, or *borsholder*. Besides being required, as stated above, to attach himself to some lord, every freeman, from the age of twelve years and upwards, was bound to be enrolled in a tithing.

Townships.—It is easy to see that the four concurrent divisions mentioned above would naturally tend, in the majority of cases, to coalesce and become conterminous. The parish was generally identical with the lordship; for the great majority of the country churches were built by wealthy landowners for the convenience of themselves and their dependants, and were endowed by them with the tithes of the district under their control, in short, of their lordship; which thus became the parish attached to the church : while they in return received the right of nominating the incumbent. The convenience of having the township of the same dimensions as the parish and lordship would be obvious. And when the tithings in process of time exchanged their original numerical limitation for territorial bounds, they would for the most part be accommodated to the existing divisions. Enrolment in the tithing and commendation to the lord of the township, would take place conjointly. In fact, in some cases the obligation to pay the fine, in case a criminal fled from justice, was transferred from the tithing to the lord. The town-moot would become for many purposes the court of the lord: it would be held under his authority, and the town-reeve would preside as his subordinate. When a lord acquired the jurisdiction over a township, and, as he sometimes did, over a whole hundred, the district was called his *sithessocna*. Again, the office of town-reeve would be united to that of tithing-man. In most cases where there was a resident lord, the right of appointing to the office fell into his hands; but in the townships which were directly under the king, as their hlaford, the freemen retained their old privilege of electing their own magistrate. The duties attached to the office came to be the decision of petty disputes between the inhabitants of the township, and the awarding of amends when one wronged another; the leading of the townsmen to the *fyrd*, the collection of the taxes due from them, and the exercise of a general supervision over them. It was further the business of the town-reeve to attend, with four other inhabitants, for the purpose of representing the township, at the *hundred-gemots* and *scir-gemots*.

Hundreds.—For besides forming part of the shire, the townships were early grouped together into *hundreds*, or, as they were called in the north, *wapentakes;* a further division into *rapes*, *lathes*, or *trithings* (ridings) being sometimes interposed between the hundreds and the shire. Every freeman was required to be enrolled in a hundred as well as in his tithing. Whatever may have been originally the case, the hundred soon lost all connection with the number from which its name is derived. The hundred-gemot was held once every month; and in addition to the town-reeve and four men from each township, was attended by the thegns of the hundred. It was convened and presided over by the hundred-gerefa or hundred-man, and took cognizance of all matters arising within the hundred.

Courts-leet.—Once a year the courts of the lordship and hundred were constituted into courts-leet for examining the frith-borgas, and ascertaining that all the freemen were duly enrolled in them. The sheriff and bishop attended in rotation the courts-leet of the different hundreds; and when they were present, the court was called the sheriffs' tourn. It was natural that all the important business of the lordships and hundreds should be postponed from the ordinary meetings of their courts until the holding of the courts-leet; and it seems that ultimately much of the judicial business which at first came before the sheriff and bishop in the county court was transacted by them in the tourn in the different hundreds.

Shire-moots.—Appeals from the ordinary hundred-gemots, and questions or causes which, as affecting more than one hundred, could not be brought before those

courts, were decided by the shire-gemot, or folk-moot—the
general assembly of the people of the shire, which met
twice a year, and was composed of the bishop, ealdorman
and shire-reeve, the hundred men, with twelve representatives from each hundred, the town-reeves, and four representative men of the townships, and the clergy and other
thegns of the shire. Probably the other freemen of
the county were allowed to be present without the right
of voting.

Ealdormen.—Originally the ealdorman and bishop sat
side by side as presidents of the shire-moot, the former
taking the lead in civil, and the latter in ecclesiastical
matters. Whether or not the prolonged conflicts with
the Danes rendered necessary the separation of the civil
from the military headship of the shires, it is at any rate
certain that the civil position of the ealdormen gradually
gave way to that of the sheriffs, and their duties became
almost entirely confined to leading the freemen of the
shire on military expeditions. And in this office they
were, towards the close of the Pre-Norman period, subordinated to the five *eorls* appointed by the central authority,
among whom the supervision of the kingdom was divided.

Municipal Government.—Such was the nature of
local government in the rural districts. A very similar
arrangement existed in the *burhs* or towns; the burh-
gerefa, or in the case of a seaport town the port-gerefa,
taking the place of the shire-reeve, and the burh-gemot
that of the shire-moot. The principal towns, and particularly London, early received peculiar trading privileges
and rights of self-government, and their affairs were
regulated by special laws and customs.

Encroachments of the Central Authority.—After
the establishment of a central government, its natural tendency was to encroach more and more upon the local

institutions, making laws which would override the resolutions of the scir-gemots, and deciding causes properly cognisable by them. This tendency to increase the central at the expense of the local authority, and therefore the power of the king and nobility at the expense of that of the people, received a strong and constant impetus from the exposure of England to the continued attacks of the Danes. It was necessary, as it always must be in a time of war, particularly of war within the country, to sacrifice private rights and privileges for the sake of the community at large, and to invest the central authority with a power which is incompatible either with full personal liberty or with a powerful local autonomy.

2. Effects of the Conquest.—The introduction of feudalism, and the immense power and influence which under that system a noble could acquire over his sub-tenants and the rest of the people dwelling on his estates, gave rise to a danger that in England, just as on the continent, the nobility might grow strong enough to defy the king, and the mass of the people might be led astray from their paramount duty to the sovereign, by the nearer demands of allegiance to their local lords. It was, doubtless, a sense of this danger which induced the early Norman kings to attempt to neutralise the power of the barons, by preserving to a certain extent the old English local institutions which were favourable to the independence of the people at large. It is true that, in furtherance of the ecclesiastical policy of Rome, William I. authorised the bishops to hold courts of their own, and prohibited them from sitting in the shire-moots and hundred-moots, thereby much diminishing the importance of those assemblies. Moreover, for the sole benefit of himself and those to whom he granted his forestal

privileges, he introduced the galling forest laws, and
established the forest courts in the extensive districts
which were laid waste for the royal hunting grounds. In
those districts verderors and regarders were appointed,
who, with the stewards of the forest, held courts of
wood-mote and *swein-mote* (at the latter of which, it is
true, the swains and freeholders within the forest were
the judges) for inquiring into any injury to the sward and
timber or deer of the forest, or any evasion of the laws
which prohibited the keeping of arms or dogs other than
mastiffs as house-dogs within the district, and required
the expeditation or maiming of the fore-feet of all the
mastiffs, to prevent their chasing the deer. In other
respects, however, the Conqueror and his sons retained
and confirmed the old laws as codified under Eadward the
Confessor; and under these laws the holding of the old
courts and assemblies of the people was continued. But so
far was it from being possible to rely on these for resisting
the growing influence of the barons, that they speedily fell
almost completely under that influence. The political
organisation of the township, and to a great extent that
of the hundred also, became practically subject to the
feudal lord of the land within the one and the other
respectively. The township was merged in the *manor*,
the tun-gemot being superseded by the *halimote* (hallmoot or court baron), the court of the lord of the manor,
at which he or the steward, his deputy, presided. The
freemen or tenants of the manor assisted as judges in this
court. It was held every three weeks; and, besides the
determination of disputes as to rights in the land of
the manor, questions of debt, and of injury to person or
property, where the amount involved was less than 40s.,
might be tried in it. As the customary court of the
manor, it was also the tribunal for all matters connected

with the lord's villeins and the demesne land occupied by
them; but in these matters the freeholders, though present,
had no voice. Moreover, in places where the franchise or
liberty of holding such a court had been granted to the lord,
it once a year formed the court-leet, where the frith-borgas,
at this period called frankpledges, were examined, oaths
of allegiance and fealty were taken to the king and the
lord, inquiries were held into nuisances, violations of
boundaries, rights of way and water, false measures, treasure-trove, and thieves and idlers within the district, and
various other local matters were transacted. In other cases
the court-leet was annually held in the hundred-gemot,
or hundred-court, which was similar in its powers and
procedure to the court-baron, but was held for the whole
hundred instead of a single manor. Its presiding officer,
the hundreder, was now a deputy of the lord of the
hundred, and farmed the office from him for the sake of
its emoluments. But the hundred-courts gradually fell
into disuse, their business being transferred to the shire-
moot or, as it came to be called, the county court, which
was thenceforth held once every lunar month, like the
old hundred-courts, instead of only twice a year. The
control over this court, too, fell in many cases into the
hands of the barons. For the bishop, who might have
formed an element of independence, had been withdrawn
from it, and the office of sheriff, the chief county magistrate,
had in not a few shires become hereditary; and assisted
by his subordinate officers, the constables and bailiffs, this
magistrate often wielded his powers in a manner equally
regardless of the king's authority and of the liberties and
rights of the common people.

Counties Palatine.—In a few cases the Crown itself
sanctioned and augmented the local political power of the
nobility by the creation of *counties palatine*, the lords of

which had full royal rights within them. They might pardon treasons, murders, and felonies; they appointed all judges and justices of the peace; all writs and indictments ran in their names, and all offences were said to be done against their peace. The object of creating these counties palatine seems originally to have been the protection of the frontiers exposed to invasion. William I. founded three—Durham, Chester, and Kent. Of these the first and the last belonged to bishops, and therefore did not add to the power of the barons; and the earldom of Chester, to which the second was attached, was united to the crown by Henry III. Royal rights over the Isle of Ely, with full criminal and civil jurisdiction, were granted by Henry I. to the Bishop of Ely; and Pembrokeshire and Hexhamshire (which is now united to Northumberland) were also made counties palatine.

Franchises.—It was further not unusual to grant to a seignory or lordship, whether a manor or a hundred, special liberties or rights of trying and punishing resident offenders and persons committing offences within it, beyond what the common law allowed. The statute book of Edw. 1 contains many enactments directed against excesses and abuses in the exercise of these private jurisdictions or franchises.

Control of the Crown.—But the barons, powerful as they were, never succeeded in wholly excluding the king from interference in local matters. His position as their feudal lord and as owner of crown lands in many of their counties, gave him a footing for exercising his authority. His court and council continued to be the supreme court of appeal from the local tribunals; and as early as Hen. I's reign the latter were brought more directly under the control of the king by the union of several counties under one of the king's judges or justices, who made a circuit in his assigned district for the purpose of arranging the assessment and collection of the king's revenues. Henry II. went much further in the same direction. Besides destroying many of the baronial castles, and deposing sheriffs who had abused their office, he limited the power of the barons by several new political institutions. One of these, the establishment of regular circuits of the king's judges throughout the country, not only for fiscal but also for judicial purposes, formed a crisis in the history of our local judicature, resulting eventually in its virtual extinguishment, and the almost entire subjection of the whole country to the one central judicial system, which will be described in ch. viii.

Decline of the old Courts.—A decrease, in fact, very rapidly took place in the importance of the old local courts. The statute of Marlborough or Marlbridge (52 Hen. 3), in 1267, exempted the clergy and nobility from attendance at the sheriff's tourn and leet, and thus necessarily deprived that tribunal of much of its importance. The power of removing all causes from the courts baron and hundred courts, and trying them before the justices on circuit (see ch. viii.), caused the jurisdiction of these courts to fall gradually into disuse. Nor did the county court itself maintain its original prestige. Before the Conquest it had sustained a blow in the neglect of the ealdorman to attend it, and the devolution of his duties upon the sheriff. The Conqueror had inflicted upon it another by excluding the bishop. And when the king's justices came on their circuit into the county, they claimed, as their peculiar province, the determination of all pleas of the crown, matters in which the king's revenues or authority were interested. Magna Carta confirmed this claim, and expressly prohibited sheriffs, constables, coroners, and bailiffs from holding pleas of the Crown. But, on the other hand, it contained a clause restraining the removal of suits respecting land into the king's courts; and even after the civil jurisdiction of the justices in eyre became settled, the county court continued able not only to try real actions or suits respecting land, but also to hold pleas of debt or damages under the value of 40s.; and might even entertain all personal actions to any amount, by virtue of a special writ called a *justicies*, which empowered the sheriff, for the sake of despatch, to do the same justice in his own county court as might otherwise be had at Westminster. Moreover, the county court of course remained for many purposes the general assembly for the transaction of county business. All Acts of Parliament at the end of every session were wont to be there published by the sheriff; all outlawries were there proclaimed; all popular elections at which the freeholders had votes—as of sheriffs, coroners, verderors, and knights of the shire—were made in full county court. The great changes brought about by the establishment of the circuits must, like the other alterations which took place during the period between the accession of Hen. 2 and that of Edw. 1, be looked upon as having conferred a substantial benefit on the people at large. It is true that in the local courts the freeholders were theoretically themselves the judges; the duty of the sheriff, or other presiding officer, being merely to superintend the proceedings and carry the decisions of the court into execution. But the same freeholders who had composed the county court were summoned to attend the courts of the king's justices; and in these courts, while they were freed from the undue influence of powerful lords which had biassed their decisions in the local courts, that share in judicial functions, which they had of old possessed, was reserved to them by the mode in which Henry II. appointed that causes should be brought before and tried by his justices—a mode which will be described in ch. viii., and of which it is enough to say here that it contained the germs of both our grand jury and our common jury.

The Charters.—The Great Charter contained provisions for an inquiry by twelve sworn knights of every county into the evil forestal customs, and customs as to the jurisdiction of sheriffs and river wardens, which might have sprung up there; and for disafforesting recently made forests, and so reducing the limits of the districts subject to the despotic forest laws: and a prohibition of any increase in the customary liability of a district or its inhabitants to make and repair bridges under the old *trinoda necessitas*. The Forest Charter further limited the forests and the jurisdiction of the forest courts, and regulated the mode of procedure in the latter.

Coroners.—In the course of carrying out the process of judicial centralisation an important political right was conferred on the people. In order to insure that pleas of the Crown were brought before the king's justices, it was deemed expedient in the reign of Hen. 2, or of his successor Ric. 1, to constitute a new county office, that of *coroner*, who was so called from his having to deal with those pleas. The lord chief justice of the King's Bench was, by virtue of his office, chief coroner throughout the kingdom; but in each shire county coroners, usually four in number, consisting of three knights of the shire and a clerk, were to be elected by all the freeholders of the county in the county court. This was the earliest revival of the practice of real popular election which every change up to this time had tended more and more to banish from the constitution. In 1275 the habit of electing to the office persons of insufficient qualifications rendered it necessary to enact that they should be chosen

from among the most loyal and wise knights of the shire
(3 Edw. 1, c. 10;) and in the following year the duties
of the office were regulated by statute. The coroners
were to hold inquiries when any one was slain or wounded,
or drowned or died suddenly, or when houses were
broken into; and the murderers or persons found guilty
of violence in the matter inquired into were to be
delivered to the sheriff and committed to gaol or bailed
till the coming of the judges. They were also to inquire
into cases of treasure-trove or of wreck, both of these
species of property being royal perquisites.

Sheriffs.—Nor was the creation of a royal officer
deemed sufficient to limit the power which the barons
exercised through the office of sheriff. Henry II. attacked
the hold they had obtained on that office by displacing
the sheriffs in many counties, and appointing lawyers and
soldiers instead of local lords to fill it. The assize of
1194 prohibited the sheriffs from acting as justices in
their own counties, and in the latter part of Edw. 1's reign
an Act was passed granting to the people the election of the
sheriff where the shrievalty was not hereditary, and thus
assimilating the appointment of sheriffs to that of coroners.

High Constables.—In the same reign a new local
office was established, the holders of which were to be
directly responsible to the king's justices. Two high
constables were to be chosen in every hundred and franchise to see that the inhabitants were duly armed, and that
strangers, for whom no security was given, were not harboured in upland districts, and to report defaulters to
the justices (13 Edw. 1, *Stat. Wynton.* c. 6).

Borough Charters.—The existence, before the Conquest, of *burhs* or boroughs, with a peculiar organisation
and officers of their own, has been already noticed. These
boroughs (including *cities*) were not handed over by the

Conqueror to his barons with the counties in which they were situate, but were retained by him as part of his own demesne, or specially granted to some lay or spiritual noble. The lord, whether king or noble, required from the burgesses an annual rent besides various dues and customs, and, to insure punctual payment to himself, generally farmed out these revenues, like those of the hundreds, for the highest price he could get. The man who paid this price became, under the title of bailiff, chief magistrate of the borough in lieu of the old borough-reeve or port-reeve, and used the powers delegated to him by the lord for the oppression and extortion of the inhabitants. The object of the lord, however, being to derive as much profit as possible from the borough, he was easily induced, on payment of an adequate sum, to grant a charter of liberties and privileges to the burgesses either in perpetuity or for a limited period, thus restoring their self-government in whole or in part. The plan was also generally adopted of farming out the boroughs to the burgesses themselves, as being more conducive to their own contentment and prosperity, and equally profitable to the lord. In such cases they were said to hold their town in fee farm. One of the earliest of such arrangements is extant in the charter granted by Henry I. to the citizens of London. By that charter he granted to them the county of Middlesex to farm in perpetuity for three hundred pounds, with the privilege of appointing their own sheriff and justiciary, and exemption from the jurisdiction of any other, and from liability to be impleaded without the walls of the city. They were also to be relieved from the payment of *scot* and *lot*, *Danegeld*, *murder-money*, and various custom-duties, and from the obligation to accept *trial* by *battel*. They were also to have their weekly *husting-courts*, their *wardemotes*, and their *folk-motes*, from which there was to be no removal of suits into the king's courts. Other borough charters were granted in Hen. 1's reign; but they were almost all superseded by those of the time of Hen. 2 and his sons, which conferred increased privileges, extending eventually to the right of the burgesses to choose annually their own mayor or chief officer. This right was accorded to London by a charter of John in 1215. In some cases, as a special favour, the king granted to a corporate town the additional privilege of being a county of itself, governed by its own sheriffs and other magistrates, and wholly independent of the surrounding rural county. The Great Charter (c. 13) confirmed to the city of London, and all other cities, boroughs, towns, and harbours, the enjoyment of their liberties and free customs.

Special Jurisdictions.—It would be beyond the scope of the present work to notice certain special jurisdictions which prevailed in particular places or districts, such as the Cinque Ports, with the two ancient towns (Winchelsea and Rye), and their members (i. e., districts attached to them), possessing their courts and lord-warden; and the Stannaries in Cornwall, with not only courts but also a local Parliament.

3. Sheriffs.—In 1315 the right of choosing their own sheriffs was withdrawn from the county freeholders, and the appointment of sheriffs and hundreders was vested in the chancellor, treasurer, barons of the Exchequer, and judges. The persons appointed were to have sufficient land in the shire to answer to the king and the people, and were not to lease their office to another; the sheriffs were not to be the stewards or bailiffs of a great lord, and the hundreds were to be farmed out at such a reasonable rent as would not render necessary any extortion on the people (9 Edw. 2, st. 2). In the following reign the

tenure of the shrievalty was limited to one year, and the
morrow of All Souls' Day and the Exchequer were fixed
as the time and place of the annual election. The mode
of appointing sheriffs thus prescribed has continued substantially the same down to the present day.

Parish Constables.—About the reign of Edw. 3
ramifications of the recently-created military organisation
of the counties and hundreds (see p. 83) were extended
into the different townships by the appointment in each
of a *petty* or *parish constable*, to act under and assist the
high constable of the hundred. He was to be chosen at
the court-leet of the township; and in general the office
of petty constable, and the old one of head-borough or
tithing-man, were filled by the same person.

Justices of the Peace.—The office of justice of the
peace, which was destined to occupy the most prominent
place in our local administration, was established on a
definite and permanent basis in the reign of Edw. 3.
Even before that time there had been occasionally
appointed local conservators of the peace, independently
of those who, like the sheriffs, coroners, and others, were
such by virtue of their office. And the agitated condition
of the country, which followed upon the deposition of
Edward II., gave rise to a distinct enactment by the king
and Parliament that in every county good and lawful men
should be assigned or appointed to keep the peace (1
Edw. 3, st. 2, c. 16). These conservators of the peace
were a few years later invested with judicial powers, and
their position and duties were gradually defined during
the reigns of Edw. 3 and his successors. In every county
there were to be assigned by the king's commission, for
the keeping of the peace, one lord and three or four of the
most worthy of the county, with some learned in the law.
Their numbers quickly became unduly increased, but

were limited, in Ric. 2's reign, to eight in each county, who were required to be residents in the county, and to possess lands of the annual value of £20. They were authorised to imprison and punish rioters and offenders, to arrest and imprison vagrants, and take security for good behaviour from persons of bad character; to hear and determine felonies and trespasses at the king's suit; and to enforce the laws as to labourers (see p. 21). They were assisted in their duties by a subordinate officer, called the clerk of the peace of the county. They were to hold their sessions four times a year, and oftener when needed, with 4s. a day as wages, and 2s. to the clerk of the peace. The sessions were to be held before *two* justices at least; and it became the practice to insert in the commissions what was called, from its opening word, the *quorum* clause, specifying certain of the justices by name, and requiring that at least one of these, who were called justices of the quorum, should be present. The power given to the justices in Ric. 2's reign of summarily arresting rioters and detaining them in prison without bail until the next assizes, was petitioned against by the commons. And doubtless their authority was in many cases no less abused than had been the special jurisdictions granted to the lords of certain manors and districts. In fact, in the following reign we find an Act which complained that divers constables of castles were assigned to be justices of peace by the king's commissions, and by colour of the said commissions took people to whom they bore ill-will and imprisoned them within the said castles till they had made fine and ransom with the said constables for their deliverance; and the Act declared that none should be imprisoned by any justice of the peace, but only in the common gaol; saving, however, to lords and others who had gaols, their franchise in this respect.

Custos Rotulorum.—Contemporaneously with the office of justice of the peace was instituted that of custos rotulorum, or keeper of the rolls and records of the county, who was always a justice of the quorum as well, and was deemed the highest civil officer of the county. Previously to 1545 he was appointed by the lord-chancellor, and had the right to appoint the clerk of the peace; and persons wholly unfit in point of learning and integrity had held those offices without liability to be removed; a state of things which caused miscarriages in the administration of criminal justice, and frauds in the transfer of landed property in the county. To remedy these evils, st. 37 Hen. 8, c. 1, enacted that the custos rotulorum should, except in counties palatine, be appointed by the king's sign manual, and hold office during the king's pleasure, and that he should appoint the clerk of the peace to continue during his own tenure of office or during good behaviour; and empowered either officer to perform his functions by a competent deputy.

Power of the Central Authority.—The effect of the new county institutions which have been noticed, as dating from Edw. 3's reign, was rather to bring under the king's control, than to diminish, the paramount influence of the nobility and great landowners in local affairs. The independent franchises of the lords were, where they existed, always reserved to them by the statutes which gave authority to the justices of the peace. And Edward III. even established a new local sovereignty by making Lancashire a county palatine under the Duke of Lancaster; but from the time that Henry IV. ascended the throne, the duchy was always held with the crown, and was permanently united to it on the accession of Henry VII.

Municipal Government.—The encroachment of individuals upon popular rights, which had already taken place in the local county courts, gradually extended itself to the municipal institutions of the boroughs. At first, after the grant of their charters, the whole body of burgesses elected their mayor or other chief officer, and assembled in person for the transaction of business. But as commerce and the size of the towns increased, and the number of the burgesses became augmented by the admission of persons connected with the town by birth, marriage, apprenticeship, or trade, and others to whom the right of being a burgess was given or sold, the more convenient practice of representation was introduced for municipal, as for parliamentary government. The most wealthy and influential inhabitants being chosen as the governing body or town council, gradually usurped the privileges of the inferior townsmen, assumed all municipal authority, and substituted self-election for the suffrages of burgesses and freemen. In spite of many struggles, the change had, at the close of the 15th century, been successfully accomplished in a large proportion of the corporations of England. In those in which it did not take place spontaneously, it was effected by the grant from the Crown of a charter either conferring or reviving the privilege of returning members to Parliament, and at the same time vesting all powers of municipal government in the mayor and town council,—nominated in the first instance by the Crown itself, and afterwards self-elected. Charters of this kind were granted by the Tudor sovereigns, and by many of them the governing body thus appointed was entrusted with the exclusive right of returning members to Parliament. And in order to bring municipalities under the direct influence of the Crown, a high steward was often appointed. The office was usually filled by a nobleman who became the patron of the borough, and dictated the members to be returned by it to Parliament.

4. Local Rates.—About the time of the Reformation, a new and important feature was introduced into local administration. This was the imposition of an organised local taxation in the shape of rates. The county rate appears in the mode prescribed in 1530 for the repair of bridges. These had previously to that time been repairable by the hundreds or parishes; but the repairs were now thrown upon the county at large, and the justices were empowered to convene the constables or two of the inhabitants of every town and parish in the shire, and with their assent to tax all the inhabitants for the repair of the bridges. Two collectors of the tax were to be appointed in each hundred, and two surveyors of bridges in each shire. A similar provision was at the same time made for the repair of bridges in cities and towns corporate (22 Hen. 8, c. 5). In the following year the imposition of another local rate was authorised. St. 23 Hen. 8, c. 5, empowered the lord-chancellor, lord-treasurer, and the two chief-justices to issue commissions in the king's name to commissioners of sewers in certain districts which, owing to the encroachments of the sea or the want of proper drainage of the land and outlets for the river water, were suffering from inundations. The commissioners were entrusted with ample powers for remedying the evil, and were authorised to levy rates on the owners of land in the district for which they were appointed, in order to meet the expenses incurred by them in the discharge of their duty.

Justices of the Peace.—Besides the new powers given to the justices in reference to the county rates, a further important step was taken in the reign of Hen. 8 towards consolidating their authority. In 1542 an Act was passed which, after reciting that certain laws as to vagabonds, gamesters, victuallers, innkeepers, and others, had up to that time been very negligently enforced, required the justices of counties to divide themselves into districts with at least two justices to each district. The justices of each district or division were to hold a sessions every quarter in addition to the quarter sessions, and were authorised at such divisional sessions to try offences against the above-mentioned laws, and also to correct the lists of jurymen (33 Hen. 8, c. 10). Such was the origin of *petty sessions*, the jurisdiction of which was thenceforward continually increased by new statutes giving additional powers to divisional justices either at their ordinary sessions, or at special sessions to be held by them for the purpose specified in the particular Act which gave the authority.

Highways.—The measure for the repair of bridges was followed not long afterwards by another for the repair of highways. But the liability to this latter duty was continued in the parishes, and its due performance was provided for, not by taxation, but by obligatory labour. By st. 2 & 3 Ph. & Mar. c. 8, two inhabitants were annually to be appointed surveyors of highways in every parish at a meeting convened by the constables and church-wardens; who were also to appoint four days between Easter and Midsummer, when the parishioners, according to their means, were either to furnish horses and carts, with labourers and implements, or were themselves to work on the road with their own tools. This requirement was called *statute duty*, and its neglect was to be punished by the stewards of the courts-leet by fines, which were enforceable by the bailiff and high constable of the hundred.

Poor Law.—But the importance of the measures as to bridges and highways is insignificant compared with that of another element of our local organisation which dates from the same period. Upon the dissolution of the

monasteries, which had up to that time alleviated distress
in an irregular manner by the distribution of alms, it
was deemed necessary to establish in their place a civil
machinery for the relief of the poor. St. 22 Hen. 8, c.
12, accordingly required all beggars and vagrants—both
the aged and impotent, and also the able-bodied—to
repair to the place of their birth: and St. 27 Hen.
8, c. 25, directed the authorities in all cities, counties,
towns, and parishes to maintain by voluntary alms the
aged and impotent poor coming there as required by
the former Act, and to set the able-bodied to work;
and imposed a punishment on beggars, and persons
refusing to work when able to do so. And the clergy
were to exhort their people to give alms for the purposes of the Act. This Act was followed in the same
and the succeeding reigns by other ineffectual measures
for the relief of the deserving poor, and the suppression
of rogues and vagabonds, as they were called; until at
length in 1601 st. 43 Eliz. c. 2, was passed, which is the
foundation of our modern poor law. It provided for
the appointment in every parish of overseers of the poor,
consisting of the churchwardens, and from two to four
householders, nominated annually by justices of the neighbourhood. These overseers were required to levy a rate
upon the landed property in the parish, and apply the
money so raised (1) in setting to work indigent children,
and able-bodied persons who were without employment and
means of subsistence; and (2) in relieving the impotent,
blind, aged, and other poor who were unable to work,
and had no parents, grand-parents or children able to support them. If any parish was unable to furnish the
money for these purposes, the justices might raise it out
of any other parish within the hundred. The Act gave
an appeal against the rates to the justices in quarter ses-

sions, who might also, if the resources of the hundred failed, impose a rate to supply the deficiency out of another part of the county, and might likewise, out of the rates imposed by them, erect houses of correction for rogues and vagabonds. The overseers were further empowered to put out pauper children as apprentices, and, with the consent of the lord of the manor, to build houses for the reception of the poor on waste land in the parish. The powers which the Act gave to rural justices were to be exercised in boroughs and cities by the mayors, bailiffs, and other head officers.

During the half century which followed the passing of the Act of 43 Eliz., its provisions were in some places very imperfectly carried out, and, where this was the case, the poor were reduced either to perish of want, or else to migrate to another parish where the law for their relief was better observed. This migration, of course, imposed a heavy and unfair burden upon the well-regulated parishes, and its evils appear to have been especially felt in London and Westminster. Accordingly in 1662, st. 14 Cha. 2, c. 12 provided that within forty days after the coming of any person to settle in a parish in a house under the yearly rent of £10, he might, by an order of a justice on complaint of the churchwardens or overseers of the parish, be removed back to the parish in which he was born or was last settled for at least 40 days, subject to an appeal from all such orders to the justices in quarter sessions. Thus was imported into the poor law the doctrine of *settlement*, upon which, as upon other details of the law, a vast amount of legislation and litigation has since taken place. It was also enacted that, in the city and metropolitan boroughs, there should be corporations and workhouses for the relief of the poor.

Decline of old Institutions.—The Act of Cha. 2 just cited furnishes a striking illustration of the disuse into which the old local courts and organisations had then fallen, and of the manner in which they were superseded. Under the early laws against rogues and vagabonds important duties had been devolved upon the parish constable; and this Act, after complaining that the want of due execution of these laws had been sometimes owing to want of officers, by reason of the lords of manors not keeping courts-leet every year for appointing them, proceeded to authorise two justices to fill up temporarily a vacancy in the office of constable, head-borough, or tithing-man in any parish until the lord should hold a court, or until the next quarter sessions; and the person whom the justices in quarter sessions should confirm in the office or appoint to it, was to remain in it until the holding of a court-leet. Similarly the high constables, originally appointed at the courts-leet of the hundred or franchise over which they were to preside, were, when those ceased to be regularly held, appointed by the justices at quarter sessions.

The same tendencies towards an extension of the influence of the crown or central authority, and an augmentation of the power of the wealthier or more influential few at the expense of the mass of the community, which were previously in progress, continued after the Reformation. The counties palatine, with the exception of the two in the hands of the Crown, those of Chester and Lancaster, and the episcopal palatinate of Durham, were abolished during the 16th century; and in the reign of Edw. 6 or of Mary the power of the Crown in the counties was strengthened by the establishment in each county of a new office—that of lord-lieutenant, who was appointed directly by the Crown, and was entrusted with the supreme military command in the county. As among the early English tribes, it was frequently the case that the same individual was aldorman and heretoga, so now the post of lord-lieutenant and the civil office of custos rotulorum were often held by the same nobleman. The attempt made by Charles I. and his advisers to revive the old forest laws and jurisdiction of the Crown over rural districts, which had long ceased to be subject to them, met with signal failure; but the policy of subjecting boroughs to the control of the Crown through the medium of high stewards, which has been noticed as adopted by the Tudor sovereigns, was continued until the Revolution; the last two Stuarts invading the liberties of the few corporations which then still retained a popular constitution. Moreover, the administration of parochial affairs in many places passed out of the hands of the whole body of rated parishioners into those of a few inhabitants self-elected and irresponsible, who were termed a *select vestry*, and as such imposed and administered the parochial rates, and exercised all parochial authority. On the other hand, an important step in the popular direction was effected by the abolition, which took place immediately after the Restoration (see p. 27), not only of the feudal tenures, but also of the court of wards and liveries, in which matters connected with those tenures had been decided, and which had afforded facilities for undue interference and oppression on the part of the king and the other feudal lords.

5. **County Rates.**—Towards the close of Will. 3's reign the justices of each county were empowered to levy a rate for the erection and repair of gaols within the county (11 Will. 3, c. 19), and early in the following reign the absolute power of fixing the rate for the repair of bridges was given to the justices in quarter sessions (1 Ann. c. 12).

Up to the year 1739 the prison rate and bridge rate, the county poor rate to make up deficiencies in destitute districts, and some other county rates which the justices in quarter sessions had been by various acts empowered to levy for building houses of correction for rogues and vagabonds, relieving poor prisoners and setting them to work, and kindred purposes, had all been levied separately —a system productive of great expense and inconvenience, and in many cases, absolutely impossible to work. To remedy this, the justices were empowered by st. 12 Geo. 2, c. 29, to make one general county rate sufficient to answer all purposes, which was to be defrayed out of the poor rate, and paid by the churchwardens and overseers of each parish to the high constable of the hundred, and by him handed over to a county treasurer appointed at the quarter sessions. Where there was no poor rate, the Act required the parish constable to collect the county rate and pay it to the high constable; but by a later Act (55 Geo. 3, c. 51) this duty was to be performed by overseers specially appointed by justices.

Lunatic Asylums.—An Act of 1808 added another to the possible items of expenditure, towards which the county rate might be applied, by empowering the justices of the county at quarter sessions to erect, or join with another county in erecting, a lunatic asylum, and to appoint visiting justices for superintending its management. The expense of the asylum was to be defrayed out of the county rate, and the justices might borrow money upon the security of the rate to meet the costs of its erection. This Act was followed by others on the same subject, and at length by st. 9 Geo. 4, c. 40, which repealed all the previous enactments; but even this last statute did not go the length of making the erection of a lunatic asylum obligatory in every county.

Highways.—The liability to the repair of highways was still retained in the separate parishes, but by an Act of 1773 (13 Geo. 3, c. 78) the justices, at special petty sessions held annually for the purpose, were required to appoint for each parish a surveyor of highways for the ensuing twelve months out of a list of at least ten persons drawn up by the constable, churchwardens, and ratepayers of the parish, and submitted to the special sessions for the purpose. Power was given to the justices to control the conduct of the surveyor, and punish him for neglect; and also to enforce the performance of the statute duty, and the proper repair of the highways, and to try and punish offences committed upon them. Besides these powers in reference to parish highways, an Act of the same year, consolidating the laws as to turnpike roads, gave to the justices in quarter sessions and petty sessions—and as to some matters, to a single justice—jurisdiction over various points connected with the management of that class of highways.

Poor Law.—In the period between the Revolution and the Reform Act of 1832, considerable alterations and amplifications took place in the machinery of the poor law. The institution of workhouses and unions dates from 1723, when the churchwardens and overseers of parishes were empowered, with the consent of the vestry, to purchase or hire houses, or contract with any person for the lodging and employment of the poor. Three small parishes might unite in establishing a single poorhouse; and persons who declined to submit to the lodging provided for them were not to be entitled to any relief (9 Geo. 1, c. 7). Sixty years later, Mr Davies Gilbert's Act (22 Geo. 3, c. 83) introduced the office of guardians in parishes where the adoption of the Act was agreed upon by two-thirds in number and value of the owners or occupiers of landed property in the parish assessed to the poor-rate to the amount of at least £5 per annum, or if there were not ten persons in the parish assessed to that amount, then by the same proportion of all the assessed owners or occupiers. Two or more parishes deciding to adopt the Act were authorised to unite for the purpose of carrying out its arrangements. Where the Act was adopted, a paid guardian was appointed for each parish by the local justices, from three persons recommended to them by a meeting of the qualified ratepayers. All the former powers and duties of the churchwardens and overseers with respect to the relief of the poor were then transferred to the guardians, except that of making and collecting the rate. A governor for each poorhouse was to be annually appointed by the justices from persons recommended to them by the parish; and also a visitor of each union poorhouse, in the case of parishes united under the Act. The guardians of such united parishes were to meet monthly, and settle the accounts of the union, and adjust the amount of the expenses to be defrayed by each parish, which was to be proportionate to the average sum paid by each for the relief of the poor during the three years preceding the first monthly meeting. The guardians were empowered to borrow money for the erection of a poorhouse on the security of the poor-rates. They were to send to the poor-house only the aged, sick and infirm, and children, providing them with suitable clothing; were to prosecute idle and disorderly persons, able to work, who neglected to maintain themselves and their families; and were to make provision for the labour of persons willing but unable to get work, applying the wages of such labour towards their maintenance, and making up the deficiency, if any. If a guardian failed in his duty, an order might be obtained from a justice enforcing the performance of it, under pain of a fine. The unions formed under this Act were called Gilbert Unions; but where it was not adopted, the relief of the poor continued to be regulated by st. 9 Geo. 1, c. 7. Various small amendments in the law were, however, made from time to time. Among other things, justices were empowered to visit parish workhouses, and if they were in an improper condition, the matter might be remedied by an order of quarter sessions. Moreover, the entire exclusion of out-door relief was modified for places not subject to the Gilbert Act; the overseers being authorised, with the consent of the vestry or of a justice of the district—and even compelled, upon an order of a justice—to give relief to persons in their homes under peculiar circumstances of temporary illness or distress, or otherwise. And in 1819, an important Act was passed, which empowered the vestry of any parish to establish a *select vestry* of not more than twenty nor less than five substantial householders, for the concerns of the poor of the parish; upon the establishment of which the overseers were to conform to its directions, and, except in urgent cases, give no relief without its order.

Local Courts.—Towards the end of Geo. 4's reign, the quarter sessions of a county were empowered to alter the existing petty sessional divisions and constitute new divisions. This measure was rendered necessary by the great multiplication of the duties assigned to the justices. For it was not in matters of county taxation and administration alone that the powers of justices of the peace were during this period largely increased. Various Acts were from time to time passed, authorising them in petty sessions to try divers small offences in a summary way; so that by degrees the petty sessions was constituted into a court of criminal jurisdiction, from which, in most

cases, an appeal to the quarter sessions was permitted.
At the same time, the kind of tribunal resorted to for the
decision of small civil matters was undergoing a change.
As late as Edw. 6's reign these matters had usually been
brought before the county courts; and, in order to prevent
the delay of justice, an Act of 1548 (2 & 3 Edw.
6, c. 25) directed that no county court should be
adjourned for longer than one lunar month: but since
that time recourse to them had been gradually becoming
less frequent. One of the chief reasons for this was the
great dilatoriness and expense of proceedings taken in
them; which were liable to be further protracted and
rendered more costly by being removed into the superior
courts on a writ of *pone* or *recordari*, or of false judgment.
The objections felt to the procedure of the county courts
led to the establishment from time to time, in various
towns, parishes, and places, by special local Acts, of
courts of requests or of conscience, for the more easy and
speedy recovery of small debts. The earliest of these courts
was that for the city of London, which was instituted in
1517 by the civic authorities, and the jurisdiction of which
was confirmed by Acts of Ja. 1 and Geo. 2. It was to be
held twice a-week, by two aldermen and four commoners
appointed monthly by the Lord Mayor and aldermen, and
its powers of adjudication were afterwards extended to
debts not exceeding £5. The small debts court, established
in Middlesex by st. 23 Geo. 2, c. 33, took the form
of a special county court to be held by the county clerk,
with freeholders as a jury, at least once a month, in every
hundred of the county, for the trial in a summary way of
causes not exceeding 40s. in value, from which there was
to be no appeal. In order to ensure recourse being had
to the various small debts courts when established, it was
the practice to insert in the Acts under which they were

erected a provision, that a plaintiff having a cause of action for a small matter, for which he might have obtained satisfaction before the newly-constituted tribunal, should forfeit his right to costs if he sued in the superior courts instead.

Municipal Government.—After the Revolution, the rights of municipal corporations were no longer subject to be overridden by stretches of the royal prerogative, but they had come to be regarded as close governing bodies, and had for the most part lost all traces of their original popular character. The charters of George III. favoured the municipal rights of burgesses as little as those of Elizabeth and James I.; and, as a matter of fact, whether by the original charter or by the progress of events, municipal government had become almost universally restricted, either to the town council alone, or to that body jointly with the freemen, who were in a great part its own nominees. The members of the council were in many cases self-elected; they usually held office for life, and took advantage of their position to advance and consolidate their own interests and those of their families. They acted without any sense of responsibility, and their proceedings were generally secret; secrecy being even sometimes enjoined by an oath. To this exclusive municipal power was added, in some boroughs, the enjoyment of exclusive trading privileges, which had an injurious effect upon commerce. The fact that the corporations were the strongholds of parliamentary interest and intrigue secured them from the reforms to which they would probably otherwise have been subjected. As it was, in many places, owing to their mismanagement, important municipal powers were entrusted, under local Acts, to independent trustees or commissioners, in whom the inhabitants had confidence.

Vestries.—It was natural that in parishes, where

select vestries became established (see p. 95), various irregularities should creep into the administration of affairs. One of these, that of transacting business without notice, was remedied by Mr Sturges Bourne's Act in 1818 (58 Geo. 3, c. 69). The same Act effected an important alteration in the mode of voting in the case of those vestries which had remained open. Up to that time every person entitled to attend had enjoyed an equal right of voting, but this Act multiplied the votes of vestrymen in proportion to the value of their rated property; limiting, however, the greatest number to be given by one vestry-man to six votes. The power to appoint select vestries for the administration of the poor-law has been noticed above (p. 99). In 1831, Sir John Hobhouse obtained the passing of a permissive measure (1 & 2 Will. 4, c. 60) for the reform of vestries in populous places; which might be adopted in any town parish, or any rural parish having upwards of 800 rated householders, if a certain majority of the ratepayers voted in favour of it. Upon its adoption, the ratepayers of the parish were thenceforth annually to elect vestrymen and auditors of parish accounts; the vestrymen were to vary in number between 12 and 120, according to the number of ratepayers in the parish, and were to hold office for three years, one-third of their number retiring every year. Few parishes adopted this Act, which had, consequently, a very limited operation.

Preservation of the Peace.—In the preceding year the principle of *plural voting*, introduced by Mr Sturges Bourne's Act, was recognised in the Lighting and Watching Act of 1830, the provisions of which might be adopted by any parish by a majority of three-fourths of the votes of the inhabitants meeting in vestry to consider its adoption; at which meeting the number of votes possessed by each inhabitant was to vary from one to six, according to 'he amount at which he was assessed for the poor-rate. This act was rendered necessary by the inadequacy of the old institution of the parish or petty constables to keep proper watch and maintain the peace in the augmented state of the population. The same cause had already led to the establishment of paid watchmen and constables in many places under local Acts, and in the previous year London and its neighbourhood had been formed by Mr Peel into a Metropolitan Police District, and the old watchmen superseded by a new system of police. In places where the Act of 1830 was adopted a certain number of substantial resident householders were to be appointed as inspectors for three years, with power to levy a watch-rate, which was to be collected, like the poor-rate, by the overseers, and the maximum amount of which was to be fixed by the inhabitants when they decided to adopt the Act. The inspectors were to appoint watchmen, sergeants of the night, and patrols, who were to be sworn in as constables, and were to guard against fires, robberies, and breaches of the peace. The Act also provided for the supply of fire-engines, and for lighting the streets with gas. In 1831 an Act was passed empowering any two justices, in cases of apprehended disturbance, to appoint special constables to assist in maintaining order, and to make allowances to them out of the county rate.

6. **Local Courts.**—The decline of the old forms of local administration, and the erection of new institutions in their place, has proceeded at an accelerated pace since the Reform Act of 1832. In the first place, the anomalies connected with the existence of the remaining counties palatine have now been almost entirely removed. One step in this direction was taken before 1832. For in 1830 the jurisdiction of the court of session of the county palatine of

Chester was abolished, and that county was subjected in all things to the jurisdiction of the superior courts at Westminster. In 1836, the secular authority of the Bishop of Ely over the Isle of Ely was abolished. In the same year the palatine jurisdiction over the county of Durham was taken from the Bishop of Durham, and vested as a separate franchise and royalty in the Crown. It is true that both that county and Lancashire still retain their own Palatine Courts of Chancery and Common Pleas; but the practice and proceedings in those courts have been now made, for the most part, conformable to those of the superior courts of Westminster. Again, the old local courts have been now formally superseded. The trial of suits affecting land in the courts baron, hundred courts, and county courts had, as we have seen, long fallen into disuse. It continued, however, to exist in theory until 1833, when it was taken away by the abolition of writs of right and the other old forms of actions in respect of landed property, and by the substitution of other modes of proceeding which were only admissible in the superior courts. In the same year, however, an attempt was made to reinvigorate the jurisdiction of the county courts in matters of debt. This attempt was abandoned in 1846 in favour of a system of new courts with all the jurisdiction and powers of the county courts for the recovery of debts and damages, the judges of which were to be barristers of experience appointed by the Lord Chancellor, and removable by him for inability or misbehaviour (9 & 10 Vict. c. 95). The establishment of the system in different districts was at first left in the discretion of the Queen in council, but it has now been extended throughout the country. There are at present 58 county court judges, each of whom, at frequent intervals, holds courts at prescribed places within the

district assigned to him; and the total number of places
where such courts are held is upwards of 500. The
judges are assisted by registrars, who transact the more
formal and less responsible part of the business. The
new courts have usurped the title of the old tribunals of
the shire, and are known as *county courts;* no suitors,
however, have any jurisdiction in them. The judge ordinarily decides all questions, as well of fact as of law; but
where the amount in dispute exceeds £5, either party
may require a jury of five to be summoned to try the
action.

The Act of 1846 limited the jurisdiction of the new
county courts to actions or contracts for not more than
£20, or for damages for not more than £5. But their
powers have been much enlarged by subsequent Acts,
and they have now a jurisdiction in common law actions
to the extent of £50, in suits affecting the title to landed
property of which the annual value does not exceed £20,
and in many equity matters to the amount of £500.
Some of them have also been constituted the local bankruptcy courts, and have been entrusted with a limited
jurisdiction in Admiralty and testamentary matters, and
with various other powers. Recourse to the county courts
in matters within their jurisdiction is enforced by the
enactment that a plaintiff who might have resorted to
them, if he sues in a superior court, in many cases loses
his costs even if successful; while, on the other hand,
parties who have a matter in dispute beyond the statutory
jurisdiction of the county court may by agreement procure its trial there. An appeal is allowed from the county
courts to the superior courts, but when the amount in
dispute is small, the leave of the county court judge must
be previously obtained. Upon the establishment of the
new county courts the former jurisdiction of the old

county courts and statutory courts of request as to small debts was to cease. But with regard to courts in respect of which there were private rights, the Act of 1846 merely empowered any lord of a hundred, honour, manor, or liberty, who had any court in right thereof in which debts or demands might be recovered, to surrender to the Crown the right of holding such court in respect of such debts or demands; and from and after the surrender the court was to be discontinued, and the right of holding it to cease, so far as related to the recovery of debts and demands. In 1867, however, it was enacted that no action or suit which could be brought in any county court should be maintainable in any hundred or other inferior court, not being a court of record; and provision was made for the compensation of persons entitled to any franchise or office in respect of these courts, who might be losers by the abolition of their jurisdiction. Manor courts are still held once or twice in the year, but only as customary courts for controlling and registering dealings with copyhold land. And a shadow of the old constitution of the court is maintained by the requirement that the homage or freeholders of the manor shall be represented at its sittings by at least two individuals. The machinery of the new county courts was not at first extended to the city of London, but in 1852 a city of London court for the recovery of debts, damages, and demands not exceeding £50, was constituted in connection with the Sheriff's court in London, with much the same powers, regulations, and mode of procedure as the county courts.

Constables.—The old offices of high and parish constable have also considerably dwindled in importance. In fact the latter, with the attendant pre-Norman office of head-borough or tithing-man, has almost become extinct.

The appointment of high constables was in 1844 transferred from the quarter sessions to divisional special seasions, and an arrangement was made for the cessation of their duties with respect to the collection of the county rates. And in 1869 certain other of their functions were transferred to the clerks of justices; and the quarter sessions were authorised, if they thought fit, to discontinue the office altogether in any hundred of the county. The first direct step towards the abolition of parish constables was made in 1839, when the justices of any county in quarter sessions, if they considered the existing staff of officers for the preservation of the peace in the county to be insufficient, were empowered to appoint a chief constable, who, with the concurrence of two or more justices, might appoint superintendents for the divisions of the county, and any number of petty constables to act under him. The expenses of the force were at first charged on the county rate, but afterwards on a police rate to be levied with the county rate. The establishment of a county police was not to interfere with the right possessed by municipal boroughs to appoint their own constables; but in the following year the justices of any county, and council of any borough, were empowered to agree together to consolidate their constabulary. County justices were also authorised to divide the county into police districts, with a different number of constables in each; the several districts in that case paying for their own constables. It was not at first contemplated that the county constabulary should supersede the old system of unpaid parish constables, for in 1842 an Act was passed requiring justices throughout the county to hold special petty sessions for the appointment of the latter in the parishes of their divisions; the power of appointing them being formally taken away from the courts-leet. It was, however, provided, that where the vestry of a parish desired it, the justices might appoint paid instead of unpaid constables, the expenses of the force being in that case defrayed out of the parochial poor-rate. In other places the persons appointed to be parish constables continued liable to a penalty if they neglected to serve, unless they found a substitute. In 1856, however, the establishment of a county police force was made obligatory throughout the whole of every county in the country, and power was given to the Queen in council to require the division of a county into police districts, and arrange the terms of consolidation of the police of a county and borough; and the development of the county police force which has since taken place has rendered the appointment of parish constables and tithing-men in general unnecessary. It was therefore provided by an Act of 1872 that none should be henceforth appointed for any parish, unless the court of quarter sessions of the county should decide that such appointment was necessary, or unless the vestries of the parish should resolve upon the appointment.

Justices of the Peace.—Since the first establishment of county justices, we have hitherto seen the augmentation of their powers and duties proceeding in an uninterrupted course. But in 1842 the criminal jurisdiction of their court of quarter sessions, which had previously extended to almost every offence (including the most heinous, such as murder), was limited to lesser crimes. With this exception, however, the increase of their powers has continued since the Reform Act. Additional offences have been made triable by summary proceedings at the petty sessions, so that the number of these is now very great. In the Metropolitan Police District, however, and in some of the larger towns, many of their criminal duties have been transferred to police magistrates and other stipendiary magistrates. We have noticed the duties which have been thrown upon them of providing a county police, and taxing the county for the purpose. In respect of providing county lunatic asylums and raising rates for the purpose, their powers and duties have also during Queen Victoria's reign been considerably increased. We shall see further traces of their powers in the other local institutions which it remains to discuss. In one respect their position is unique. They are now the sole non-representative body who have the power of taxing their fellow-countrymen. Considering the large figure at which the county taxation stands, this state of things would not be acquiesced in, were it not for the fact that the justices, being chosen on account of their position and character from among the land-owners of the county, retain the confidence as well as the respect of the whole county. It has, however, since 1860, been deemed desirable that the Imperial legislature should be accurately informed as to the state of county as well as parochial taxation; and, accordingly, all clerks to corporations, justices, commissioners, district and other boards, vestries, inspectors, trustees, and other bodies and persons authorised to levy rates, taxes, tolls, and dues, for the purposes of local government and improvements in England, are required to make an annual return of the amount and expenditure of the sums levied to the Home Secretary, who is to lay an abstract of the returns before Parliament. But the returns of the poor-rate continue as before to be made to the central Poor Law authority.

Municipal Government.—A reconstitution of the municipal corporations followed soon after the Reform Act of 1832. By the Municipal Corporations Act of 1835 (5 & 6 Will. 4, c. 76), the exclusive rights of trading existing in certain boroughs were abolished; and the council of the borough, composed of a mayor, aldermen, and councillors, was thenceforth to be elected by the burgesses, who were to consist of the persons occupying houses and paying rates in the borough. The councillors were to be themselves burgesses, and their term of office was ordinarily to be three years, one-third of their number retiring on every 1st November, when an election was to be held to supply their places. The aldermen were to be one-third of the whole number of councillors, were to be chosen by the latter out of their own body, and while in office were to be exempt from the liability to retire from the council in rotation. They were to hold office for six years, one half of their number retiring every third year. The mayor was to be elected annually on the 9th November by the council from among themselves. The larger boroughs were divided into wards, and the right of electing a certain number of councillors was given to the burgesses of each ward. The burgesses were likewise to elect annually two auditors, and either two assessors for the whole borough, or where there were wards, two assessors for each ward. The council were empowered to appoint a town-clerk, a treasurer, and other officers, and make bye laws for the government of the borough, and were to constitute out of their own body a watch committee, who should have the appointment and control of a body of constables. The expenses of municipal government were to be defrayed out of the income of any corporate property belonging to the borough, the surplus, if any, of such income being devoted for the benefit of the inhabitants and improvement of the borough; while, if the income from this source was inadequate to meet the expenditure, the deficiency was to be supplied by a borough-rate leviable in the borough in the same way as the county-rate was leviable in a county. Nor did the Act omit provision for the local administration of justice in the boroughs. In most cities and towns corporate there had previously been quarter sessions, held before the mayor and resident justices, for the trial of minor offences committed within the municipal boundaries; and in performing their judicial duties these magistrates were usually assisted by a barrister who acted as assessor to the mayor, and was called a recorder. Moreover, in former times sundry special rights of criminal jurisdiction had, by local Acts, letters patent, or charters, been granted to the mayors, bailiffs, aldermen, recorders, and other officers of divers boroughs. By the Act of 1835 these rights were abolished, and the Crown was empowered to appoint separate justices for any borough, either unpaid, or, if the council made a bye law to that effect, with a stipend out of the borough funds; and also, upon a petition from the council, might constitute in the borough a separate court of quarter sessions of the peace, with all the criminal and many of the civil powers of a court of quarter sessions for a county, to be presided over by a barrister of not less than five years' standing as recorder, who was to be *ex officio* a justice of the peace for the borough. The Act extended to those cities and towns which were counties of themselves, as well as to others; but the city of London was exempted from its operation.

Poor Law.—The mal-administration of the Poor Law, always a subject of complaint, had, at the time of the Reform Act of 1832, attained an unprecedented notoriety. Within the preceding fifty years the poor-rate had been quadrupled, and then reached the total annual sum of £8,600,000. At the same time grievous abuses prevailed in the modes of giving relief, partly in consequence of the wide-spread practice, where a Gilbert Union was not constituted, of farming out the lodging and maintenance of the poor to contractors, who made the utmost possible profits out of the transaction, and partly owing to the fact that there was no superior body to keep a watch over and control the proceedings of the parishes and their mismanagement in reference to poor relief. This unsatisfactory state of things led to the appointment in 1833, upon the recommendation of Parliament, of a royal commission to inquire into the subject. On the report of this commission was based the Poor Law Amendment Act of 1834 (4 & 5 Will. 4, c. 76), by which, though its details have been considerably modified by subsequent amending Acts, our system of poor relief has ever since been mainly regulated. It placed the administration of the Poor Law for five years under the control of a board of three Poor Law Commissioners who were to be nominated by the Crown, and were to have power to appoint assistant commissioners, secretaries, and other officers, and to make regulations for the management of the poor, the government of workhouses, and the guidance and control of guardians, vestries, and parish officers, with respect to the relief of the poor. But all regulations made by them were to be submitted for the approval of the Home Secretary, and were to be laid before Parliament at the earliest opportunity. The duration of this board was afterwards from time to time extended till 1847, when it was superseded by a board, consisting of the Lord-President of the Privy Council, Lord Privy Seal, Home Secretary, and Chancellor of the Exchequer for the time being, as well as of other commissioners appointed by the crown, one of whom was to be the president of the board, and was after 1849 a member of the ministry, and after 1859 of the cabinet. This board, to which the title of "Poor Law Board" was afterwards given, was originally established for five years, but by subsequent Acts was prolonged until 1871, when its powers were transferred to the local government board (see p. 118). By the Act of 1834, and subsequent Acts, the board was authorised to require the erection and enlargement of workhouses, into which the able-bodied paupers should be obliged to enter; to consolidate several parishes into one union with a common workhouse, under the management of a joint board of guardians, consisting of the resident justices as *ex officio* members, and of other persons elected by the rate-payers and owners of property in the different parishes; to dissolve or alter the limits of unions; and to direct that in any single parish the poor law should be administered by a board of guardians, constituted in a similar manner to the board of guardians of an union. At the election of guardians owners of property were to have the same number and proportion of votes as provided by st. 58 Geo. 3, c. 69 (see p. 102), and ratepayers were to have one, two, or three votes, according as they were rated under £200, between that sum and £400, or above £400. Wherever a board of guardians was appointed they were to be the sole dispensers of relief, except only that an overseer might give it in case of urgent necessity, and justices might order outdoor relief to the aged and infirm, and medical relief. Masters of workhouses, assistant overseers, and other paid relieving officers of unions and parishes were to be removable by the poor law board, who were also empowered to appoint inspectors to visit workhouses and attend meetings of guardians. The Act of 1834 provided for a proper audit of the accounts of the overseers; and to assist them and the churchwardens in levying the poor-rate the appointment of collectors and assistant overseers has been authorised. By an Act of 1836 (6 & 7 Will. 4,

c. 96), the power of deciding on complaints by individuals against the amount of the rate levied upon them was in the first instance vested in the justices in petty sessions, who were to hold quarterly special sessions for the purpose; but an appeal was permitted from their decision to the quarter sessions. In any union formed by the board the parishes were to contribute to a common fund for the erection and maintenance of the union workhouse, in a proportion calculated upon an average of the annual amount spent by each parish in poor relief during the three years preceding the formation of the union; but each parish was to remain separately chargeable for the maintenance of its own poor, whether relieved in or out of the workhouse. The beneficial effects of the Act of 1834 are shown in the fact, that while relief was in consequence better administered, and the really deserving poor better cared for, the annual expenditure for the relief of the poor was in three years reduced to the extent of three millions. With the great increase that has since taken place in the population and aggregate wealth of the country, it has now risen to nearly the same figure as that at which it stood before the Act of 1834. Though this of course represents a far less heavy burden on the resources of the country than it did then, there is no doubt still room for improvement in the difficult subject of the administration of poor relief.

Highways.—The subject of highways occupied the attention of the reformed Parliament in the same year as that of municipal corporations. By st. 5 & 6 Will. 4, c. 50, provisions were made for the annual election of unpaid or paid surveyors of highways by the vestry of every parish which maintained its own highways. Power was given to the county justices at quarter sessions, or special petty sessions, upon the

application of a parish vestry to constitute two or more
parishes into a highway district, and to select a surveyor
of highways for the district out of persons nominated to
them by the different parishes for the purpose. The Act
also authorised in parishes with a population exceeding
5000, the appointment of a highway board, consisting
of from five to twenty resident ratepaying householders,
who should act as surveyors of highways for the parish,
and might appoint an assistant surveyor, clerk, and
treasurer. Surveyors of highways were to make up
annual accounts, and lay them before their parish vestry,
and before the justices of the division, who were to hold
annually at least eight special petty sessions for the purposes
of the Act, and were invested with many powers
and duties in reference to highways. The old statute
duty for the repair of highways was abolished, but the
ratepayers keeping horses were empowered to agree to
apportion among themselves the labour of carrying
materials for the purpose, for which they were to be paid
after a rate fixed at the special sessions. Since the Act
of 1835 the subject of the local management of highways
has much increased in importance, owing to the gradual
abolition of turnpike trusts and consequent transfer of
those roads to the highway authorities, a process still in
progress: and in 1862 an Act was passed empowering the
justices of a county to divide it into highway districts
under the management of highway boards, consisting of
the county justices residing in the district and of waywardens
elected annually by the parishes within the
district.

Public Health.—Besides the police districts, the poor
law unions, and highway districts already mentioned,
certain further divisions of the county have been made in
recent times for particular purposes. Both before and

since 1832, numerous local Acts have been passed, constituting large towns and their immediate neighbourhoods and other places into districts for specific purposes, such as public waterworks, docks, and harbours, under the regulation of elected and responsible boards. In 1847, the general provisions usually contained in town improvement Acts were consolidated into one Act, which provided for the exercise by the commissioners, trustees, or other authority appointed by the local Act, of divers powers respecting the appointment of a surveyor and inspector of nuisances and officer of health, the maintaining of sewers and drains, the paving, repair, and cleaning of the streets, the prevention of nuisances and other matters, and the levying of rates to defray the expenses incurred.

In 1848 the first step was taken towards the general establishment of a local organisation throughout the country for preserving and promoting the health of the people. An Act of that year (11 & 12 Vict. c. 63), established for five years a General Board of Health, consisting of the First Commissioner of Woods and Forests as president, and two other persons appointed by the Crown, with power to appoint clerks and officers and superintending inspectors. The board were authorised, in their discretion, where a certain proportion of the ratepayers in any place petitioned to that effect, or where the annual death rate was above 23 per 1000, to direct a preliminary inquiry into the sanitary condition of the place, and in case the results of the inquiry justified such a course, to order all or any of the provisions of the Act to apply to the place in question. In any district to which the Act was applied a local board of health was to be constituted. This board was, in the case of municipal boroughs, to be the borough council, and elsewhere was to consist of substantial householders of the district (the number being fixed by the general board), who were to hold office for three years, so that one-third of the board should retire every year, and were to be elected by the ratepayers of the district, who were to vote by signed voting papers, and were to have from one to six votes in the election, according to the value of their rated property. The local boards might appoint surveyors, inspectors of nuisances, medical officers of health, and other officers. Various duties and powers were reposed in them as to maintaining sewers, regulating the erection of buildings, cleansing the streets, removing nuisances, and as to other matters connected with public health. Wherever a local board was formed, they were to be the surveyors of highways within their district. They were empowered to make bye laws, which, however, were not to come into force till approved by the Home Secretary; and the consent of the general board was by the Act made necessary to many of their proceedings. The expenses incurred by them were to be defrayed by rates levied on the same persons and in the same proportions as the poor-rate, an appeal to the quarter sessions being permitted against the rate. They were also empowered to borrow money on the security of the rates. The General Board of Health was continued in existence till 1858, when its powers were transferred to the Privy Council, and in the same year the Public Health Act of 1848 was amended by The Local Government Act 1858 (21 & 22 Vict. c. 98), which allowed the councils in boroughs, the improvement commissioners in places under the jurisdiction of a board of improvement commissioners, and in other places a meeting of owners and ratepayers, to resolve on the adoption of the Act and the consequent constitution of a local board.

Instead of carrying out the principle of local boards of health throughout the country, the legislature, when in 1855 it was deemed necessary to make further provision for the removal of nuisances and prevention of disease, constituted for the purpose, in places where there was no available local authority under any previous Act, a nuisances removal committee, consisting of the surveyor of highways *ex officio*, and of other members chosen annually by the parish vestry. The expenses incurred were, however, to be defrayed not by a new rate, but out of one of the existing local rates.

The Sewers Act of 1833, while regulating the powers of commissioners of sewers, did not alter the districts for which they were appointed under the Act of Hen. 8 (see p. 90); but the Land Drainage Act of 1861 authorised commissions of sewers to be issued for inland as well as maritime districts, and permitted the establishment of drainage districts, with elected drainage boards, who, as respects those districts, were to supersede the commissioners; and ample powers, including that of levying rates, were given to the commissioners and boards.

In 1871 and 1872, the first steps were taken towards simplifying the management of local affairs, particularly in respect of sanitary matters, by reducing the number of the authorities charged with the duty of attending to them. In 1871, st. 34 & 35 Vict. c. 70, reciting that it was expedient to concentrate in one department of the government the supervision of the laws relating to the public health, the relief of the poor, and local government, abolished the Poor Law Board, and established in its place a board, to be called the Local Government Board, consisting of a president, appointed by and holding office during the pleasure of the Crown, and of the President of the Privy Council, all the principal Secretaries of State, the Lord Privy Seal, and the Chancellor of the Exchequer. Its members being all ministers, its composition is entirely altered on a change of ministry. It is empowered, with the sanction of the Treasury, to appoint secretaries, assistant secretaries, inspectors, clerks, and other officers. To it are transferred not only all the powers and duties of the Poor Law Board, but also those of the Home Secretary with reference to the registration of births deaths and marriages, public health, returns of local taxation, drainage, improvement of towns and kindred matters, and those of the Privy Council with reference to vaccination and the prevention of disease. The Public Health Act of the next session (35 & 36 Vict. c. 79) has further transferred to the new board the powers of the Home Secretary and the Board of Trade respecting highways and turnpike roads, bridges, metropolitan water works, and, various other heads of local administration. The Act of 1872 has also entirely reconstituted the various sanitary authorities. The whole country is now divided into sanitary districts; boroughs, and any districts formed under a previous improvement Act and local government districts, being constituted urban sanitary districts; while in other parts of the country the poor law unions are constituted rural sanitary districts. The sanitary authority of the district is the municipal council, the improvement commissioners, the local board, or the board of guardians as the case may be; and to it are intrusted all powers previously vested in the local board, nuisance authority, sewer authority, or local authority under any former Acts. Each sanitary authority is to appoint a medical officer of health; and the rural authorities are also to appoint inspectors of nuisances, clerks, treasurers, and other necessary officers. The rural authorities may at any time delegate their powers for the current year to a committee composed of some of their own members; and may in any parishes within their districts form parochial committees, composed in like manner, with or without the addition of competent ratepayers of the parish. The expenses of the urban sanitary authorities are to be defrayed, where the Local Government Acts are in force, in the manner directed by those Acts, and elsewhere, out of the borough fund or borough rate, or out of the rate leviable by the Improvement Commissioners as the case may be; and those of the rural sanitary authorities are to be defrayed in part out of the poor-rate of the constituent parishes, according to their rateable value, and in part by a separate rate specially levied on the parish or drainage district, for the particular benefit of which an outlay may have been incurred. Provision is made for the appointment by the Local Government Board of special sanitary authorities in ports, and for altering the boundaries of districts, converting a rural into an urban sanitary district, and uniting two or more districts into one, under a joint board, upon application by the district authority. The Local Government Board is also intrusted with the extraordinary power, upon a similar application, of repealing, altering, or amending, with certain few exceptions, any local Acts relating to sanitary matters which may be in force in any district.

Metropolis.—The present local government of the metropolis was organised in 1855. The affairs of each of the metropolitan parishes (exclusive of those in the city) are now managed by a body of vestrymen proportionate in number to the population of the parish, and consisting of substantial ratepayers, who are elected by the ratepayers of the parish, or, where the parish is large and divided into wards, by the ratepayers of the different wards; a certain number of vestrymen being assigned to each ward according to its size. Auditors of accounts are also elected annually for each parish or ward. Some of the parishes are grouped into districts, for each of which there is a board of works composed of members elected by the parochial vestries of the districts. Besides these, there is a Metropolitan Board of Works, composed of members elected by the council of the city of London, by the district boards, and by the vestries of parishes not included in any district. The members of the Metropolitan Board, district boards, and vestries, unless elected to supply an intermediate vacancy, hold office for three years, and one-third of each of these bodies goes out of office annually.

The Metropolitan Board is intrusted with the management of the main drainage of the metropolis, and with the power of making various improvements, and of controlling the action of the district boards and vestries, and is authorised to levy metropolitan rates to defray its expenditure. To the district boards, and the vestries of parishes not included in a district, is committed the branch drainage, and the general control over the buildings, streets, water supply, lighting, and sanitary arrangements of their district or parish, with power to levy local rates to meet the requisite expenses.

Education.—The subject of education, which was originally dealt with exclusively by the central executive, has by recent legislation been brought within the domain of local administration. The matter was first taken in hand by the State in 1834, when a small grant was made by Parliament to aid in building school-houses. The fund was to be distributed by the Treasury, and was to be appropriated, in part to Church Schools through the medium of the National Society, and in part to the schools supported by the British and Foreign Schools Society, in which the religious teaching was of no distinct denominational character. In 1839 Lord Melbourne's Government vested the management of the annual education grant in a committee of the Privy Council, who administered it in aid of schools erected and supported in part by voluntary contributions. Owing to the liberality with which these latter were given, this theoretically imperfect scheme provided to a very tolerable extent for the education of the poor; but in 1870 it was deemed necessary to supplement it by more direct legislation. While the semi-voluntary semi-State-supported system has been left to go on as before, the Elementary Education Act of that year has established by its side a local organisation to supply its deficiencies. The metropolis, the boroughs, and rural parishes are constituted school districts. In every district there is to be provided sufficient accommodation in public elementary schools (including those supported wholly or in part by voluntary efforts) for all the children of the district for whose elementary education provision is not otherwise made. A school board is established in the metropolis, and in every other school district in which the committee of the Privy Council on Education, or, as it is called, the Education Department, authorise its establishment; which they are empowered to do if, after an inquiry and due warning, they find a deficiency of elementary school accommodation in the district, or if an application is made to them for the purpose by the council in case of a borough, or elsewhere by the ratepayers. The department have power to unite two or more school districts into one, or to make one district contribute towards elementary education in another district. The Act of 1870 limited the term of office of members of school boards to three years, at the expiration of which there was to be a new election. The details of the election were left to be settled almost entirely by the Education Department; but it was enacted that in the case of the metropolis members should be elected to represent certain specified divisions, and that the novel practice of *cumulative voting* should be employed, that is to say, each voter should have as many votes as there were members to be elected in his division, and might give them all to one candidate or distribute them among the candidates as he should think fit. The Education Department extended cumulative voting to the election of borough school boards, and while in these it prescribed the use of signed voting papers, it introduced into the elections for the London School Board, except in the city of London, the additional novelty of secret voting. The electors were to be in boroughs the burgesses, in the city of London the persons entitled to elect the Common Council, and elsewhere in the metropolis the body of ratepayers. The School Boards for London and for many of the larger towns were elected at the close of 1870. The boards are to erect and maintain sufficient schools; they may accept the transfer (if made to them by the managers) of schools hitherto supported voluntarily, and may pay the fees of children of indigent parents at voluntarily supported schools.[2] They may also make bye-laws rendering it compulsory on parents to send their children between 5 and 13 years of age to school, unless prevented by good cause. Their expenses are defrayed by the school fees, and the share of the Parliamentary grant which their schools receive; and the deficiency is made up out of the local rates, upon the security of which the board may borrow money for the erection of school buildings.

[2] St. 18 & 19 Vict. c. 34. (Denison's Act) had already authorised guardians to assist persons receiving out-door relief in the education of their children. But this Act had practically remained a dead letter.

Where a school board neglects its duty the Education Department may supersede it by temporarily themselves appointing a new board, or may at once dissolve the board, and direct a new election.

The Act of 1870 provided that the Parliamentary grant should be given in aid of voluntary and board schools alike, but should in no case exceed the amount of the income of the school derived from voluntary contributions, school fees, or other sources. It required that no denominational religious teaching should be given in board schools, and that in them, as well as in other schools receiving the Parliamentary grant, religious observances and instructions should be confined to the beginning or end of school, and no child should be required to attend any religious observance or instruction objected to by the parents; and it at the same time discontinued the examination in religious subjects by the Government Inspectors which had been previously held.

By an Act of 1873, amending the Act of 1870, the granting of out-door relief to poor persons is made conditional upon their sending their children to school; and guardians are required to furnish them with the means of doing so. By the same Act, the method of secret voting, prescribed by the Ballot Act of 1872 (see p. 175), is extended to the elections of all school boards.

PART II.

Constituents of the Central Authority.

CHAPTER IV.

THE KING.

1. Origin of Royalty.—Although the kingly office was not at the time unknown among the Teutonic tribes on the Continent, the various bands of Angles, Jutes, and Saxons appear to have settled in this country under the leadership of a *heretoga* as chief military commander, and an *ealdorman* as highest civil magistrate; the same individual in many cases holding both offices. Very soon, however, owing perhaps to the increase of dignity and power which would accrue to the leader from the very act of conquest, we find the heads of the principal tribes assuming the title of king. As the name seems to imply,[1] the individual holding this position was from the first looked upon as the representative of the whole nation,

---

[1] "*Cyning*, by contraction *king*, is probably closely connected with the word *cyn* or *kin*. ... The king is representative of the race [or kin], the embodiment of it in its national being; the child of his people, and not their father." Freeman's "Norman Conquest," I. 82. Others, however, like Carlyle (see "Heroes and Hero-Worship," Lects. I., vi.), connect the word, the German form of which is *könig*, with "can" (Germ. *können*), and understand it to mean the canning or able man.

and the process of his elevation to the dignity, and his duties and powers when holding it, were in accordance with this idea.

In Teutonic communities the possession of the highest office of the State in the first instance depended, as did that of property in land, on the will of the community at large, who assigned the office to a particular individual for his life, with the power of revoking the gift at any time for misconduct. But the idea of something more than this seems to have been very early attached to the title and dignity of king.[2] The possession of this office was looked upon as conferring a right which was more than merely personal, and did not altogether cease with death; but was transmissible to the king's descendants or nearest of kin, and subsequently even became liable to be disposed of by his testament. The feeling of reverence with which the office was regarded, is shown by the prevalent tradition that the royal family was descended, as among the early Greeks, from the national gods. The same feeling was expressed and perpetuated by the solemnities with which the ceremony of coronation was attended, and particularly the use, in Christian times, of the anointing oil.

Pre-Norman Kings.—From the first settlement of the Angles and Saxons in Britain, down to the accession of William the Conqueror, a combination of the elective and hereditary principles regulated the succession to the throne of the most powerful kingdom in the country. The extent to which the hereditary principle grew, is seen from the fact that persons of royal blood received as such the special title of Ætheling. And we, in fact, find that from the establishment of the kingdom of Wessex by

---

[2] Tac. Germ. c. 7. *Reges* ex nobilitate, duces ex virtute sumunt.

Cerdic in 519, until within fifty years of the Norman conquest, the West Saxon crown first, and then the imperial English crown, was always worn by his descendants. After the intrusion of three monarchs of the Danish royal family, it reverted once more to his race, to be transferred for one brief year to a stranger in blood, and then to pass to a successful invader.[2] But during all this time that crown was never placed on the head of any one, whether a descendant of Cerdic, or, like Harold, a claimant under the will of the preceding king, or a Danish or Norman conqueror, unless his accession had been previously sanctioned by the Witenagemot, or general council of the nation. The granting or withholding of this sanction was a vital matter; not a foregone conclusion, as was the second election by the clergy and people, who, during the coronation ceremony, responded by affirmative acclamations to the demand whether they would accept the proposed individual as their king. The exercise of the power of election by the Witenagemot enabled a minority to be averted by the choice of a brother of the deceased king instead of his infant child. It was thus that the great Ælfred obtained the throne. In consequence of this, we find only two instances—and those immediately following each other, and owing to the same circumstances—of minors being raised to the English throne before the Conquest. Upon the death of Eadgar, in 975, leaving two sons, aged thirteen and seven years respectively, there was no near male kinsman of full age who could be chosen to succeed, nor any man of commanding pre-eminence in the nation in whose favour the hereditary principle could be

---

[2] In the person of Henry II., through his mother Matilda, the crown was restored to a descendant of Cerdic in the female line, and has ever since been worn by individuals having the blood of the West Saxon king in their veins. This, however, is obviously accidental, and is not due to the hereditary principle in the succession.

set aside, as it was later in the case of Harold. Accordingly Eadward, the eldest son of Eadgar, was chosen king, though not without a dispute whether his younger brother Æthelred should not be preferred to him; and upon his murder three years later, that brother, though then only about eleven years old, was accepted as his successor. The Witan also possessed the right of deposing the king,—a right which they asserted in the cases of Sigeberht of Wessex (A.D. 755) and Æthelred II. (A.D. 1013), whom they restored to the throne in the following year. In one instance they took part in the settlement during the lifetime of the king of the subsequent succession, for they confirmed the will of Æthelwulf, which affected to dispose of his regal dignities among his sons. The same king also procured his youngest son Ælfred to be anointed king by the Pope during his life. The order of succession prescribed in the royal testament was not, however, implicitly observed; nor did the premature coronation of Ælfred avail to place him on the throne before his elder brothers. On the other hand, on the death of Eadward the Confessor, the Witan followed his last wishes respecting the succession, by choosing, as king, Harold, to whom he had upon his deathbed committed the kingdom.

2. **Early Norman Kings.**—At the Norman Conquest the due succession to the crown suffered a violent interruption; but in the accession to the throne of the members of the new royal family, we find that the hereditary principle, though great stress is always laid upon it, is yet controlled, as before, by other considerations, among which that of election continues to hold a prominent place. After King Harold had fallen on the field of battle, and the English Witan had found it impossible to sustain their choice of Eadgar Ætheling as his successor, they, a

few weeks later, practically revoked that choice by sending an invitation to William to ascend the vacant throne. It was only after this invitation, and after the ceremony of coronation had been performed in the old English form, when the unanimous voice of the assembled people accepted him as their king, that William assumed the regal dignity. Upon his death his second son Rufus, with no shadow of hereditary right, succeeded, not so much by virtue of his father's arbitrary bequest, as by the consent of the nobility of the land, and of the Archbishop Lanfranc, who possessed and exercised the power of performing over him the solemn rite of coronation. His successor, Henry I., owed the crown to the choice of the barons and prelates assembled at Winchester, supported by the mass of the people there,—a choice confirmed a few days afterwards by the acclamations of assent at his coronation in Westminster Abbey. It was upon this title of election that he as well as the next king, Stephen, relied[4]; and John's right to the throne depended upon the same title.

To form an estimate of the degree of weight which a previous settlement by the king for the time being, with the consent of the great council of the nation, was considered to carry, we may adduce, on the one hand, Henry I.'s unsuccessful endeavour to secure by that means the succession of his daughter Matilda and her son Henry; and, on the other, the effectual arrangement made in Stephen's reign in favour of Henry, which led to the unresisted accession of the latter upon Stephen's death.

The importance attached to the solemn act of coronation itself, with the rite of anointing which formed part of it, is indicated (i.) by the desire of Stephen that his son

[4] Henry styles himself, "Ego nutu Dei a clero et a populo Angliæ electus." And Stephen, "Ego Stephanus Dei gratia assensu cleri et populi in regem Anglorum electus."

Eustace should during his lifetime be anointed by the
Archbishop of Canterbury, whose refusal to comply with
it was visited by banishment from the country; (ii.) by
the fact that Henry II. procured the coronation of his
eldest son, whom, however, he outlived; and, (iii.) by the
hurried performance of the ceremony over Henry III.,
when at the age of nine years he was left heir to the
throne by the death of his father John. Until Edward
I., the reigns of our kings, both before and after the Conquest, dated from the day of their coronation, there being
no recognition in those times of the maxim subsequently
imported into our law, that "the king never dies;" by which
is meant, that the next heir ascends the throne at the very
instant of the death of the previous sovereign. The
change of practice in Edward I.'s case, whose reign dates
from the day on which the barons swore fealty to him in
his absence four days after his father's death, was due to
his being in the Holy Land when his father died, and to
the inconvenience that would have arisen had the throne
been deemed vacant until his return.

3. **Growth of the Hereditary Principle.**—In the
fourteenth century the power of the national assembly to
depose the king, of which we have noticed instances
before the Conquest, was again exercised in the cases
of Edward II. and Richard II. But from the latter
a previous, and from the former a subsequent, resignation
of the crown was extorted; and, while in the case of
Richard II. the greater weight seems to have been attached
to the act of deposition, in that of Edward II. it was
the king's own resignation which was publicly put forward
as the ground for the accession of his son. At the same
time the principle of a strict hereditary succession was
gradually becoming stronger. It cannot be said that the

Act of 1350 (25 Edw. 3, st. 1), which placed the children of the king born out of England on the same footing with those born within the realm as regarded the right to succeed to inheritances, did much to advance it. But it received a decided development in the succession, on the death of Edward III., of his *grandson* Richard, as representing his deceased eldest son, the Black Prince. On the other hand, the accession of the Lancastrian dynasty was in violation of it, and depended on the acquiescence of the Parliament and people; but Henry IV. showed his appreciation of hereditary right by dwelling on his own descent from Henry III., and also by obtaining an Act of Parliament (7 Hen. 4, c. 2) to the effect that the inheritance of the crown should remain in him *and the heirs of his body issuing*. This arrangement was altered by a Parliament in 1460, which declared that Henry VI. should wear the crown for life, and that after his death it should devolve on Richard Duke of York, who possessed the better title by birth. The duke was shortly afterwards defeated and slain at Wakefield, and when in the next year his son Edward entered London after his victory at Mortimer's Cross, first the lords assembled in council, and then the acclamations of the people, decided that Henry should no longer be king, because by making war on Duke Richard he had violated the arrangement made by himself and Parliament as to the succession of the crown, and that Edward IV. had good right to the crown,—first, as son and heir of Duke Richard, the lawful inheritor of it; and secondly, by authority of Parliament and the forfeiture committed by King Henry. In the Acts of Edw. 4's reign, the monarchs of the rival line are always referred to as "late in deed, and not of right, kings of England." Richard III. was declared king by the popular voice in a somewhat similar way to his brother. In

Hen. 7's reign we find another settlement of the crown by Parliament, namely, that the crown should remain in Henry VII. and the heirs of his body for ever, and in none other (st. 1 Hen. 7, Tit. Reg.) This settlement has been so far observed to the present day, that every subsequent English monarch has been a lineal descendant of Henry VII.

Disposition of the Crown by Parliament.—The coronation of Henry VIII. appears to have been the last occasion in which the assent of the people to the performance of the rite was formally asked during the service. In the reign of this king the power of Parliament to regulate the succession was twice exercised,—first, by an Act (28 Hen. 8, c. 7) entailing the crown on the king's sons by Jane Seymour or any other wife, and then on the king's legitimate daughters, and giving power to Henry, in case of default of such sons and daughters, to dispose of the crown by letters patent or will as he should please; and secondly, by st. 35 Hen. 8, c. 1, which introduced into the succession Henry's two daughters, Mary and Elizabeth, and their issue, with such conditions as Henry should impose by letters patent or by his will.

4. Successors of Henry VIII.—Edward VI. united a strict hereditary to a parliamentary title. His attempt to exercise in favour of Lady Jane Grey, without the authority of Parliament, the power of appointing a successor which Parliament had granted to his father, was repudiated by the nation, who accepted as his successors his two sisters, one or other of whom had clearly no claim on strictly hereditary principles. In the reign of the second, Elizabeth, an Act was passed declaring it to be treason either to deny the right of Parliament to direct the descent of the crown, or to affirm in writing that any person, other than the queen's issue, was her lawful successor, until the point should be settled by Parliament. The latter enactment virtually amounted to a retrospective repeal of the power given to Henry VIII. to appoint a successor, failing the issue of his children, which he had exercised in favour of the children of his sister Mary, Queen of France. And this appointment was openly set aside when James I., the descendant of Henry's eldest sister, Margaret, was accepted and crowned king on the strength of his hereditary right as lineal heir of Henry VII., backed by considerations of expediency. But after his coronation it was deemed proper to confirm his title by Act of Parliament (1 Ja. 1, c. 1). In the first year of Mary's reign it was laid down as law, that when the kingly office devolved upon a female, she became invested with the royal prerogatives equally with a king, and that all statutes in which the latter was named applied equally to a queen (1 Mar. sess. 3, c. 1).

The Stuart Monarchs.—The fact that, after the restoration of Charles II., the years of his reign were reckoned from the death of his father, was a distinct recognition of his inherent right to the crown by birth alone. Yet even in his reign it was by no means generally admitted that an hereditary claim to the succession was absolutely indestructible. The exclusion Bill for omitting James Duke of York from the succession, and transmitting the crown as if he were dead, which in 1679 and 1680 actually passed the House of Commons, was an attempt to exert, against the wish of the king, the parliamentary control over the succession, which had at the instance of the reigning sovereign been exercised in the reign of Hen. 8, and asserted in that of Elizabeth.

The conduct of James, when on the throne, produced

another crisis in the history of the monarchy. After his second flight, the Convention Parliament, while it undoubtedly in fact committed the act of deposing him and selecting his successor, veiled the transaction under the fiction of a voluntary abdication. They resolved "that King James the Second, having endeavoured to subvert the constitution of the kingdom by breaking the original contract between king and people, and, by the advice of Jesuits and other wicked persons, having violated the fundamental laws, and having withdrawn himself out of this kingdom, has abdicated the government, and that the throne is thereby vacant." Of course, looking to the hereditary principle alone, an abdication by James would have transmitted the crown immediately to his son.[5]

5. **Acts of Settlement.**—In the following reign occurred the two latest instances of parliamentary legislation upon the succession to the crown. Upon the accession of William and Mary the crown was settled on them during their joint lives,[6] and on the survivor after the death of either; then on the lineal heirs first of Mary, then of Anne, and lastly of William. But it was at the same time enacted that, whereas experience had shown "that it is inconsistent with the safety and welfare of this Protestant kingdome

[5] In Scotland, where the government was carried on without the presence of the king, so that his flight carried with it no appearance even of abdication, the Convention assembled by William plainly declared, "That James VII., being a professed Papist, did assume the royal power, and acted as king without ever taking the oath required by law, and had, by the advice of evil and wicked councillors, invaded the fundamental constitution of the kingdom, and altered it from a legal limited monarchy to an arbitrary despotic power, and hath exerted the same to the subversion of the Protestant religion and the violation of the laws and liberties of the kingdom, whereby he hath forfaulted" (i.e., forfeited) "his right to the crown, and the throne has become vacant."

[6] But the regal power was to be exercised by William alone in the joint names of both.

to be governed by a Popish prince, or by any king or queene marrying a Papist," persons who should either be themselves members of the Church of Rome, or should marry a Papist, should be incapable of holding the crown; which should, in any such case of incapacity, descend to the nearest Protestant in the line of succession (1 Will. & Mar., sess. 2, c. 2). On the death of Mary without issue, and of the Duke of Gloucester, the last surviving child of Anne, who, like his brothers and sisters, died at a very early age, it was enacted that, on failure of the lines included in the succession by the previous Act, the crown should devolve on the Princess Sophia of Hanover, daughter of James I.'s daughter Elizabeth, and the heirs of her body, being Protestants. Besides a repetition of the provision disqualifying a person who should become or should marry a Papist, it was now enacted that all future sovereigns should join in communion with the Church of England as by law established (12 & 13 Will. 3, c. 2). And by 6 Ann. c. 41, s. 2, it was enacted that if any person should maintain that "the kings or queens of this realm, with and by the authority of Parliament, are not able to make laws and statutes of sufficient force and validity to limit and bind the crown, and the descent, limitation, inheritance, and government thereof," such person should incur the penalty of *præmunire*.

6. **Present Succession.**—Happily for the country, the limitation of the succession made in 12 & 13 Will. 3, has been maintained to the present day without having ever required, and without, according to present appearances, being likely to require a further supplement; nor has the necessity ever arisen for passing over an heir to the crown on the ground of religious disqualification.

CHAPTER V.

PARLIAMENT.

I. THE WITENAGEMOT, GREAT COUNCIL, AND PARLIAMENT.

1. **Witenagemot.**—When several of the Teutonic shires became amalgamated into one kingdom, a new assembly, called the *Michelgemot* or *Witenagemot*, was formed for regulating the affairs of the united people. It may be presumed that originally the same persons had the right to attend it, who were entitled to take part in the shire-moots; but the size of the kingdom and the distances to be travelled would effectually prevent this right from being generally exercised. Accordingly, we find that the Michelgemot became practically changed into a Witenagemot; that the assembly, in fact, was attended almost exclusively by the *wise men*—the caldormen, and other officers of the kingdom, the king's thegns and the higher ecclesiastics, viz., bishops, abbots, and priors. The occasional traces which exist of the presence of other thegns, and even of ceorls, at its deliberations, may be accounted for by supposing that the ordinary thegns and citizens of London, Winchester, Exeter, or of any other city in which the witan happened to meet, and of the surrounding country, still exercised the privilege which had once belonged to their whole class. It cannot, however, be supposed that they exercised any appreciable influence in the proceedings. The principle of the whole body of freemen taking part in the deliberations by deputy in the persons of representatives, though adopted for the shire-moots (see p. 75), was not extended to the composition of the national assembly.

When the king of Wessex became monarch of England,

the witenagemots of the other kingdoms sank into the position of local deliberative assemblies, subordinate to the Witenagemot of England. The first traces of what is called Privilege of Parliament, or the peculiar immunities enjoyed by members of that body, appear in a law of Æthelberht about the close of the sixth century, to the effect that if the king summoned his people to him, and any one did an injury to them there, he should give double compensation, and pay 50 shillings (solidi) to the king besides.

2. **Great Council.**—After the Conquest the place of the Witenagemot was supplied by a purely feudal assembly, consisting of the barons and others who held immediately under the Crown, and called the *Magnum Concilium*, or *Great Council*. The lay and spiritual heads of the counties—the *comites* (counts or earls) and the archbishops and bishops—had seats in it, as in the Witenagemot; for the former were the leading barons in their respective shires; and a barony was at the Conquest attached to each episcopal see. A similar annexation of a barony to many abbeys and priories gave the privilege of attendance to the abbots and priors. Besides these, not only all the other greater barons, or, as they were afterwards simply called, barons, but also the lesser barons, or military tenants *in capite*, had the right to be present. The council was presided over by the king in person, or, if he were absent from the kingdom, by the chief-justiciary. The frequency of its meeting greatly increased in the reign of Hen. 2, who summoned it twice or thrice during every year of his stay in England. That monarch early infringed upon the purely feudal character of his Great Council by introducing the practice of sending a special writ of summons to the individuals who were to attend. The receipt of a sum-

mons, and not the possession of a barony, was now considered as conferring the right to be present, while the omission of a summons would debar a baron from attending; and the king in some cases issued summonses to persons who had not the old feudal qualification. Henry and his successors were thus able to introduce into the council lawyers and clerks, whom they desired to raise to judicial or administrative offices, and to make members of their ordinary council. We shall see at a later period of the history how the habit of receiving summonses was at length considered to confer an absolute right to receive them, not only on the individual himself, but also on his heir,—how, in short, the seats in the House of Lords, into which the Magnum Concilium had been then converted, became permanent and hereditary, and its members recovered their original right to attend independently of the caprice of the king.

Attendance at the Great Council has, in the preceding paragraph, been spoken of as a right or privilege, but it was equally looked upon as a duty. The presence of the barons at the king's court was in fact a pledge and security for their continuance in allegiance to him. Accordingly, those who did not present themselves were liable to a fine, unless they obtained the king's license to appear by a procurator or proxy. Thus originated the right of the peers to record their votes by proxy, which they continued to exercise until 1868.

While such was the origin of the position of the nobility in Parliament, the presence in it of the other two estates of the realm, the clergy and commons,[1] was secured but gradually and fitfully; and, in the case of the former, was

[1] The three estates of the realm are the Clergy, Lords, and Commons; the three estates of Parliament are at present the King, Lords, and Commons.

destined to be of but short duration. In Hen. 2's reign we read on one occasion that deans and archdeacons, as the historian has it, "without number" were present at the Great Council. At another time almost all the knights of the realm are said to have attended. But neither deans and archdeacons nor knights appear to have had any voice in the deliberations of the council.

Representation.—The system of representation first appears in the composition of the national assembly at the commencement of the thirteenth century. In 1213 the sheriffs were directed by the king's writ to send to him four discreet knights of each shire, *ad loquendum nobiscum de negotiis regni nostri*, "to hold parley with us concerning the affairs of our realm." These knights were probably appointed by the sheriff. Their number was the same as that of the knights who at that time were summoned to select the recognitors for the grand assize and the grand jury for the county. (See ch. viii.)

In the same year John summoned the town-reeve and four representative men from every township in the royal demesne, to confer with him on the affairs of his kingdom. As the boroughs were for the most part held in demesne, this summons may be said to have involved a representation of burgesses, and the assembly in which they met is styled a council. The Archbishop of Canterbury and other bishops and nobles were present, and it was presided over by the chief-justiciary, who, in the name of the king, pronounced a confirmation of the laws of Hen. 1.

Neither county nor borough representation in the national council is contemplated by Magna Carta, which prescribes that for assessing an extraordinary *aid*, or the *scutage*, the king shall summon by writ the archbishops, bishops, earls, and greater barons, and shall also summon, through the sheriffs and king's bailiffs, all who hold of the king *in capite*. But instances of the representation of the counties by chosen knights occurred on several occasions in Hen. 3's reign. Thus in 1254 the sheriffs were required to send from each county to the king's council at Westminster two qualified and discreet men, whom the county should choose as its representatives, for the purpose of determining what *aid* they would grant to the king for his expedition into Gascony. Each sheriff was to explain the king's necessity to the knights and others of the county, and induce them to consent to an adequate aid, so that the representatives might come prepared to name the amount which their county would contribute. In 1261 the confederate barons issued summonses, which were afterwards confirmed by the king, for the attendance of three knights from each shire to discuss the common affairs of the realm. The first summons of burgesses to Parliament was in 1264, when writs were issued by Simon de Montfort, in the name of the king, to the sheriffs for the return of two knights for every county, and to the cities and boroughs for the return of two citizens or burgesses from each, to deliberate on public affairs. The principle of representation continued to be occasionally recognised during the next thirty years, but it was not until 23 Edw. 1 that the Lower House can be said to have been regularly constituted. The name of Parliament appears to have been first applied to the assembly early in that reign.

The Clergy.—As regards the attendance or representation in Parliament of the estate of the clergy. In 1213 the deans attended the council as they had done in Hen. 2's reign. The practice of proctors or deputies from the inferior clergy attending Parliament began in Hen. 3's reign. There is an undoubted instance of it in 1255, and it apparently took place on a few occasions previously.

They were summoned by Edward I. in 1283 and 1294, and in 1295 (23 Edw. 1), what is called the *præmunientes* clause, because it begins with that word, was for the first time inserted in the summonses of all the bishops, requiring them to bring with them to Parliament the prior or dean of their cathedral church, their archdeacons, and one proctor for the chapter, and two for the clergy of the diocese. The *præmunientes* clause became a regular form in the summonses of the bishops, although the clergy soon ceased to attend Parliament. They met instead in their provincial convocations, to which they were summoned by the archbishops, and as they there fulfilled the object for which they were summoned to Parliament, namely, the voting of subsidies from their own order, they were excused from attendance at the national council. The discontinuance of their attendance was the more easy from the fact that, when present, they had always formed a distinct body, and voted apart from the knights and burgesses.

3. **Parliament.**—From the final division of the assembly into two houses, it will be convenient to postpone the consideration of the changes which the composition of each house has since undergone, and to deal first with matters affecting the two houses alike, or Parliament as a whole.

Meeting of Parliament.—Thrice in the course of the reigns of Edw. 2 and his son we find enactments that a Parliament shall be held annually, or twice in the year if need be, and that in a convenient place, for the maintenance of the statutes and redress of divers mischiefs and grievances which daily happened (5 Edw. 2, c. 29; 4 Edw. 3, c. 14; 36 Edw. 3, st. 1, c. 10). But the tendency on the part of our kings and their counsellors to neglect the annual assembling of Parliament, which is indicated by the necessity of repeating this enactment, continued to prevail notwithstanding its reiteration.

Privilege.—The privilege of Parliament, the germs of which we saw before the Conquest, and which had since been partially recognised, was distinctly confirmed by st. 11 Hen. 6, c. 11, which punished assaults upon members on their way to Parliament. The privilege of freedom from arrest during the session was asserted by the Commons in the following reign; and in 4 Hen. 8, Parliament by statute annulled a sentence which had been passed and penalties which had been inflicted by the Stannary Court on Richard Strode, for Bills introduced by him and certain other members into Parliament, which that court had adjudged to be destructive of the privileges of the Cornish tinners; and declared that all proceedings of a civil or criminal nature which should thereafter be brought against him or his associates on account of any Bill introduced into Parliament, or any language or arguments there used, should be utterly void.

Freedom of Debate.—The Commons had before this asserted as against the Crown their right of freedom of debate. It is not clear when the old feudal practice that the king should himself be present at the deliberations of his council or Parliament was given up; but upon the division of the assembly into two houses, the king, of course, could not be present in both; and the right of the Commons to insist on his absence from their debates was admitted by Henry IV., who also promised that the king should not receive or give any credence to reports of what passed at those debates. But this promise did not always in succeeding reigns serve to protect members who incurred the displeasure of the Crown by their conduct in Parliament. Thus, in 31 Hen. 6, Thorp, the speaker, was imprisoned; and although, on the complaint of the

Commons, the judges gave an opinion in his favour, he was kept in prison, and the Commons at the king's command proceeded to choose a new speaker.

4. **Meeting of Parliament.**—Until the middle of the seventeenth century no law existed as to the duration of a Parliament, except that it was always deemed to be dissolved on the death of the sovereign. And the frequency of its meetings, respecting which the statute-book did contain a direction, was in practice regulated less by that than by the necessities of the sovereign. But after the twelve years (1629–1640) which Charles I. had suffered to elapse without a Parliament, one of the first measures passed by the Long Parliament was the Triennial Act, by which every Parliament was to be *ipso facto* dissolved at the expiration of three years from the first day of its session, or if then sitting, at its first subsequent adjournment or prorogation, and a new Parliament was to be elected within three years from the dissolution of the last. And Parliament was not to be dissolved, nor was either house to be adjourned without its own consent, within fifty days after its meeting. This Act, however, which had been infringed by the very Parliament which had passed it, was repealed after the Restoration at the request of Charles II., and one of his Parliaments sat for seventeen years. Nor was the annual assembling of Parliament invariably observed by the two later Stuarts.

Irregular Assemblies.—In the summer of 1640, Charles I. being unwilling, after his unsuccessful experiment of a Parliament in the spring, again to convene the representatives of the Commons, and at the same time being reduced to the greatest pecuniary straits, reverted to old feudal precedent, and convened a great council of peers at York. This assembly voted him £200,000 out of their own resources, but were of course unable to give him any other assistance.

In the case of the conventions of Lords and Commons, which met at the Restoration and Revolution, some of the strict parliamentary forms were wanting. For the peers had never received the royal summons, and the whole body had met without royal authority. It was therefore deemed necessary on both occasions that the assembly should pass an Act, declaring itself to be a Parliament (12 Cha. 2, c. 1 ; 1 Will. & Mar., c. 1). This, of course, could not, from a strictly legal point of view, remedy the defect ; nor on the later occasion was the blot entirely removed by the fact that the succeeding Parliament, convened by the authority of the sovereigns who owed their title to the Convention of 1688, solemnly ratified the Acts which the latter had passed (2 Will. & Mar., c. 1).

Privilege.—From the time of Hen. 8 it became the practice, at the commencement of every new Parliament, for the speaker of the House of Commons, immediately after his election, to claim from the king, on behalf of members of the house, their ancient privileges of access to the king's person, freedom of speech, and freedom from arrest. The possession of these privileges by both houses, together with the power of enforcing respect to them, became of great importance in the struggles between Parliament and the Crown in the seventeenth century. Privilege from arrest was at that time extended to the servants of members ; and it was held a breach of privilege not only to serve any sort of legal process on members, but also to commit any civil injury against them which would put them under the necessity of seeking redress at law. The only cases in which it did not apply were those of members accused of treason, felony, or refusal to give surety for the peace. The privilege, in the case of peers, was perpetual; and in the case of members of the other House, existed during the session, and for a certain time before and after.

Charles I. set at defiance the privilege of the Upper House in 1625, by the imprisonment of Lord Arundel; and that of the Lower in the following year, by the arrest of Sir John Eliot and Sir Dudley Digges for words spoken in debate. There was no such justification for this proceeding, as there was for the imprisonment of Sir John Eliot and others, three years later, when (as was dispassionately resolved by the Commons after the Restoration) they had, in detaining the Speaker in his chair, been guilty of a riot, from the consequences of which privilege could afford them no protection, inasmuch as it does not extend to acts, but only to words. But the most flagrant violation of parliamentary privilege by Charles was his personal visit to the House of Commons in 1641, for the purpose of seizing the five obnoxious members in their places. This proceeding, though it proved unsuccessful, and though he apologised for it, was one of the chief causes which brought about the final alienation between himself and his Parliament and people.

Privilege of debate was reasserted after the Restoration. In the Act of 1661, which imposed penalties on persons making malicious or detrimental allegations respecting the king or the established government, or advancing certain political opinions, care was taken to introduce a proviso that nothing in the Act should extend to deprive either House of Parliament, or any of their members, of their just ancient freedom and privilege of debating any matters or business propounded in Parliament, or touching the repeal or alteration of any old, or the preparing of any new law, or the redress of any public grievance. And at the same time that the Commons came to the resolution

respecting Sir John Eliot's case, they laid down that the
Act of 4 Hen. 8 was to be taken as a general law establishing the privilege of Parliament, and that the judgment given by the King's Bench in 1629 against Sir John Eliot and others, though right as regarded the riot, was illegal and erroneous in extending to words spoken in Parliament; and the judgment to that extent was solemnly reversed by the Lords.

Punishment of Members.—While the two Houses claimed peculiar exemptions from the jurisdiction of the ordinary tribunals, they asserted their own right to punish the misconduct of their members. From the Journals of the Commons during the reigns of Edw. 6 and Mary, it appears that on more than one occasion the Commons, through the Speaker, passed a censure upon disorderly or indecent behaviour in the House; and in the former reign they committed one member to the Tower. In 1581 they inflicted fine, imprisonment, and expulsion on one of their members, Arthur Hall, for printing a libel derogatory to them as a part of the Legislature. In 1677 the Lords committed Lord Shaftesbury and three other peers for a high contempt in calling in question, during the course of a debate, the legal continuance of Parliament after a prorogation of more than twelve months; and the judges of the King's Bench refused to grant a *habeas corpus*, on the ground that they had no jurisdiction in the matter, notwithstanding a technical informality on the face of the committal.

Publication of Debates.—The Long Parliament, in 1641, permitted a publication of its proceedings under its special sanction, but prohibited the unauthorised publication of speeches. They even expelled Sir E. Dering, and imprisoned him in the Tower, for printing a collection of his own speeches, and ordered the book to be burnt by

the common hangman. The prohibition to publish the
debates continued after the Restoration; but, to ensure
accurate records of the business done, the House of Commons, in 1680, directed its "votes and proceedings,"
without any references to the debates, to be printed under
the direction of the Speaker.

5. **Meeting of Parliament.**—The principle affirmed
by the Bill of Rights, "that for redresse of all grievances,
and for the amending, strengthening, and preserveing of
the lawes, Parlyaments ought to be held frequently," has
been since strictly observed. Owing in part to the necessity of passing the annual Mutiny Act, and of obtaining
annually votes of money to meet the largely increased
public expenditure, and in part to the closer connection
established between Parliament and the executive through
the existence of a responsible ministry, no year has
elapsed since the Revolution without at least one session
of Parliament. Nothing was laid down at the Revolution respecting the duration of a Parliament; and previously to 1694, when once elected, it continued in being
till the demise of the reigning sovereign, unless it was
previously dissolved by the Crown. In that year William
acceded to the Triennial Bill, which had once before
passed both Houses, but had been lost through the withholding of the royal assent; and the duration of Parliament was thenceforth limited to three years. The period
was extended to seven years by the Septennial Act (1 Geo.
1, st. 2, c. 38), passed in 1715; and this arrangement has
continued in force ever since, though frequent attempts
have been made, both in the last and in the present century, to obtain a return to triennial Parliaments. In Anne's
reign, the rule that Parliament was *ipso facto* dissolved by
the death of the king was relaxed, and it was permitted to

sit for six months afterwards. And this restriction was swept away by the Reform Act of 1867, so that a demise of the Crown will in future have no effect whatever on the continuance of the Parliament then in being (30 & 31 Vict., c. 102, s. 51). Apart from the limitation imposed by the clause in the Bill of Rights already referred to, and by the Septennial Act, the discretion of the Crown to summon, prorogue, and dissolve Parliament at its pleasure remains unrestricted; and neither House can do more than present addresses to the Crown, praying for a dissolution. The legality of such addresses, and also of petitions by the people requesting the king to summon or dissolve Parliament, though not allowed to pass unquestioned, has been more than once affirmed since the Revolution.

Privilege.—Before the Revolution privilege of Parliament had been almost invariably asserted on the side of the rights and liberties of the people, to the establishment and protection of which its maintenance, and even its extension, may be said to have been absolutely essential. But when those rights and liberties had become firmly secured, privilege of Parliament, instead of being a check on the Crown, became in some cases oppressive to the public at large. Accordingly, during the century which followed the Revolution the exemption of members from the jurisdiction of the ordinary tribunals was gradually restricted, until at length in 1770 an Act was passed which permitted actions and suits to be commenced and prosecuted at all times against members of either House and their servants, with the sole reservation to members themselves of an immunity from arrest or imprisonment. Nor was it by statute alone that the limits of privilege were narrowed. Cases of treason, felony, or refusal to give surety of the peace have been already mentioned as at one time the only recognised exceptions to the privilege possessed by members of freedom from arrest. But upon the publication by Wilkes, member for Aylesbury, of the *North Briton*, No. 45, in 1763, containing a virulent attack upon the king's speech on the prorogation of Parliament, the House of Commons resolved " that privilege of Parliament does not extend to the case of writing and publishing seditious libels, nor ought to be allowed to obstruct the ordinary course of law in the speedy and effectual prosecution of so heinous and dangerous an offence." And the Lords agreed to this resolution, although seventeen peers protested against the surrender of the privilege of Parliament " to serve a particular purpose *ex post facto, et pendente lite* in the courts below."

Down to the year 1795 members of both Houses enjoyed the privilege of sending and receiving post-free an unlimited number of letters. This privilege, objectionable in itself, became the subject of great abuse, being fraudulently employed by persons connected with members to secure the gratuitous transmission of their own letters. It was therefore subjected to restrictions by Mr Pitt, and was wholly abolished in 1839.

Privilege of Debate.—The privilege of freedom of debate in Parliament was reasserted after the Revolution in the Bill of Rights, which laid down " that the freedome of speech and debates or proceedings in Parlyament ought not to be impeached or questioned in any court or place out of Parlyament." Though no attempt was afterwards made by the Crown to punish members for words spoken during a debate by imprisonment or legal proceedings, yet, as will be mentioned later (see ch. ix.), instances occurred in which George III. visited conduct in Parliament with substantial marks of his displeasure. The exercise of freedom of debate was assisted by the right, which both

Houses had possessed from very ancient times, of excluding strangers from their debates. The enforcement of this right, which had previously been very strictly maintained, was gradually relaxed after the Revolution, though it was still occasionally exercised.

Notwithstanding the endeavours of both Houses during the first half of the seventeenth century, by frequent resolutions and punishment of offenders, to restrain news-letter writers from giving any report of their proceedings, the appearance of regular though imperfect accounts of the principal debates in one or two of the magazines of the year began at the accession of George I. The initials only of the speakers were given, and the publication was withheld till after the session. And when publication even during the recess was prohibited, and more rigorous measures were taken by the House of Commons against offenders, the debates were disguised as the proceedings of the Senate of Great Lilliput or of the Political Club. The last attempt on the part of the House of Commons to punish the publication of its debates was in 1771, and led to a conflict between that House and the Lord Mayor and aldermen of the city of London, who in the Mayor's Court had declined to treat the printers of the debates as guilty of any offence, and were ultimately committed to the Tower by order of the House for the rest of the session. Though the publication of the debates remains in theory a breach of privilege, it has since proceeded with impunity; and it has been found that the misrepresentation of speeches, which was so much complained of when the publication of the debates was carried on under disguise and in constant fear of punishment, and which was advanced as one of the strongest arguments for its total suppression, entirely ceased when all interference and restraint were abandoned. Reporting, however, still continued a matter of difficulty. The taking of notes was prohibited, and no places being reserved for reporters, they had to wait sometimes for hours to secure seats in the limited space allotted to strangers. And the way in which members voted still remained, generally speaking, a secret. The Houses themselves recorded merely the numbers in the division; and in 1696 the Commons declared the printing of the names of the minority a breach of privilege destructive of the freedom and liberties of Parliament.

6. **Presence of Strangers.**—The power of a single member of either House to require at any time the exclusion of strangers still remains, and was exercised in the Lower House in 1849, and again in 1870, 1872, and 1873. But after the destruction of the two houses by fire in 1834, the presence of strangers in the galleries and other parts of the House of Commons not appropriated to members was recognised by the orders of the House, and separate galleries were assigned in both houses for the accommodation of reporters. Since 1853 strangers have been permitted to remain in the House of Commons during a division, and the same liberty has been allowed to them in the Upper House since 1857.

Publication of Proceedings.—Notwithstanding the declaration of the Commons in 1696, the lists of the minority, and latterly of the majority also, were occasionally published in the case of important divisions; but it was not until 1836 that the practice was begun in the Lower House of recording the votes of the members, and publishing them daily as part of the proceedings of the House. The daily publication of the division lists of the House of Lords dates from 1857. Moreover, the Commons since 1839, and the Lords since 1852, have printed the names of members present on select committees, with their votes upon every point, and the questions addressed by them to witnesses.

It is characteristic of the altered state of feeling, that whereas in the last century the House of Commons were in conflict with the courts of justice respecting their right to uphold the secrecy of their proceedings, the last instance of a similar conflict was owing to their assertion of the right to publish their proceedings for the benefit of the nation. In 1835 they directed all their papers to be publicly sold at a cheap rate, and in the following year certain reports were by their order published by Messrs Hansard, containing reflections on a book by an author named Stockdale, who thereupon brought an action for libel against the publishers. In this action the judges of the Queen's Bench held that the order of the House of Commons was no justification to Messrs Hansard for publishing the libel, and notwithstanding a resolution of the House condemning this decision, Stockdale brought another action, and the sheriffs proceeded to levy the amount of the damages upon Messrs Hansard. Thereupon the House retaliated by committing Stockdale and his attorney and the sheriffs to the custody of their serjeant-at-arms, and an Act of Parliament was passed to protect all persons publishing papers by order of either House (3 & 4 Vict., c. 9). That the publication of the debates of both Houses, even without their order, is privileged on the ground of public policy, was laid down in 1868 by the Court of Queen's Bench, which decided, in the case of *Wason* v. *Walter* (8 B. & S. 671), that an action for libel could not be maintained against the proprietor of the "Times" for matter published in the course of a fair and faithful report of proceedings in Parliament.

Privilege.—In 1812 bankruptcy was made a disqualification for sitting in the Lower House (see p. 167). Until 1869, however, members of both Houses, though liable to be made bankrupts, continued as bankrupts to enjoy the privilege of Parliament. But in that year the new Bankruptcy Act abolished all the benefit of privilege of Parliament as regarded bankruptcy in England, and similar provisions as to Ireland were inserted in the Irish Bankruptcy Act of 1872.

II. THE HOUSE OF LORDS.

3. Members.—After the constitution of a new House to represent the interests of the commons, the Upper House, the lineal successor of the Witenagemôt and Great Council, became in process of time confined to the nobility of the land by the gradual elevation to the peerage of some of the tenants *in capite* or lesser barons, and the omission to summon the rest to Parliament. The abbots and priors who held baronies continued to sit until Hen. 8's reign, and with the bishops considerably outnumbered the lay peers. The latter consisted chiefly of barons *by tenure*—lords who held a barony under the Crown. But there were others who had been summoned to Parliament without possessing the qualification of tenure, and who were therefore called barons *by writ*; and with respect to these, it was, in the 14th century, a common practice for the king to omit to summon them or their descendants to subsequent Parliaments. At this time, too, knights bannerets were often summoned to the Upper House. In the early part of Ric. 2's reign cases occur of peers being created by Parliament. And the first instance of their creation by letters patent was in 10 Ric. 2.

Number of Peers.—In the Parliament of 1454, the

last before the civil war, the names of 53 lay peers are recorded as in attendance. Their numbers were reduced by the struggle of the Roses, and Henry VII. summoned only 29 to his first Parliament. This number included some whose attainder had never been judicially reversed. The greatest number summoned by Henry VIII. was 51. By the dissolution of the monasteries about 36 abbots and priors were withdrawn from the Upper House, and the spiritual peers were reduced to a minority of the whole body, and formed about one-third of the house; their total number being thenceforward 26. This included the bishops of the 5 newly created sees, to which, although no baronies were attached to them, the right of a seat in the Upper House was annexed.

Chancellor.—Among the incidents connected with the office of chief-justiciary, which upon its abolition in Edw. I's reign devolved on the chancellor, was the position which that functionary had held in the council or Parliament. The chancellor therefore became, and has ever since continued to be, the prolocutor or speaker of the House of Lords. He may, however, speak and vote like the other peers, and has no casting vote; equality of votes having the effect of negativing the question before the House.

4. Status of Peers.—About the end of Eliz.'s reign, the receipt of a writ of summons to the Upper House was held to confer an inheritable peerage, descendible, as was subsequently decided, upon heirs female as well as male; and conversely in 1626, it was recognised as a fundamental principle that every peer of full age is entitled to his writ of summons at the beginning of a Parliament, and that the House will not proceed with business if any peer is denied it. The number of peers, which Elizabeth

maintained at a very low figure, was considerably augmented by James I. and Charles I., both of whom adopted in several cases the practice of selling peerages. The number of temporal peers who sat in the first Parliament of James I. was 82. That king created 62 new peerages, and Charles I., 59. But at the same time many old peerages became extinct, so that not more than 139 peers received summonses to attend the Parliament of 1661. For the same reason, although Charles II. added 64, and James II. 8 new peers, the number of temporal peers, exclusive of minors, Roman Catholics, and non-jurors, was in 1696 only about 140.

Protests and Proxies.—About the time of the Reformation peers obtained the privilege of recording, if they pleased, in the journals of the House, their dissent from a measure which they had unsuccessfully opposed. The right of adding the grounds of their dissent was first asserted towards the middle of the seventeenth century. In the same century it became a rule that proxies which had previously been held by persons not members of the House, should, in the case of a spiritual lord, be entrusted only to a spiritual lord, and in that of a lay peer, only to another lay peer; and the number of proxies to be held by any one peer was limited to two. Before this restriction, the Duke of Buckingham had in one Parliament held 14.

5. Increase of Peerage.—After the Revolution the augmentation of the peerage continued with greater rapidity than before. In 1711, Anne created 12 in one batch for the purpose of obtaining a majority in the House in favour of the Crown. The Act of Union with Scotland in 1706 added to the house 16 representative peers for the latter kingdom, elected at the commencement of every Parliament by the Scottish peers, who at that time numbered 154.[2]

In the years 1719 and 1720, attempts were made to restrict the increase of its members. It was proposed that the existing number of 178 peerages should not be augmented by more than 6, though new peerages might be created in lieu of any which became extinct; and instead of the 16 representative peers, 25 hereditary peers of Scotland were to have permanent seats. The scheme met with favour in the House of Lords, but was rejected by a large majority of the Lower House. In Geo. 3's reign, peerages were granted with a profusion previously unparalleled, amounting to no fewer than 388. In this number, however, are included some promotions of existing peers to a higher rank in the peerage. The House was further augmented in 1801 by the 28 representative peers for Ireland, chosen for life by the nobility of that country. In order to reduce the excessive number of that nobility, the Act of Union with Ireland provided that only one new Irish peerage should be created for every three which should become extinct, until the reduction of the number to 100, when it might be maintained at that figure. Irish peers, not being chosen representatives, were permitted to sit in the House of Commons as representatives of any constituency in Great Britain. The Act of Union with Ireland

[2] Soon after the Union the Lords resolved that no Scottish peer, on being admitted to the peerage of Great Britain, obtained a right to sit in Parliament or upon the trial of peers. This resolution, while it lasted, was evaded by creating the eldest sons of Scottish peers peers of Great Britain, who having thus obtained seats in the House of Lords did not lose them on succeeding to their Scottish titles. In 1782, however, the restriction was removed, the judges having given an unanimous opinion that it was not contemplated by the Act of Union. The principle was shortly afterwards established, that a Scottish peer on being raised to a peerage of Great Britain loses his right to vote for Scotch representative peers, and, if one himself, at once ceases to be so.

also gave seats in the Upper House to four Irish bishops. They were to pass to the different bishops by rotation of sessions, but one was to be always filled by an archbishop.

Creation of Peers.—The circumstances which attended the passing of the Reform Bill of 1832, proved the importance of the unlimited prerogative of the Crown to create new peerages. Sixteen new members were thus actually added to the Upper House in order to assist the progress of the Bill. And the mere fact that there existed a power of effectually overriding the opposition of the peers to the measure, by the creation of a further number adequate for the purpose, notwithstanding the extreme repugnance to the exercise of that power, and the dread of its consequences which the king shared with all who valued our constitution, was sufficient to give force to the circular letter of the king, by which, without the knowledge of his ministry, he prevailed on a number of the opposition peers to abstain from continuing to resist the measure.

6. Spiritual Peers.—During the reigns of Queen Victoria and her predecessor, one or two unsuccessful attempts have been made to exclude the bishops from the House of Lords. In 1834, and again in 1836 and the following year, the House of Commons, by majorities of more than two to one, refused to entertain the question of depriving them of their seats in Parliament. On the other hand, upon the creation of the bishopric of Manchester in 1847, it was determined that the episcopal element in the house, although of insignificant proportions as compared with former times, should not be increased, but that the bishop last appointed to any of the English or Welsh sees, except those of Canterbury, York, London, Durham, and Winchester, should wait for his seat in

Parliament until the occurrence of another vacancy. It was naturally provided by the Irish Church Act of 1869 that, upon the disestablishment of the Church of Ireland, her bishops should cease to have seats in the House of Lords.

Life Peerages.—Before the meeting of Parliament in 1855, the Crown, on the advice of the ministry, issued letters patent to Sir James Parke, who had been a baron of the Court of Exchequer, giving him a peerage for life with the title of Baron Wensleydale. When Parliament met, the House of Lords referred this patent to a committee of privileges, which, while they did not question the power of the Crown to confer such a peerage on its subjects and thereby give them rank and precedence, reported that the life-peerage could neither of itself, nor with the addition of the writ of summons founded upon it, entitle the grantee to sit and vote in Parliament. The House agreed to the report, and the Crown, in deference to its decision, issued a new patent conferring on Lord Wensleydale an hereditary peerage. Shortly afterwards a bill was brought in to authorise the Crown to grant life-peerages to two judges of at least five years' standing, who should sit with the Lord Chancellor as judges of appeal and deputy speakers; but, after passing the House of Lords, it was lost in the Commons.

Proxies.—The practice of giving proxies having been found to diminish the personal attendance of peers in Parliament, was discontinued by a resolution of the House in 1868.

Number of Peers.—The total number of peers, lay and spiritual, having seats in the House at the close of 1872, was 481. The number of Scotch peers which, at the time of the Union, was 154, has now by extinction and absorption into the peerage of the United Kingdom, dwindled down to one-half of that number; and as no new members of the order can be created, the whole body may possibly at some future period altogether disappear, being incorporated into the national nobility.

III. THE HOUSE OF COMMONS.

3. Early Composition.—The regular and unvarying attendance in Parliament of representatives from both counties and boroughs dates from 1295. In that year the number of knights who sat was 74, and the number of burgesses 200. The knights seem to have been originally chosen only by the military tenants *in capite*, but as their election took place in the county court, in which all freeholders had a voice, it probably soon fell into the hands of the whole body of freeholders. The deputies for a borough were probably elected originally by all the burgesses or resident householders, but when a poorer class of householders sprang up, unable to discharge he duties attaching to full citizenship, the franchise became limited in some towns to the inhabitants who paid taxes under the name of *scot and lot*, and in others to those who held houses or land in the town by *burgage* tenure.

From the fact that the rates of taxation for the counties and boroughs were in Edw. 1's reign often different, it may be inferred that the knights and burgesses in many cases voted separately. But in Edw. 2's reign they were permanently united together in one House, although an instance occurs so late as 6 Edw. 3 of the knights taxing themselves at a less rate than the burgesses.

In the reign of Edw. 3 and the three following reigns, about 180 burgesses and 74 knights sat in the Lower House. In 46 Edw. 3 complaints were made of the number of lawyers returned as knights for counties, and an ordinance was passed rendering them ineligible as such. This ordinance, after having been long disregarded, was formally repealed in 1871.

Imperfect Representation.—The representation in the Lower House was in early times exceedingly imperfect. Not only was the attendance of the elected members very defective, but in the holding of the elections themselves great irregularity prevailed. The Crown exercised the right of from time to time summoning deputies from new boroughs, and omitting other boroughs which had been previously represented. Moreover, the obligation to pay a salary to their representatives, which amounted to 4s. per diem for a knight and 2s. for a burgess, caused considerable gaps in the representation; for the sheriffs were prevailed upon by some boroughs to pass them over on account of their poverty, while others on the same ground obtained express dispensation from sending deputies. Others again, when the writ for the election was issued to them, refused to comply with it. Sometimes, too, the sheriffs fraudulently omitted to return deputies for boroughs within their bailiwick. And in both counties and boroughs they frequently, at the instance of the Crown, or for their own private interests, exercised undue influence over the elections. In general, the king and his privy council had at this time exclusive jurisdiction over disputed elections. But in the reigns of Hen. 4 and Hen. 6 statutes were passed punishing sheriffs for making false returns. And st. 7 Hen. 4, c. 15, alluding to the malpractice, enacts that the elections of knights shall be made in the full County Court by all there present freely and indifferently, notwithstanding any request or commandment to the contrary. This Act probably did not create any new privilege, but merely declared the existing right of *all* the freeholders to take part in the election.

In 1429, however, it was found necessary to curtail
this right, owing to the riots that took place at the
elections; and the possession of a freehold of at least 40s.
clear annual value was thenceforth fixed as a qualification
for a county vote. St. 8 Hen. 6, c. 7, by which this
was effected, also repeated, as to knights of the shire, the
qualification of residence which had been required by an
Act of 1 Hen. 5, for the eligibility of representatives of
both counties and towns. The election of deputies for
cities and boroughs gradually fell into the hands of the
corporations. At first they obtained the concurrence of
the whole community in the choice, but ultimately they
acquired exclusive control over it.

4. **Members.**—The first instance of an heir to the
peerage sitting in the Lower House was in 1549, when,
upon the Earl of Bedford succeeding to the peerage, it was
ordered that his son, who was then a member, should
continue in the House. The second occurred in 1575,
in favour of the son of the individual in whose case the
point had been first decided. Since that time it has
become a usual practice.

The payment of members by their constituencies, and
the necessity of their being resident in the counties or
towns which they represented, fell into disuse about the
time of Elizabeth; and it was in her reign that the first
instance occurred of punishment for bribery. About the
same time the House successfully asserted its right to
determine all cases of contested elections. It is true that
in the following reign the royal proclamation for the
meeting of Parliament in 1604 arrogated a control over
the elections; but the case of Fortescue and Goodwin's
election in that year was the last attempt to dispute the
exclusive jurisdiction of the House in the matter. The

right of the House to expel one of its members, which was asserted in the case of Arthur Hall in 1581 (see p. 146), was frequently exercised by the Long Parliament.

New Boroughs.—The control exercised by the Crown over the constitution of the Lower House by the arbitrary creation of new parliamentary boroughs was continued by the successors of Henry VIII. Under Edward VI. the privilege of returning members was granted to fourteen additional towns, and restored to ten who had lost it by disuse. Mary added twenty-one, Elizabeth sixty-two, and James I. twenty-seven new members to the Lower House. Many of the so-called decayed boroughs, the scandal of which was one of the causes of the Reform Act of 1832, were thus created, when their condition was no better than it was three centuries later. Some of them received the franchise at the same time as their charters of incorporation, in the hope, which proved illusory, that prosperity would follow. To others it was granted merely on account of their being part of the ancient demesne of the Crown, or subject to its influence. The practice was especially carried out in Cornwall, where the Stannary Court was a ready engine of royal coercion. Thus, between the accession of Edward VI. and the death of Elizabeth the number of Cornish boroughs returning members was increased from five to twenty-one. In 1563 eight new boroughs at once were created by charter, a measure which was acquiesced in by the House of Commons, though not without question. In the reign of Ja. I the Commons resolved that every town which had at any time returned members to Parliament was entitled to a writ as a matter of course. And in accordance with this resolution, the privilege was, upon their petition, restored to fifteen boroughs during that and the following reign.

The County Palatine and city of Durham were first admitted to the franchise in 1673.

5. **Members.**—After the Revolution the Crown and its ministers being unable any longer to coerce the House of Commons, endeavoured to secure a majority within its walls by a large distribution of places, pensions, and titles of honour. With the prerogative of the Crown in granting the last of these attractions the House never took upon itself to interfere, and thwarted an attempt of the Upper House to do so. But when William III. began to multiply offices for the purpose of controlling Parliament, the Lower House in 1693 passed a Bill to prohibit all members thereafter elected from accepting any office under the Crown. This Bill having been thrown out by the Lords, a similar measure was introduced in the following year and passed both Houses, but was lost from a refusal of the royal assent. The Act of Settlement in 1700 enacted that, after the accession of the House of Hanover, no person holding an office or place of profit under the king, or receiving a pension from the Crown, should be able to sit in the House of Commons. This enactment, if carried out, would have brought Parliament into hopeless conflict with the executive, but it was repealed in Anne's reign before it came into operation, and the Act for the Security of the Crown and Succession (6 Ann. c. 41), contained clauses instead to incapacitate from sitting in the House the holders of any new office created after the 25th October 1705, as well as persons in receipt of a pension from the Crown during pleasure, and to oblige members to vacate their seats on accepting any of the existing offices, though they were allowed to be immediately re-elected. Even in the preceding reign certain Government officials, such as the Commissioners of Stamps and

Excise, had been expressly excluded from the House, and to these others were now added. But owing to the reservation in favour of old offices the House was still liable to be swamped with placemen, and previously to 1742 we find upwards of 200 officials actually holding seats. In that year, however, a short Act was passed, which excluded at one sweep a vast number of commissioners and clerks in public offices, and the number was forty years later still further reduced, when Lord Rockingham's Civil List Act suppressed many superfluous offices which had been usually held by members. Further special disqualifications of particular offices have since been added. The common law judges had been from the earliest times incapable of sitting in the Lower House. This incapacity was from time to time extended by statute to the Scotch and Irish judges, and to the holders of newly created judicial offices in England; so that the only judge now capable of sitting in the House is the Master of the Rolls. An exception from disqualification has always been made in favour of the holders of naval and military commissions; and officers of the militia, yeomanry, and volunteers, enjoy the same privilege of sitting.

The provision in 6 Ann. c. 41, with reference to persons receiving pensions from the Crown, which was a few years later extended to pensions for a limited term of years, proved ineffectual to restrain the undue influence thus obtained by the Crown, owing to the practice adopted by ministers of granting secret pensions out of the large sums annually voted by Parliament as secret service money, to be applied for purposes which it was against the interests of the nation to disclose. This abuse was at length checked by Lord Rockingham's Act, already alluded to, which restricted the grants of secret service money to a small amount, and contained stringent provisions to prevent its being applied in pensions (22 Geo. 3, c. 82). Moreover, the purchase of the support of members by entrusting them with lucrative Government contracts extensively prevailed, until an Act of the same year prohibited contractors for the public service from sitting in the House (22 Geo. 3, c. 45).

Nor did the ministers of the Crown content themselves with obtaining by these means the general support of members of the House. They did not scruple to offer special sums of money for votes on particular occasions when an important measure was at stake. This bribery of members was commenced in Cha. 2's reign, and was largely resorted to by the ministers of Will. 3. It was partly with a view to secure the return of members who would be free from temptation of this kind, and partly in order to exclude rich commercial men, that a measure passed both Houses in 1696, and, after failing to secure William's assent, became law in the following reign, which imposed as a qualification of membership the receipt of an annual income from land to the amount of £300 in case of a burgess, and £600 in case of a knight of the shire. But even persons holding this amount of property were found venal, and bribery of members was reduced to an organised system under the administration of Sir Robert Walpole, and was continued by his successors. The dispensing of the bribes was popularly known as the "management of the House of Commons" and was entrusted to an experienced ministerial agent. Little or no secret was made of the practice, and correct reports were not unfrequently circulated of the sum which a division of importance had cost the Government. Besides the payment of actual sums, bribery sometimes took the form of a distribution of shares in public loans and lotteries under their market value. It is said that by this latter means the country sustained a loss of £385,000 in 1763, and of as much as £900,000 in 1781. The direct bribery of members of Parliament appears to have ceased about the close of the American war. It is at any rate certain that Mr Pitt, though he employed it to obtain the consent of the members of the Irish Parliament to the Act of Union, never resorted to it in the English House of Commons, and no minister has since ventured to do so. Mr Pitt, moreover, in his first year of office began the practice of receiving sealed tenders for the public loans, which enabled him to accept the most favourable terms offered; and he distributed the lottery tickets among the subscribers to the loan in proportion to the sums which they lent. The change thus effected was of hardly less importance than Lord Rockingham's Contractors' Act in restraining the indirect bribery of members of Parliament by the Government.

Exclusion.—In 1714 Sir Richard Steele was expelled from the House for writing a pamphlet called the *Crisis*, reflecting on the ministry. Fifty years later the Commons expelled Wilkes for publishing the *North Briton*, No. 45 (see p. 149); and when in 1768 he was returned for Middlesex to a new Parliament, he was again expelled. Being immediately re-elected, he suffered a third expulsion, accompanied by a resolution of the House, that his expulsion rendered him incapable of being elected a member to serve during the continuance of that Parliament,—an extension of their right of exclusion which was of very doubtful legality. In defiance of the House he was again re-elected, but the election was of course declared void; and upon a new election, when the constituency persisted in placing him at the head of the poll, the House gave the seat to the candidate who obtained the next largest number of votes. The contest was thus for a time ended, but

Wilkes was returned in a subsequent Parliament, and at length obtained from the House a resolution that all the proceedings connected with the Middlesex election should be expunged from its records.

Insolvency was first recognised as a disqualification for a seat in the House of Commons in 1812, when it was enacted that upon the bankruptcy of any member he should be debarred from sitting and voting for twelve months; and if at the end of that time the bankruptcy was not annulled, or his debts paid in full, his seat should be deemed vacant, and be filled up by a new election.

Elections.—The Bill of Rights affirmed that elections of members of Parliament ought to be free. But after the Revolution the independence of the elections, like that of the House itself, though in no risk of forcible infringement, was liable to a danger of a different kind. It was natural that members who took bribes themselves should not scruple to employ the same means in order to retain a position which they could turn to personal profit. Bribery of electors like that of members existed in the reign of Cha. 2, and increased after the Revolution. At the beginning of Geo. 2's reign its prevalence had excited such alarm, as to lead in 1729 to an Act which inflicted severe penalties on persons receiving bribes. But notwithstanding this measure, and others on the same subject, the practice continued to increase. The validity of a disputed election was at this time determined by the whole House, and it was found almost impossible to obtain a vote adverse to the election of a member of the dominant party. To remedy this scandal, Mr Grenville in 1770 obtained the passing of an Act, which transferred the jurisdiction over all cases of controverted elections to a sworn committee of thirteen members.

Acts of Union.—The Act of Union with Scotland

(6 Ann., c. 11) provided that 45 representatives of that kingdom should sit in the Lower House in the Parliament of Great Britain, of whom 30 should be chosen by the shires, and 15 by the royal burghs. And by the Act of Union with Ireland in 1800 (39 & 40 Geo. 3, c. 67), the number of Irish members in the House of Commons of the United Kingdom was fixed at 100, being two for each county, two for each of the cities of Dublin and Cork, one for Trinity College, and one for each of the 31 principal boroughs.

Representation.—The three chief defects in the representation of the people in the House of Commons arose—(i.) from the number of parliamentary boroughs which had either been originally rotten, or else had decayed through migration of the population; (ii.) from the fact that the elections had in nearly all the boroughs fallen into the hands of the corporation; and (iii.) from the growth of wealthy and populous commercial towns, which possessed no right of sending members to Parliament. The existence of these defects led Lord Chatham to advocate the reform of the House of Commons as early as 1766. The subject was taken up by his son, after having been agitated in the interval by Wilkes and others; but the king being averse to it, Mr Pitt did not press the matter, and on the outbreak of the French Revolution all idea of it was abandoned. After the close of the war in 1815, proposals for reform were again started, and were brought almost annually before Parliament. Some of these were of a very advanced character, extending to manhood suffrage, and even to the female franchise, together with equal electoral districts, vote by ballot, and annual parliaments. Towards the close of Geo. 4's reign the agitation for reform received an impetus from the disclosure of corrupt practices of a flagrant character in some of the close corporations and rotten boroughs. The accession of Will. 4 was soon followed by the advent to power of Lord Grey and a Whig ministry, by whom a reform bill was introduced early in 1831. After carrying the second reading in the Commons by a majority of one in a house of 608, they were beaten upon the Bill in committee, and dissolved Parliament. In the new House of Commons they had a decisive majority, and passed the Bill in the month of September. But it was thrown out by the Lords in the following month, upon which Parliament was prorogued till December, and when it met again the Bill was brought in anew with improvements founded on the recent census and on statistics obtained in the interval. This Bill having passed the Commons in March, was read a second time in the Upper House by a small majority. When, however, the Bill went into committee, the ministry met with an adverse vote, and resigned; but it being impossible to form any other administration, they were speedily recalled, and the Reform Bill passed both Houses, and became law on the 7th June 1832.

By its provisions 56 rotten boroughs, with less than 2000 inhabitants, and returning 111 members, were swept away. Thirty boroughs, having an aggregate of less than 4000 inhabitants, lost each a member, and Weymouth and Melcombe Regis were in future to return two between them instead of four. Thus 143 seats were left to be apportioned between the different towns and counties in the United Kingdom requiring additional representation. The right of returning two members was granted to 22 large towns, including metropolitan districts, and that of returning one to 21 more; and at the same time provision was made for altering the boundaries of the parliamentary boroughs. The number of county members was increased from 94 to 159, the larger counties being divided into distinct representative divisions, and a third member being given to others. The occupation of a house of the yearly value of £10 or upwards was fixed as the qualification for the franchise in boroughs, the rights of freemen of corporate towns being alone reserved. The county constituency was enlarged by the admission of persons holding copyhold or leasehold land of a certain value. And an endeavour was made to lessen the expenses of elections by the registration of electors, the division of counties and boroughs into convenient polling districts, and a reduction of the days of polling (2 & 3 Will. 4, c. 45).

In the same session a Scotch Reform Bill was passed, by which the number of Scotch representatives was increased from 45 to 53, 30 of whom were given to counties, and 23 to cities and boroughs. The county franchise was extended to owners of property of £10 a year, and to certain classes of leaseholders, and the burgh franchise to all £10 householders (2 & 3 Will. 4, c. 65).

The disfranchisement of rotten boroughs in Ireland had been effected at the Union, but a Reform Act was passed for that country, which took away the right of election from the corporations, and vested it in the £10 householders, and made large additions to the county constituencies. The number of Irish members was at the same time increased from 100 to 105 (2 & 3 Will. 4, c. 88).

The effect of the three Acts was thus to leave the total number of members at its former figure, 658.

6. **Members.**—As the result of the measures already noticed for restricting the tenure of offices and pensions by members, there were in the reformed House of Commons of 1833 only 60 members who held civil offices and pensions from the Crown. The requirement of 6 Ann. c. 41, as to vacation of seat and re-election on the accept-

ance of any office under the Crown, has been dispensed with by the Reform Acts of 1867-8 in the case of the transfer of a member of the ministry from one office to another.

The property qualification of members, after being altered at the commencement of Queen Victoria's reign, was altogether abolished in 1858.

Exclusion.—The right of the House to expel and exclude its members has more than once been the subject of discussion in the reformed Parliament. In 1849, when Smith O'Brien, M.P. had been adjudged guilty of high treason, the House ordered the Speaker to cause a writ to be issued for a new election to supply his place; and in 1870, when O'Donovan Rossa was returned for Tipperary, while under sentence of penal servitude for life for treason-felony, they prefaced a similar order with a resolution that Rossa, by his conviction and sentence, had become and continued incapable of being elected or returned a member of the House. In the same year, any doubts which might have existed as to the legality of this proceeding were set at rest by a provision in the Act which abolished forfeiture for treason and felony, that persons convicted of those offences should, while undergoing punishment, be incapable of sitting or voting as a member of either House, or of exercising any parliamentary or municipal franchise.

Representation.—In 1850 the borough franchise in Ireland was extended to £8 householders, and a reduction was made in the qualifications required for the county franchise in that country. During the years 1850-60 several measures for further reform in England were unsuccessfully proposed. Lord Palmerston, who became prime minister in 1859, was disinclined to move in the matter, and after the abandonment of the Bill of 1860, it made no progress during the remainder of his tenure of office, which lasted till his death in October 1865. Meantime the demand for the lowering of the franchise and a redistribution of seats had been strengthened by the vast increase of the population, and the growth of new towns of large dimensions not possessing the franchise; and in the session after Lord Palmerston's death, Earl Russell's Government brought in a Reform Bill, upon the details of which they were defeated, and resigned office in consequence. In the following year, 1867, Lord Derby's Conservative ministry, by the management of Mr Disraeli in the House of Commons, and with the help of their opponents, who were in a large majority in that House, succeeded in carrying a comprehensive measure of reform in England, which they supplemented in the following year by similar Acts for Scotland and Ireland (30 & 31 Vict. c. 102; 31 & 32 Vict. c. 48; 31 & 32 Vict. c. 49).

By these Acts the borough franchise was given in England and Scotland to every man of full age after a residence of twelve months within the borough, either as a householder paying the poor-rate, or as a lodger in lodgings which would let unfurnished for at least £10 a year. A similar franchise was accorded to Ireland, but instead of the household franchise, votes in the Irish boroughs were given to occupiers of houses or land within them rated at a net annual value of not less than £4. The county franchise in Great Britain was at the same time extended to all persons possessed of land in the county of the clear yearly value of £5 and upwards, except persons holding under short leases, and to all owners or tenants paying the poor-rate, and occupying land in the county of the rateable value of at least £12 in England, and £14 in Scotland. As the qualifications for the county franchise in Ireland had been already reduced by the Act of 1850 to almost exactly these figures, no alteration of it was con-

sidered necessary. Nor as regards Ireland was any
change made in the shares of the representation allotted
to the boroughs and counties. In Great Britain, however,
and more particularly in England, these underwent considerable modification. Several boroughs were deprived
of one of their members; and on the other hand, new
boroughs were created, old boroughs received a third
member, and large and populous counties, which had previously formed one constituency, were divided into districts with a distinct representation for each district.

At the same time a totally new principle, that of the
representation of minorities, was in a very imperfect and
partial manner introduced into our representative system,
by the provision that at contested elections in a constituency returning three members, no person should vote
for more than two candidates, nor in the city of London,
which returns four members, for more than three candidates. The effects of this is, that in these constituencies
at a general election the party who are in the minority
can usually secure one of the seats; but in the rest of the
country the elections are left as before, altogether in the
hands of the majorities of the constituencies; and even in
the favoured places themselves the minority may lose
their representation if their candidate happens to die or
vacate his seat during the continuance of the Parliament,
since in the election to supply the vacancy the majority
can assert their numerical superiority without restraint.
This, however, is of course also the case where elections are
conducted with the cumulative vote (see p. 123).

The total number of members was left unchanged by
the Reform Acts of 1867-8; but seven seats were transferred from English to Scotch constituencies, so that at
present England and Wales return 493, Scotland 60, and
Ireland 105 members.

The Reform Act of 1832 has been followed at intervals by measures for simplifying and improving the registration of electors, for increasing the number of polling places, and for reducing the time of polling to one day in counties and boroughs, and to five days in the Universities. The proceedings at University elections were further altered in 1861, by the power then given to persons entitled to take part in them, to record their votes by voting papers, instead of coming up from all parts of the kingdom to exercise the franchise.

Many measures have been taken during the last forty years with a view to the suppression of bribery at Parliamentary elections, but hitherto with only partial success. Several boroughs have been disfranchised on account of its prevalence in them; and in 1854 an Act was passed, limited in its duration to one year, but annually renewed ever since, which made the offer or acceptance of a bribe a misdemeanour punishable with fine, imprisonment, and forfeiture of franchise; and prohibited treating, cockades, colours and music at elections. And since experience proved that the committees before whom elections were impugned on the ground of corruption, were apt to look on the case with too lenient eyes, the House in 1868 surrendered in favour of the courts of law its long-cherished privilege of exclusive jurisdiction in cases of controverted elections. The present mode of questioning the validity of an election is to present a petition against it, which is tried before one of the judges of the superior Courts of common law. The judge certifies the result of the trial to the Speaker, and at the same time reports any corrupt practices which have been proved before him, and the House takes the requisite action on his certificate and report.

The existence of bribery and intimidation was one of the main reasons adduced for the Ballot Act of 1872.

The proposal to substitute voting by ballot for the old English method of open voting was made in almost every session after 1832, and was actually carried in the House of Commons in 1848. But it subsequently fell into disfavour, and its chance of becoming law was very small until Mr Gladstone's Government took it up in 1871. The Ballot Bill of that year was thrown out by the Lords, but in the following session an Act was passed abolishing the open nomination of candidates on the hustings, and imposing a secret ballot as the method of polling at all parliamentary and municipal elections, except in the Universities (35 & 36 Vict. c. 33). The Act was to continue in force till the 31st December 1880.

CHAPTER VI.
THE KING'S COUNCIL.

1. Pre-Norman Period.—It is almost impossible to conceive of any monarch, however great his power and intellect, being able to exercise dominion over a considerable community without receiving continual advice and assistance from at least a few of his subjects. Accordingly, we find that the early English kings, besides consulting the Witenagemot, kept certain counsellors permanently attached to their court for the purpose of discharging the functions of government. They had their *stallere* or *constable*, their dish-thegn, their bower-thegn or chamberlain, and their chancellor—officers originally charged, as their names imply, with menial duties in the palace, but in process of time entrusted with the military, financial, and general administration of the realm.

2. Concilium Ordinarium.—It was shown in the last chapter, how, at the Conquest, the Witenagemot was

superseded by a feudal assembly—the council of the king's
barons or vassals. This, according to the feudal theory,
was the proper council from which the king should seek
and receive advice, and ought to have been assembled
by him thrice in the year. But attendance at the
king's court involved on the part of its members, who
were scattered throughout the country, an interruption
of their domestic and local affairs, and the performance of
an arduous journey; so that they were probably by no
means dissatisfied with the fact, that the king, instead of
convening the whole body, resorted to the advice of a
select number of the members of the Great Council, consisting of those nobles, both lay and ecclesiastical, who
held permanent offices of state, and were therefore more
or less constantly about the king's person, and of a few
others who were specially summoned by him. This
smaller body was called the *Concilium Ordinarium*, or
Permanent Council. Like the Great Council it was,
before it parted with its judicial functions, and even for
some time afterwards, called the *Aula Regia* or *Curia
Regis*, and was presided over by the king, or in his
absence by the chief justiciary (see p. 137). Its regular
members under the early Norman kings were the chief
justiciary, lord chancellor, lord treasurer, lord steward,
chamberlain, earl marshal, and constable. But besides
these, there were sometimes present in it the comptroller
of the household, the chancellor of the exchequer, the
judges, the king's serjeant, and other officials. While its
members in their different official capacities attended to
different branches of the royal and public business—the
justiciary, for instance, to judicial matters, the chancellor
to the king's grants and appointments, the constable and
marshal to military and foreign affairs, the treasurer to
the public finance, and the steward and chamberlain to

the management of the king's palace and private property
—all in their position of counsellors united in deliberating on public affairs, and took part in the administration of them. At first the *Concilium Ordinarium* was merely a sort of standing committee of the Great Council. It held its meetings at the times of the year when that body ought, strictly speaking, to have been summoned; and whenever the latter was convened, the Ordinary Council sat with it, and became merged for the time being in the larger assembly. Gradually, however, just as it became separated from its offshoots, the law courts, on the one hand (see below, ch. viii.), so on the other it became a defined institution distinct from the Great Council or Parliament; and it eventually met at all times of the year according to the exigencies of state affairs. Yet even so late as Hen. 4's reign, we find a resolution that nothing should be transacted in the council out of term-time, except matters which would not admit of delay.

3. **Origin of Privy Council.**—At first the only avenue of admission to the council which was open to commoners lay through the Church; but in Hen. 4's reign, in 1404, we find, as the members of his council, three bishops, nine peers, and seven commoners, of whom six were knights—making nineteen in all. The councillors at this time held their office for a year only; but not long afterwards they were appointed for life, though they continued removable at the king's pleasure, or at their own wish. During the minority of Henry VI. they were nominated by Parliament, but ordinarily, like all other officers of state, they held their appointments from the Crown. They, or at least those of them who attended regularly, were bound by a special oath to advise the king according to the best of their ability, to

keep the king's counsel secret, and to assist in the execution of what should be resolved on, and were paid salaries of considerable amount. About the time of Hen. 6 a distinct line of demarcation was drawn between the sworn and paid counsellors and the occasional members of the council, the former being constituted into the Privy Council, and monopolising all the administrative and executive duties.

4. The Council under the Tudors and Stuarts. —The distinction between privy councillors and ordinary councillors is met with in Hen. 8's reign, and it is one which, in fact, exists to the present day; for although all persons appointed to the council are sworn and considered as privy councillors, they do not attend the council board unless specially summoned. The ordinary councillors of Hen. 8's time and subsequent reigns were qualified to take part in the judicial business of the council in its court of Star Chamber, but not in its administrative functions. In Hen. 8's reign increased importance was given to the office of president of the council, and an Act was passed to fix the order of precedence in Parliament, and in the council, of the person who held this position, and of the other principal officers of state (31 Hen. 8, c. 10). In Edw. 6's reign the council consisted of 40 persons, of whom 22 were commoners, and was divided into five commissions or committees, to which different judicial and administrative functions were assigned. Under this arrangement the committee "for the state," composed of one-half of the whole number, was in fact the Privy Council, while those who were not upon it were in the position of ordinary councillors. The numerical proportion and influence of commoners in the council was maintained by Elizabeth, but declined in favour of the

nobility in the reigns of the first two Stuarts. After the
Restoration, when the Star Chamber, and with it the
judicial functions of the Privy Council, had been abolished, the reason for the existence of ordinary as distinct
from privy councillors no longer existed. From that time,
therefore, all the councillors were sworn as privy councillors; but, while Charles II. largely increased their
number, he introduced the practice of summoning only a
limited number of them to deliberate on state affairs.
Thus was originated the Cabinet, of which more will be
said in ch. ix.

5. The Council since the Revolution.—Although,
since the Revolution, the whole administrative functions
of the council have been monopolised by the Cabinet,
the council has continued to exist as the legally recognised
body to which those functions are entrusted, and of which
the Cabinet is, in the eye of the law, merely a committee,
like the committee "for the state" of Edw. 6's reign.
Thus it was against a foreigner, even though naturalised,
becoming a privy councillor, and not merely against his
being a member of the Cabinet, that a clause of the Act
of Settlement of 1700 was directed; it was a privy councillor, an assault upon whom when in discharge of his
duties was made felony, without benefit of clergy, in Queen
Anne's reign; and it was the whole Privy Council, and
not the Cabinet only, which, by a statute of the same reign,
was empowered to continue and act for six months after
a demise of the sovereign, having previously been *ipso
facto* dissolved upon that event.

6. Committees of the Council.—The Cabinet, as
at present constituted, usually consists of the 15 leading
members of the ministry for the time being. There are,

besides, other committees of the Privy Council for dealing with special subjects. After the suppression, in 1782, of the Commissioners of Trade and Plantations, the supervision of mercantile and colonial affairs, formerly entrusted to them, was transferred to a committee of the council called the Board of Trade. In 1833, when appellate judicial powers of large extent were restored to the council, it was provided that they should be exercised by a committee called the Judicial Committee of the Privy Council. And, early in Queen Victoria's reign, when the practice had been commenced of making annual parliamentary grants for educational purposes, a "Committee of Council on Education" was appointed by the Crown to superintend the distribution of the money voted. A few years afterwards, the Poor Law Commissioners, appointed in the preceding reign, were superseded by the Poor Law Board, of which four cabinet ministers were to be ex-officio members. This Board, however, was not obliged to be exclusively composed of privy councillors; but in 1871 it was in turn abolished, and its functions, as well as the powers previously vested in the Privy Council at large, the Board of Trade, and the Home Secretary, in reference to public health and other matters, were transferred to a new committee of the council, consisting of cabinet ministers, and styled "The Local Government Board." All privy councillors, whether at the time serving on any of its committees and boards or not, are distinguished by the title of "Right Honourable." The fact that they enjoy this title in common with the peers, the members of the Upper House, which, as has been stated, is the present representative of the old Great Council, is a vestige of the close connection which formerly existed between that body and the king's smaller council.

PART III.

Central Government.

CHAPTER VII.

LEGISLATION.

1. Pre-Norman Legislation.—In the English constitution the king has ever theoretically been vested with the supreme legislative as well as executive powers. But in the exercise of his legislative functions a certain number of his subjects have been almost always, at least nominally, associated with him. In the early times the king frequently, perhaps in the majority of cases, took the initiative in legislation; but all the laws were expressed as made with the counsel and consent of the *witan*. Ælfred, for instance, in the preface to his code, states that he had introduced into it many former laws which appeared to him good, while those old laws which he disapproved he had rejected by the counsel of his witan; and that, having made his compilation, he had shown it to all his witan, who had expressed their approval of it. The above remarks apply to ecclesiastical and civil legislation alike; for the king, with the advice of the lay and spiritual members of the Witenagemot, made laws upon religious no less than upon secular subjects.

2. Early Norman Legislation.—During the reigns of the Conqueror and his sons the laws were put forth in the form of charters granted or promulgated by the king, which, however, always contained an expression to the effect that they were made with the counsel and consent of the nobles. The same was the case with the assizes or constitutions, as they were called, of Hen. 2's reign. Magna Carta was granted by the counsel of the archbishops, bishops, and nobles, and other faithful subjects; and we know that as regards this instrument such was the actual fact: but probably in many of the enactments of John's predecessors the expression of *consent* was no more than a form, or if the consent of the nobles was actually asked for, it was granted as a matter of course, without any option on their part to withhold it. And in many cases the utmost that the words can be taken as implying is, that the decree received the assent of the *Concilium Ordinarium;* for whilst the meetings of the Great Council were infrequent, the former body no doubt possessed considerable legislative as well as executive power. This is evident from the fact that in Edw. 1's reign, when Parliaments, which had taken the place of Great Councils, began to meet regularly, and enact statutes in due form, there were issued, distinct from these parliamentary statutes, articles and ordinances expressed as made by the king and his council. There are a few laws in our statute book in which the mention even of the council is omitted, and which therefore ostensibly rest on the authority of the king alone.

Early Parliamentary Legislation.—The admission into Parliament of all three estates of the realm[1] did not at once lead to the distribution of the legislative power among all. The main object of the presence of the clergy

[1] See note I, p. 138.

and the commons being to sanction taxation, the latter were until 1295 sometimes summoned not *ad faciendum,* "in order to enact," but only *ad consulendum et consentiendum hiis quæ comites, barones et proceres ordinaverint,* "in order to give counsel and consent to such things as the earls, barons, and nobles shall ordain." Occasionally, as in 1290 and 1294, all the legislation of the year was transacted by the barons before the representatives of the commons had assembled. In 1290 the important statute *Quia Emptores,* which put an end to the subinfeudation of land, was thus passed without their concurrence. But from the year 1295 their enacting functions were always recognised in the language of the writs by which they were summoned.

3. **Growth of Power of Parliament.**—Edward II., in the third year of his reign, was prevailed upon to empower the lords of the realm to choose a body of persons called ordainers, who should make ordinances for the government of the royal household and of the kingdom in general. These ordinances having imposed considerable restrictions on the king's prerogative were repealed in 1322; and it was at the same time expressly enacted that all matters concerning the estate of the king, the estate of the realm, and of the people, should be treated of and established in Parliaments by the king, and by the assent of the prelates, earls, and barons, and the commonalty of the realm, according as it had been theretofore accustomed. The principle thus laid down became fully recognised in the course of the following reign. The continuous practice of expressing in Acts of Parliament the concurrence of the commonalty as well as of the lords dates from 1318, a few years previously. About this time the Commons began to exercise the right of initiating legislation

by *petition*. Every petition was referred to certain spiritual and temporal lords, appointed from time to time as *auditores petitionum*, receivers or tryers of petitions, and the king returned an answer to it in accordance with their advice. Then from the petition and answer together the statute was drawn up by the judges,—a practice which, of course, involved the risk of a deviation in the Act from the intention of the Commons, and which in fact was often fraudulently taken advantage of to effect that result. The statute so drawn up was expressed as made, not by the assent of the Lords and Commons, but by the assent of the Lords and at the request of the Commons.

The clergy also, as late as the reigns of Ric. 2 and Hen. 4, either in Parliament or in Convocation, presented petitions which became law *at their request* by the assent of the Lords alone, without the concurrence of the Commons. The laws against heresy of 5 Ric. 2 and 2 Hen. 4, which were incorporated into the statute book, were of this description.

Bills.—The practice of legislating by Bills was gradually introduced in the reign of Hen. 6, and it soon became a recognised principle, that in accordance with a concession made by Henry V. in the second year of his reign, but not immediately observed, the king must accept or reject the Bill in its entirety, without qualification or alteration. But if slight alterations were made by the Lords in a Bill sent up to them from the Commons, it was not at this time held necessary that it should be sent back to the latter for assent to the amendment. The presentation by the Commons of private petitions, for which private Bills were afterwards substituted, was introduced in Hen. 5's reign, and the greater part of the Rolls of Parliament of that and the following reign was occupied with statutes founded upon them. The main features of the form now used in Acts of Parliament—" Be it enacted by the

King's Most Excellent Majesty, by and with the advice and consent of the Lords spiritual and temporal and Commons in this present Parliament assembled, and by the authority of the same," have been employed with tolerable regularity since 1 Hen. 7, from which time the statutes, formerly drawn up in Latin or French, and afterwards in duplicate in one of these languages and in English, were exclusively drawn in English. The word "assent," however, was originally used instead of "consent," and the expressions "our Sovereign Lord the King," and "the King's Highness," instead of "the King's Majesty." All the enactments made in one session were up to this time looked upon as chapters of one statute, and it was not until 7 Hen. 7 that it became customary to prefix a separate title to each particular chapter, and to treat the chapters as distinct Acts. The separation of private Acts (which are only binding upon the persons specified in them, and not upon the nation at large) from the public general statutes appears to date from 31 Hen. 8.

Legislation by King in Council.—But legislation, in certain cases, by ordinances (or laws which wanted the consent of one branch of the Legislature), and by proclamations issued on the authority of the king and his council alone, independently of Parliament, was still continued. The practice was expressly sanctioned, under certain limitations, by st. 31 Hen. 8, c. 8, which enacted that the king, with the advice of a majority of his council, might set forth at all times by the authority of that Act his proclamations, under such penalties and pains as might seem necessary, and that the same should be obeyed as though they were made by Act of Parliament; but the exercise of this power was not to entail upon any person or body corporate the loss of inheritance, possessions, offices, liberties, franchises, or goods, nor the punishment of death, except in the case of heretics, or of persons who left the realm to avoid a trial for an offence committed against any proclamation; nor should any proclamation subvert or infringe the existing statutes or customs of the realm. In the same reign the Act which established the Council of Wales (34 & 35 Hen. 8, c. 26) enabled the king to make laws for the Principality without the consent of Parliament. This power was abrogated in Ja. 1's reign.

Suspending and Dispensing Powers of the King.—In addition to this right of independent positive legislation, the king possessed an arbitrary power of a negative kind, in his prerogative of suspending a law altogether, or dispensing with its requirements in particular cases. Instances occur of the suspension of laws by Richard II. and Henry IV.; and throughout the reigns of all the Plantagenets a dispensing power in favour of individuals was recognised as belonging to the king, and was frequently exercised by him. Thus, although st. 23 Hen. 6, c. 7, after declaring that all patents to hold the office of sheriff for more than one year should be void, expressly enacted that the king should not have a dispensing power in the matter, yet all the judges in Hen. 7's reign held that the king might, by virtue of that power, grant a patent for a longer term on good grounds, whereof he alone was judge. The ancient and undoubted prerogative of pardon, which is possessed by the Crown, is in a sense a power of dispensing with the law of the land. Attempts were from time to time made to restrain it by statute, but all such enactments have been held void, and have been disregarded.

Ecclesiastical Legislation.—In the 46th year of Edw. 3 we find in the writs of summons to Parliament the declaration that Parliament is to be held "upon arduous and pressing matters .... affecting the state and defence of our realm of England and the English Church."[1] This mention of the Church, though it never occurs before, has been repeated ever afterwards; but its first insertion does not appear to have been due to any change in the relations between Church and State. On the contrary, it merely expressed the control over ecclesiastical affairs which the great national council continued to exercise after the Conquest —though in a less degree than before, owing to the connection between Church and State having been weakened by the intervention of a foreign element, the ecclesiastical dictation of the Court of Rome. When the Convocations separated from Parliament (see p. 141) they claimed and exercised a concurrent power of legislation for the clergy in Church matters.

4. **Limitation of the King's Powers.**—The Statute which had invested royal proclamations with the force of Acts of Parliament was repealed by 1 Edw. 6, c. 12, but the arbitrary issue of these proclamations was long continued on many matters in which such an interference was not authorised by the law. In Mary's reign the judges laid down that the sovereign might make a proclamation to put the people in fear of his displeasure, but not to impose any fine, forfeiture, or imprisonment, "for no proclamation can make a new law, but only confirm and ratify an ancient one." The limits thus defined were not, however, strictly observed. In the next three reigns we find proclamations against the growth of London, against the residence of the county gentry there, against the eating of flesh in Lent, or on Fridays and Saturdays, and on other matters affecting the liberty of the subject. One in 1634 fixed the price of poultry and butter. The

[1] "Super arduis et urgentibus negotiis .... statum et defensionem regni nostri Angliæ et Ecclesiæ Anglicanæ contingentibus."

violation of them was frequently punished by fine or imprisonment through the medium of proceedings in the Star Chamber. In 1610 a remonstrance by the Commons against them led to a reaffirmation by Sir Edward Coke and some members of the council, whom the king consulted on the subject, of the principles laid down by Queen Mary's judges. Notwithstanding this the practice was not abandoned, a few instances of it being found as late as Cha. 2's reign. The illegal proclamation of James II. on the subject of the customs is noticed in ch. x.

On the other hand, after the shock which the constitution sustained by the later proceedings of the Long Parliament, and the establishment of the Commonwealth, it was deemed necessary by express enactment (13 Cha. 2, st. 1, c. 1, s. 3), to deny the existence of any legislative power in either House of Parliament, or both Houses, without the king, and to impose the penalty of a premunire on a person who ventured by writing, or in speech, to affirm its existence. But while the inability of the separate branches of the Legislature to make laws without the concurrence of all three was being thus gradually established, the claim on the part of the king, not only to dispense with laws already made in favour of particular individuals, but also to suspend their operation as regarded the whole community, was not finally surrendered without a struggle.

In the reign of Cha. 2, in the course of a private suit, the legality of the king's dispensing power came under the consideration of the judges. It was then held that the power could not be exercised with regard to the common law, or any statute prohibiting a thing which was in itself wrong or injurious, nor so as to prejudice the rights or interests of an individual or corporation.

The deliberate employment, by James II., of the royal powers of dispensing with and suspending laws, in order "to subvert and extirpate the Protestant religion, and the lawes and liberties of this kingdome," was questioned in the courts, and formally declared to be legal by the judges of that day. A collusive action was brought against Sir Edward Hales, who, in defiance of the Test Act, had accepted the commission of colonel without having received the sacrament in the Church of England. A royal dispensation was pleaded in defence, and eleven judges out of twelve affirmed the king's right to dispense with the Test Act. Not content with this dispensing power, James, by his Declarations of Indulgence, took upon himself to suspend altogether the operation of the penal statutes which had been enacted in former reigns against Roman Catholics and Protestant Dissenters. It was evident that the assumption of this despotic prerogative, by which laws, however fundamental or important, could be abrogated at the mere will of the king, was inconsistent with a limited monarchy; and the exercise of it was one of the main causes which led to the Revolution, and one of the first points upon which care was taken after that event to obtain a clear legal definition.

Passing of Bills.—The method of passing Bills through the Legislature had, before the Revolution, become settled in the form in which it now exists. According to this method the Crown can initiate no Bill, except Bills for a general pardon. The Lords possess the exclusive right of originating Bills affecting the peerage, such as for restitution of forfeited honours and reversal of outlawries; while, with the Commons alone can begin Bills imposing any tax or burden on the community. All other Bills may commence with either House indifferently. Except in the case of Bills of grace, as for a general pardon, which are passed on the first reading, the progress of a Bill is as follows:—Leave is first asked to bring in the Bill, and if obtained, it is then brought in and read a first time. These, though really two distinct stages, usually in practice follow immediately the one upon the other. At a subsequent date the Bill is read a second time, and the House then goes into committee upon it, and discusses its clauses in detail, making such alterations and additions as appear desirable. All private Bills, and sometimes public measures, instead of coming before a committee of the whole House, are referred to a select committee of a limited number of members specially appointed for the purpose. When the consideration of the Bill in committee is finished it is reported to the House, and at this stage further amendments can, if desired, be introduced, and it may be recommitted for the purpose. After the report has been finally agreed to, it is read a third time, and the question is then put, "That this Bill do pass." At any one of these stages it is liable to be lost by an adverse vote, or may be withdrawn by its promoters, if alterations are introduced into it to which they cannot assent. When passed, it is sent to the other House, where it undergoes the same process; after surviving which, it is returned to the House whence it originated, in order that the latter may consider any amendments which have been introduced into it since it left them. The amendments are either agreed to or disagreed to; and in the latter case, if both Houses persist in their respective views on the subject, a conference takes place between deputed members of both Houses with a view to coming to an agreement. If this is found impossible, the Bill must necessarily be dropped. When a Bill has been passed and agreed to by both Houses, it is submitted to the Crown for the royal assent, and becomes law upon this being given in the form, "le roi le veut;" the negative, which would be fatal to the Bill, being expressed in the courteous form, "le roi s'avisera." If a Bill has been lost at any of its stages, no second Bill to the same effect can be brought into Parliament during the same session; and if the session terminates either by prorogation or dissolution before a Bill becomes law, the steps through which it has passed are thrown away, and it must be brought in and started anew in a subsequent session. The whole process thus described is well adapted to prevent hasty legislation on any subject, and to provide the opportunity of due consideration being given to every measure. At the same time, in cases of emergency it does not unduly hinder the passing of important Bills; for, when necessity requires it, all the steps can be got through in one day. Thus, on Saturday the 17th February 1866, the Bill for the Suspension of the Habeas Corpus Act in Ireland was introduced at noon, and after passing through all its stages in both Houses, received the royal assent three-quarters of an hour after midnight.

Ecclesiastical Legislation.—Since the Reformation the king and Parliament have legislated upon all Church matters in the same manner as upon secular affairs. The legislative power of Convocation was restrained by the Act for the submission of the clergy to the king (25 Hen. 8, c. 19), which prohibited them from making any new canon, or other law without the king's previous license. This was occasionally given during the remainder of the sixteenth and first half of the seventeenth centuries. But after 1664, when Convocation ceased to grant subsidies (see ch. x.), little business was done in it. In 1717 it was suddenly prorogued on account of the excitement caused by the Bangorian controversy, which had arisen out of the denunciation by the

Lower House of the Convocation of Canterbury, of a sermon on religious liberty by Dr Hoadley, Bishop of Bangor. Thenceforward it was for more than a century regularly convened every year, and as regularly prorogued immediately afterwards. But about the year 1850 the practice of sitting for debate and discussion was resumed; and in 1861 the assembly was empowered by royal license to alter the canon which prohibited parents from being sponsors to their children. Again, in 1872 Convocation was empowered, by letters of business from the Crown, to frame resolutions on the subject of public worship, which were afterwards embodied by Parliament in the Act of Uniformity Amendment Act (35 & 36 Vict. c. 35.)

5. **Bill of Rights.**—The powers of the Crown as to interference with legislation were finally determined by the Bill of Rights (1 Will. & Mar., sess. 2, c. 2), which laid down as follows:—

"That the pretended power of suspending of laws or the execution of laws by regall authority without consent of Parlyament, is illegall.

"That the pretended power of dispensing with laws, or the execution of laws by regall authoritie, *as it hath beene assumed and exercised of late*,[*] is illegall."

Abuse of Power by House of Commons.—The right which, as will be shown in ch. x., the Commons had at this time acquired, not only of initiating money Bills, but also of having them passed through the Lords without amendment or alteration, was about this time perverted so as virtually to deprive the Lords of their right of legislative interference in other matters. In

---

[*] The qualifying words in italics, which were inserted by the Lords, have reserved to the Crown the ancient prerogative of pardoning criminals, or commuting their sentence into one of a milder character.

1692, and again in 1699, the Commons inserted in a money Bill clauses on subjects of a general character, respecting which the Lords were therefore unable to make any amendments without depriving the king of his requisite supplies. Though this most unconstitutional and reprehensible artifice was on those two occasions successful, the Commons happily did not persist in the practice.

Royal Assent.—The direct share of the king in the making of laws, none of which can become binding without his consent, was of course retained unaltered at the Revolution. William III. three times availed himself of it to reject measures which had been passed by both Houses of Parliament, but since his reign the uniform repetition of the *le roi* (or *la reine*) *le veut* has never once been broken by the contrary utterance (see p. 191). This has, no doubt, been in great part due to the fact that the affairs of the country have since that time been conducted by a united and responsible ministry, acting in harmony with the king on the one hand, and Parliament on the other, as will be explained in ch. ix. Through its intervention any difference of opinion between the sovereign and the two Houses upon a proposed measure becomes known, and is settled by concession on the one side or the other, before the final step of the submission of the Bill for the royal assent is reached. We are therefore by no means to conclude that during the last 160 years the sovereign has exercised no personal influence whatever upon the progress of legislation, but rather that this influence has been exerted in a different way, and at an earlier stage in the proceedings. The sovereign, when strongly adverse to a proposed measure, has induced his ministers to abstain from bringing it forward themselves, and to procure its defeat in Parliament if brought forward by others. Thus George III. succeeded in preventing during the whole of his reign the removal of the disabilities of Roman Catholics and their admission to political privileges, by his own personal aversion to the proposition, without the necessity of exercising his constitutional veto.

Classification of Acts.—Until 1793 all Acts which were not specified to come into operation on a given day, were held to commence from the first day of the session in which they were passed. This involved, in many cases, the injustice of retrospective legislation, and was altered by st. 33 Geo. 3, c. 13, which required all Acts in future to be endorsed with the date on which they received the royal assent, and prescribed that date as the time of their commencement, if no other date of commencement was specified in the Acts themselves. Down to 38 Geo. 3, the Acts had been divided simply into public and private, the public Acts containing many of a merely local or personal nature. But from that year onward the public Acts were divided into two series, public general and public local and personal Acts, the chapters of the former being designated by Arabic, and of the latter by Roman numbers.

6. Power of House of Commons.—The course of legislation since the Reform Act of 1832 has been marked by two principal features. The first of these is the preponderating influence and power of the House of Commons, which, as now representing with tolerable exactness the wishes of the majority of the people, is felt to be that branch of the Legislature which has the best right, within due limits, to dictate the shape to be assumed by legislation on all important public matters. The function of the Upper House, as regards these matters, has been almost exclusively confined to checking for a time or modifying the proposals of the Commons—the instances being comparatively few where it has made a permanent stand in such matters against the action of the Commons, or has initiated a course of legislation of its own.

Delegation of Legislative Functions. — The second feature has been due, in a great measure, to the immense multiplication of legislative business through the augmentation of population, and the commercial and other development of the country. The feature alluded to is the increasing tendency on the part of Parliament to delegate its legislative functions on various subjects as regards matters of detail to persons, or bodies of persons, in whom it has confidence, being content itself to lay down the main principles of the new law. Thus, in the various reforms which have been made in the procedure of our law courts, the outline has been laid down by statute, and has been left to be filled up by rules made by the judges of the courts themselves, the statute having declared that such rules when made shall have the force of law. Again, large powers have been given to the Privy Council as a whole, and to the Board of Trade and Committee of Council on Education, of making regulations on various important subjects placed under their control. As an example of this may be cited the powers given to the Privy Council in 1869 of legislating as to the conveyance of and traffic in cattle, with a view to the prevention of disease. The powers with which the same body were formerly invested of framing rules for the preservation of public health, have now been transferred to the Local Government Board. And secretaries of state are occasionally empowered to make regulations on matters within their respective provinces. So far, indeed, has the practice been carried, that in certain cases Parliament has latterly authorised the formation of public companies and construction of works of public utility,—things which were formerly always the subject of private acts,—to be temporarily effected under the authority of provisional orders of the Board of Trade, requiring, however, that such orders should at an early date be confirmed by Act of Parliament. Most of the tramways now laid down in London and elsewhere were authorised by provisional orders of this description. The willingness of Parliament thus to depute its functions is intelligible, when we remember that in most cases (that of the judges, of course, excepted), the persons to whom they are deputed are either themselves ministers of the Crown, or the nominees of ministers, liable to be changed upon a change of ministry, and they are, therefore, persons who, at the time, enjoy the confidence of Parliament, and will continue to exercise those functions only so long as that confidence is accorded to them. Moreover, a check is retained over the exercise of this delegated legislation, by the practice of enacting that the rules, regulations, and orders, thus made under the authority of Parliament, shall be laid on the table of both Houses on the earliest practicable opportunity, and that if either House disapproves of them within a given time afterwards, they shall cease to be in force. A less important form of delegation of legislative powers is to be found in the authority constantly given to companies to make bye-laws for the regulation of their own property and traffic.

Simplified Form of Legislation.—The actual machinery of legislation has been much simplified since 1832, by the disuse of superfluities and redundancies in the language of the statutes, the reference to former Acts by short titles and by the numbers of chapters and sections, instead of setting out in full the enactments alluded to, and by abandoning the repetition of the formal words of enactment in every clause.

CHAPTER VIII.

JUDICATURE.

1. Judicial power of King.—With our present developed ideas on the subject of constitutional government, we are accustomed to look upon it as essential to the well-being of a state that the judicial and legislative functions should be entirely independent of each other. But in primitive political communities we usually find them lodged in the same hands. Indeed, in the formation of these communities the office of the judge has probably in most cases preceded in point of time that of the legislator, the latter office having subsequently become developed out of the former, and having for a long time remained united to it. In other words, private laws were made retrospectively in each particular case as it arose, by the decision of the judge upon it, before the idea was conceived of framing a general prospective law which should apply to a number of cases. Previously to the eleventh century many codes of general laws had been framed by the English kings and their witan, yet we gather from the coronation oath taken by the kings in the latter part of the pre-Norman period, that their judicial duties were still considered as among the most important of those attached to their office. In that oath the king promised three things to his subjects:—1st, That the Church of God and all the Christian people should always preserve true peace under his auspices; 2dly, That he would forbid rapacity and all iniquities to every condition;

and, 3dly, That he would command equity and mercy in all judgments, in order that to him and his subjects the gracious and merciful God might extend His mercy.

The judicial functions of the king consisted at this time in deciding appeals from the local courts noticed in ch. iii.; and in trying military officers, and matters in which a high officer of state or a king's thegn was concerned, such persons being exempt from the local jurisdiction. The English kings had also adopted the practice of arbitrarily calling up to their own tribunal cases which had not yet passed through the local courts. And though crimes committed in a county were charged as breaches of the peace of the sheriff and not of the king's peace, yet the latter was so far deemed to be concerned in the maintenance of order throughout the realm, that in many cases while one-third of the fine payable for the offence went to the sheriff or the ealdorman of the shire, the remaining two-thirds were remitted to the king. In the exercise of his judicial functions the king was always assisted either by the whole Witenagemot, or by some selected members of that body.

Procedure.—The mode of procedure and form of trial employed in the king's court and in the shire-moot were much the same. We have already seen the number *twelve*, which was subsequently to become stereotyped in the institution of the jury, enter into the early English judicial system in the representation of the hundreds at the shire-moot (see p. 75). We find either it, or some multiple of it, appointed as the number of judges to try particular cases which had come before that assembly. Again, when a man was accused of having committed an injury, one of the modes of defence open to him was to purge his character by the oaths of twelve compurgators, if he could find that number to swear to his innocence.

This proceeding was called *compurgation* or *wager of law*. If the accused were a king's thegn (in which case he would be tried before the king himself), his compurgators must be so likewise; if he were of a subordinate rank, it sufficed that his compurgators should be of the same rank with himself. The other mode of rebutting an accusation was by undergoing *ordeal* of either fire or water. The former consisted of taking up in the hand for a few moments a weight of red-hot iron, or walking barefoot over red-hot ploughshares, and the party was acquitted or condemned according as the blisters disappeared in three days or not. Water ordeal was confined, at any rate in later times, to defendants among the lower orders, who either were required to plunge their bare arm up to the elbow in boiling water, or were cast into a river or pond,— innocence being determined in the first case by the absence of injurious consequences, in the second, by the individual floating on the surface instead of sinking. The water ordeal was evidently of a more serious character, and afforded less opportunity for evasion or collusion than that by fire. Another mode of refuting an accusation was by *corsned*, the accused person eating a piece of barley bread, with solemn oaths and imprecations that it might prove poison, or his last morsel, if his denial of the charge were false.

It must not, however, be supposed that these methods of compurgation, ordeal, and corsned were always resorted to for the determination of judicial suits. In many cases, particularly where rights of property were in dispute, the question was decided in a rough and ready way, the judges and members of the moot deciding according to the previous personal acquaintance with the facts of the case, which they might possess as inhabitants of the district in which it occurred. The different value attached to the oaths of witnesses according to their rank has been already noticed (pp. 4, 6).

2. Jurisdiction of King. — Our judicial system underwent several important changes at the Conquest. Like every other institution of the country, it became tinged with the continental feudalism then introduced. Besides the appellate jurisdiction hitherto possessed by the English king, all matters in which his immediate vassals—the barons, higher ecclesiastics, and tenants *in capite*—were concerned, now came before him as the sovereign feudal lord, in his feudal court. A distinction was made between *placita coronæ*, or *pleas of the Crown*, cases where the interests of the king were involved, and *communia placita*, or *common pleas*, causes in which the matter was only between subject and subject. The former were very soon considered to embrace all prosecutions for crimes and offences. Where these were punishable by the local tribunal of a lord or of the sheriff, they were said to have been committed against the peace of the lord or sheriff, as the case might be. But, as has been pointed out in ch. iii., this local criminal jurisdiction was gradually abolished; and at length, except in the counties palatine, all crimes were held to have been committed against the peace of the king, his crown and dignity. The feudal court for the exercise by the king of his judicial functions, was, according to feudal theory, composed of the whole body of his vassals, who were supposed to aid him in the trial of causes. It was, in short, his *Great Council*, which thus took the place of the old Witenagemot, in judicature as well as in legislation. But the meetings of this council, which ought to have been held every Christmas, Easter, and Whitsuntide, were, in fact, during the early Norman reigns, very irregular;

and, just as before the Conquest, the judicial functions of
the witan had of necessity been deputed to a select number of their body, so now it was found impracticable to
bring all causes before the whole assembly of the Great
Council. Nor could the king himself assume in all cases his
theoretical position of presiding judge. For, independently
of his prolonged absences in Normandy, in all criminal
indictments he was named as prosecutor, and many of the
causes which came into his court were actually such as
more or less involved his own private interests, and
could not therefore with decency be decided by himself.
Accordingly, there was rendered necessary the appointment of a new officer, called Chief Justiciary, who,
besides other functions which will be mentioned hereafter,
exercised, in the place and name of the king, the highest
judicial power; the prerogative of pardon being alone
retained exclusively in the hands of the sovereign. For
judicial purposes the Chief Justiciary was placed at the head
of the *Concilium Ordinarium*, described in ch. vi., which
met at Christmas, Easter, and Whitsuntide, as the Great
Council was supposed to do, but for a longer time, and
sometimes also at Michaelmas, at the city where the king
happened at the time to be. Hence the origin of the four
law terms — Hilary, Easter, Trinity, and Michaelmas.
Not only did it decide matters affecting the Crown, but
it also entertained common pleas or suits between subject
and subject, a fine being exacted for leave to bring such
suits before it. In respect of its judicial functions the
council was called the *Aula Regis* or *Curia Regis;* and,
when required to deal with matters of revenue or finance,
it adjourned to another part of the palace, and was called
Curia Regis ad Scaccarium, or *King's Court of Exchequer*,
its members being styled in this capacity, *Barones
Scaccarii*, or *Barons of the Exchequer*.

Severance of Common Law Courts.—In the year 1178, Henry II. reduced the number of judges in the *Curia Regis* from 18 to 5, and reserved a right of appeal from the *Curia*, whose decisions had hitherto been final, to himself in his *Concilium Ordinarium*, from which the *Curia* became thenceforth detached. The latter, however, continued to follow the king and sit where he happened to be. To remedy the inconvenience which this occasioned to private suitors, there was inserted in Magna Carta the article, "Common pleas shall not follow our court, but shall be holden in some place certain." Thenceforth the *Curia* became divided into two branches—the *Curia Regis* proper, or Court of King's Bench, for pleas of the Crown, and the Court of Common Pleas for suits between subjects, which always sat at Westminster. About the same time the *Curia Regis ad Scaccarium* was formed into a separate tribunal, and distinct functionaries appointed as its judges. That this court sometimes wrongfully assumed the decision of common pleas, appears from st. 28 Edw. 1 (*Art. sup. Cart.*), c. 4, which prohibits the violation of the Great Charter in that particular. As an appeal was held to lie from all inferior courts to the *Curia Regis* proper, the latter received appeals from the Exchequer until Edw. 3's reign, and from the Common Pleas for a considerable time afterwards.

Jurisdiction of Chancellor, &c.—Other members of the *Concilium Ordinarium* were gradually entrusted with distinct judicial functions. Chief among these was the *Cancellarius*, or Chancellor, usually an ecclesiastic, and the keeper of the king's conscience as well as of the Great Seal, who, by virtue of his office, was charged with the duty of redressing, on behalf of the king, the wrongs of suitors whom the ordinary courts might, from the nature of the case, be unable to assist. He, like the judges of the King's Bench, followed the king, and held his court wherever the latter happened to be (28 Edw. 1, c. 5). After the abolition, in Edw. 1's reign, of the office of Chief Justiciary,[1] the Chancellor became the highest judicial functionary of the land, through whom the king exercised his prerogative of appointing all the other judges and justices. Again, military offences and offences committed out of the realm were tried by the Constable and Marshal of England in the Court of Chivalry; and the Court of the King's Steward and Marshal was entrusted with the decision of causes arising within the verge or limits of the king's palace; but it arrogated to itself a much more general jurisdiction, until checked by st. 26 Edw. 1, c. 3.

Justices in Eyre.—But besides all these courts, there was another way in which the royal authority was exercised in judicial matters, namely, by *justitiæ itinerantes*, or *justices in eyre*—itinerating justices, who were sent to administer justice in the different counties. The plan of circuits throughout the country, both for financial and for judicial purposes, by officers bearing the king's commission, is as old as Hen. 1's reign; but it was not until Hen. 2's reign that the practice became systematic and continuous; and for a long time the details with which it was carried out were perpetually varying. In 1168 the number of justices in eyre was four. In 1173 the kingdom was divided for financial purposes into six circuits, three justices being appointed for each. Six years later we read of a division of the country for judicial purposes into four parts;

---

[1] The office was, however, as to some of its judicial duties, continued in the person of the Chief Justice of England, the head of the Court of King's Bench.

and this arrangement was in turn superseded by others of an equally fleeting nature.

The primary judicial duty of the justices in eyre was, no doubt, the decision of causes in which the Crown was concerned. These were still tried in the county courts, but under the presidency of the justices, and not of the sheriff or other local officer; it being at length expressly laid down by the Great Charter, that no sheriff, constable, coroners, or bailiffs should hold pleas of the Crown. But the jurisdiction of the justices became gradually extended. The same charter provided that the king, or in his absence from the realm his Chief Justiciary, should send two justiciaries throughout every county four times a year, to take, with four chosen knights of the shire (see p. 207), the assizes or recognitions in suits about land. In subsequent confirmations of the Charter the circuits were limited to one a year; the assizes were to be taken only in the county where the land in dispute was situate, or, if the cause could not be finished during the stay of the justiciaries in the county, it might be concluded at some other place on their circuit; and difficult points were to be referred to the justiciaries *de banco*, the judges sitting in the Court of King's Bench. The judges on circuit had not at this time power to try common pleas; and for general business, other than the assizes of land and criminal matters, the circuits appear to have been only septennial. A change was, however, made in these respects by the statute of Westminster the second (13 Edw. 1), c. 30. Thenceforth two justices were to be appointed, who, with two of the discreetest knights of the shire into which they should come, should try *assizes* and *attaints* not oftener than thrice a year; and they were empowered to try other civil causes, such as trespasses and the like; but were required to adjourn questions of special difficulty for their personal knowledge both of the facts in question and of the credibility of the witnesses. The jurors were to be good and lawful men, and men of substance; and either party was allowed to challenge the array, or object to the panel of jurors summoned on the ground of partiality. A person tried for his life might arbitrarily challenge and strike off the panel as many as thirty-five without assigning a reason. But all these precautions were in many cases insufficient to secure a fair trial. Repeated Acts were in vain passed to check the practice of bribing the jurors; nor was the mischief effectually restrained by their liability to a writ of attaint for giving a false verdict, upon which, if found guilty by a jury of twenty-four, they were to lose all their property and civil privileges, and become for ever infamous; they were to be themselves imprisoned, to have their wives and children cast out of doors, their houses rased, and their trees cut down and meadows ploughed.

4. Ecclesiastical Courts.—At the Reformation the sovereign acquired a new judicial power, by the transfer to him of the appellate jurisdiction over the ecclesiastical courts which had formerly been exercised by the Court of Rome. St. 25 Hen. 8, c. 19 directed that appeals from the archiepiscopal and other ecclesiastical courts, from which appeals had formerly lain direct to Rome, should be made to the king in Chancery, and should be heard by commissioners appointed by the king under the great seal to try the case, whose decision should be final. These commissioners, whenever appointed, constituted what was called the High Court of Delegates. They were usually three *puisne* judges, one from each of the common law courts, together with three or more civilians or persons versed in the civil law. In special cases, how-

in the affirmative in the famous case of Warren Hastings, which, with the exception of Lord Melville's case, is the last instance of recourse to that mode of procedure. The Act of Settlement affirmed what had been clearly laid down in the case of Lord Danby, that no pardon under the great seal should be pleadable in bar of an impeachment by the Commons in Parliament.

6. **Privy Council**—In the year of the Reform Act of 1832 the once dreaded judicial functions of the Privy Council were partially revived. The loss of judicial power sustained by the council upon the abolition of the Court of Star Chamber has been already noticed. That event did not, however, affect its jurisdiction over colonial causes. For inasmuch as no tribunal for the ultimate decision of these causes had ever been constituted by legislation, the king in council was held to have a final appellate jurisdiction in respect of them, in his general capacity of head of the judicature and fountain of justice. And when appeals were presented to him from the colonies, they were usually heard before a committee of the whole council, who made a report to the king, and judgment was then given by him in accordance with the report. The same method had been occasionally adopted in entertaining and determining appeals on ecclesiastical and admiralty matters from the Court of Delegates, notwithstanding the declaration in the Acts of Hen. 8 and Eliz., that the decisions of that court should be final.

The constitution both of the committees of the council for hearing appeals and of the Court of Delegates being unsatisfactory, Lord Brougham, in 1832, procured the passing of an Act which transferred the right of hearing and finally deciding appeals in ecclesiastical and marine matters from the king in chancery (see pp. 214, 5) to the king in council. For the purpose of hearing these appeals, as well as all colonial and other appeals to the king in council, a committee was constituted in the following year, to be called "The Judicial Committee of the Privy Council," and to consist of all members of the council who held for the time being, or had previously held, the office of president of the council, or one of the leading judicial offices, such as Lord Chancellor or chief of a common law court, and also of two other privy councillors appointed by the king. The committee were to make a report or recommendation upon the appeals to the king in council for his decision, as previous committees had done. The king was also authorised to refer to the Judicial Committee such other matters as should seem expedient, and they have accordingly been invested with certain powers in reference to copyrights and patents. By a later Act, every archbishop or bishop on the Privy Council was to be a member of the Judicial Committee, for the purpose of hearing ecclesiastical appeals; and when these came before it, at least one archbishop was to be present. And the appointment of salaried members of the committee was authorised in 1871.

Central Criminal Court.—In 1834 a new court, called the Central Criminal Court, was established for the trial of offences committed in London and Middlesex, and certain portions of Essex, Kent, and Surrey. The judges who usually sit in this court are the common law judges and the recorder, common serjeant, and judge of the Sheriffs' Court of London. The establishment of this court, which may at first sight appear inconsistent with the decentralising policy adopted as to civil matters by the erection of the county courts in recent times, was primarily rendered necessary by the enormous growth of the metropolis and its suburbs.

Probate and Divorce Court.—Up to within a recent date the ecclesiastical courts possessed exclusive jurisdiction over testamentary and matrimonial matters, subject only to the interference of Parliament, which occasionally granted a divorce between parties by special private Act. But in 1857 all jurisdiction in these matters was transferred to the Crown, and a Court of Probate and Divorce was constituted to deal with them.

Parliament.—The conflict between the House of Commons and the courts of law in the case of *Stockdale v. Hansard*, has been already noticed (p. 152). In an action which grew out of it the power of the Lower House to inflict imprisonment was distinctly recognised. The action was brought by Stockdale's attorney, Howard, for assault and wrongful imprisonment, against Mr Gosset, the serjeant-at-arms, who, by order of the House, had taken him into custody. The Court of Queen's Bench decided in Howard's favour, but this decision was reversed in the Exchequer Chamber, and Baron Parke (afterwards Lord Wensleydale), in delivering the judgment of the court, affirmed what had before been laid down by Lord Camden, namely, that "the House of Commons is a part of the High Court of Parliament, which is, without question, not merely a superior, but the Supreme Court in this country, and higher than the ordinary courts of law" (*Gosset v. Howard, in error*, 10 Q. B. 456).

The power of punishment has, however, of late been very sparingly exercised by Parliament. In 1838, for a much grosser libel on the House of Commons than many for which members had in former times suffered imprisonment, O'Connell was merely reprimanded in his place in the House by the Speaker.

Contempt.—Akin to the right of Parliament to punish offences connected with itself is the power, which

Supreme Court was to be called "Her Majesty's Court of Appeal," and was to hear appeals from the decisions of the High Court of Justice, just as the appellate Courts of Chancery and Common Law, and the Judicial Committee of Privy Council, had previously heard appeals in equity, common law, admiralty, and lunacy matters. Moreover, to this division was to be transferred the jurisdiction of the Stannaries Court (see p. 85), and also that of the Judicial Committee of Privy Council in ecclesiastical matters, provision being made for the attendance of some of the archbishops and bishops as assessors to the judges when such matters were to be tried. It was further provided, that the remaining jurisdiction of the Judicial Committee might, if it seemed expedient, be transferred to the Court of Appeal. There was to be no further appeal from this new Court of Appeal, either to the House of Lords, Privy Council, or any other tribunal. The Lord Chancellor and Master of the Rolls, and the three chiefs of the old common law courts, were to retain their former titles and precedence; but the other judges were to be called judges of her Majesty's High Court of Justice, or Lords Justices of Appeal, according as they were appointed to the first or second division of the Supreme Court.

The main object of thus consolidating the courts was to produce a complete fusion between the systems of law and equity as previously administered in the Common Law and Chancery Courts respectively, and provisions to effect this fusion were inserted in the Act; but the mode in which it was to be carried out, as well as other details of the practice and procedure in the new court, were left to be laid down by rules of court to be drawn up by the Lord Chancellor, Lord Chief Justice, and other judges, during the interval between the passing of the Act and its coming into operation. The Act also empowered the queen, by order in council, to establish district registries throughout the country in connection with the Supreme Court, and to confer on other inferior courts a similar jurisdiction in equity and admiralty matters to that possessed by the county courts. It likewise directed the appointment of official referees, and enacted that the court might, under certain circumstances, refer cases to them or to special referees, and might act upon their report, instead of deciding the question itself. Another alteration consisted in the abolition of the old legal division of the year into terms, it being left to the rules of court to determine the times and duration of the vacations (36 & 37 Vict. c. 66).

CHAPTER IX.

THE EXECUTIVE.

1. Power of the King.—The executive power of the Crown has been always more absolute and less subject to control than its legislative and judicial powers. It has never, like the judicial functions of the sovereign, been delegated to distinct bodies, with whose action he has no right to interfere. The position occupied by subjects with respect to it has ever been that of counsellors and agents; and though the sovereign cannot now put forth executive power except with their advice, and through their instrumentality, yet they are absolutely incapable of exercising it independently of the person who, whether as king or regent, is for the time being invested with royal authority. It is the Crown which appoints, and may at any time dismiss, the officers to whom it entrusts the administration of state affairs and the command of the national forces. Through them the sovereign enforces the laws, collects and dispenses the public revenues, regulates the movements of the army and navy, and communicates with foreign nations, entering into treaties and making war and peace. Of course, the extent to which in these various matters the king directs, or is himself directed by the officers who wield his authority, must depend upon his and their personal character and relative abilities, and will consequently vary from time to time, and from reign to reign. In either case, however, his individual capacities exercise a most important effect upon the government of the state. The magnitude of that effect in pre-Norman times may be estimated by the fact, that an Ælfred could save the nation, while an Æthelred could reduce it to the verge of ruin.

Control of the Witan.—We are told by Tacitus that the old Teutonic tribes entrusted the administration of affairs to their nobles (see p. 2), who, in a small and compact community, were, of course, able constantly to meet together and carry it on in concert. Its transfer into the hands of the king among the tribes who settled in Britain is probably due partly to the increase of power which a victorious military leader would inevitably acquire on locating his tribe in a new territory after a successful invasion, and partly to the fact that, when several tribes, settled over an extensive tract of country, became united into one kingdom, the constant meeting of the nobility for the transaction of business would be impossible. They might be convened from time to time for legislation and judicature, which could be carried on at intervals, but the daily administration of affairs must be left to the king and the few permanent counsellors in constant attendance upon him. Yet we find that during several of the reigns before the Conquest, the Witan possessed a considerable share of administrative and executive power.

They were consulted as to the appointment of bishops, ealdormen, and other public officers, as to the making of war or peace, and the management and appropriation of the folc-land, or public land. The stronger kings, however, kept these matters under the control of themselves and their state officials. This was particularly the case in the latter part of the pre-Norman period. It was then also that, by the distribution of the kingdom among a small number of *eorls* or *earls* appointed by the sovereign, a heavy blow was given to local self-government, and a corresponding increase of the central authority effected.

2. **Power of the King.**—After the Conquest the executive power of the Crown remained theoretically the same. Everything was still nominally transacted by the king. But practically he was much controlled by his council and officers of state. That this control was a reality, and was recognised as such, is evident from the passage in Bracton, who lived in Hen. 3's reign, in which he says that the king, besides being subject to God, is also subject to the law by which he was made king, *and to his curia, or court,* that is, to the counts and barons, who, if the king is acting in an unbridled and lawless manner, ought to put a curb upon him.[1] It followed, in fact, from the ancient and fundamental maxim of our constitution, "The king can do no wrong," that whenever an injury was committed in the name of the Crown, the blame of it must rest either with the counsellors who

---

[1] "Rex autem habet superiorem, Deum. Item legem, per quam factus est rex. Item Curiam suam, videlicet comites, barones, quia comites dicuntur quasi socii Regis, et qui habet socium, habet magistrum; et ideo, si rex fuerit sine fræno, *i. e.*, sine lege, debent el frœnum ponere, nisi ipsimet fuerint cum rege sine fræno."—*Bracton* lib. 2, c. 16, § 3.

acquiesced in it, or with the ministers (*i.e.*, servants) or agents who carried it into execution.

Officers of State.—The *curia* which Bracton describes was, in fact, the *Magnum Concilium*, which met, as we have seen, at the oftenest, only three times a year. When it was not convened, the king had recourse, in the exercise of his executive as well as of his judicial power, to the aid of his *Concilium Ordinarium*. The different branches of administration were entrusted to the different officers composing this council, who were at first almost all either lay or spiritual peers. Thus the constable and marshal attended to military matters, the chamberlain to the king's private financial concerns, and the chancellor to questions respecting the grants of the Crown lands. But the greatest of all the state officers was the chief justiciary, who, besides his judicial and financial functions, was invested with a control over the other officials and over the general administration of affairs, much the same as that now exercised by the prime minister. In the early Norman reigns the chief justiciary also acted as *regent*, and represented the king during his frequent absences abroad. In this capacity the chancellor was sometimes united with him, as in Ric. 1's reign, in the case of William Longchamp, who was deposed from the office by a convention of the barons. But, in the reign of Hen. 3, instead of the justiciary assuming the regency by virtue of his office, *custodes regni* were specially appointed. The power of the justiciary, as organised and augmented by Roger bishop of Salisbury, who held the post under Henry I., at length became so great, that in Edw. 1's reign it was deemed expedient to abolish the office (see p. 203). Next in importance to the chief justiciary stood the chancellor, from the fact of his being the keeper of the great seal, the impress of which was at that time required, not only for the grants of Crown lands, but also for all the king's warrants and orders in affairs of state.

Advice of the Great Council.—But although the Ordinary Council had acquired the principal share in the administration of affairs, the Great Council was not unfrequently consulted when matters of more than ordinary importance were under consideration. Thus Henry II. consulted his Great Council on the subject of the coronation of his eldest son and the marriage of his daughter, on the circuits of the judges, on the removal of corrupt sheriffs and bailiffs and of wardens of castles, on the resumption of alienated Crown lands, and on the quarrel between Castile and Navarre.

Magna Carta.—Some of the provisions of Magna Carta imposed a control over the executive powers of the king. John was made to promise :—

"We will not make justiciaries, constables, sheriffs, or bailiffs, except of such men as know the law of the realm, and are willing to observe it properly" (c. 45.)

It was also stipulated that immediately after the restoration of peace he should remove all foreign soldiers from the kingdom. Moreover, the relations between the English and the Welsh were made the subject of distinct declarations, and John was obliged to give an assurance that he would enter into a treaty with the king of Scotland.

3. Regencies. — After the loss of the duchy of Normandy, the absences of our kings from the country became less frequent, but circumstances from time to time still rendered it necessary to appoint a regency. This was done in the form practised by Henry III., that of *custodes regni*. The Black Prince and his son Richard both held this office while still minors. Regencies occurred upon the accessions of Richard II. and Henry VI. The proceedings in the last case were more regular than on previous occasions—the Duke of Bedford, or, in his absence, the Duke of Gloucester, being appointed by Parliament protector and defender of the kingdom and English Church, and the king's chief counsellor. The Duke of York was similarly appointed in 1454, and again in the following year, when Henry VI. was deranged in mind. It seems to have been at this time recognised: (1.) That the king does not possess any constitutional prerogative of appointing a regent during the minority of his successor; and, (2.) That neither the heir presumptive nor any other person is entitled, as of course, to exercise the royal prerogative during the king's infancy or infirmity, but that the sole right of determining such persons, and prescribing the limits of their authority, rests with Parliament.

Control of Parliament.—Besides this occasional control by Parliament over the executive, it was, like the Great Council, whose place it had taken, from time to time consulted on matters of administration, such as the question of peace or war. Instances of this occur in the reigns of Edw. 3 and Hen. 7.

Power of Council.—On the other hand, the power of the Ordinary Council was continually on the increase. In Edw. 2's reign petitions were presented by Parliament to the king *and his council*, and in 1341 a complaint was made by Parliament of its growing influence. A desire to get rid of the control which it was able to exercise upon the king's proceedings, from the fact of one of its members having the custody of the great seal, led Edward I. and his successors to adopt the practice of issuing writs under a smaller or privy seal, and even at times to retain the great seal in their own hands.

But they were unable to persist long in the latter course, and the freedom, which they at first gained by the use of a privy seal for certain purposes, was soon lost, for this seal also passed into the custody of a member of the council, called the Lord Privy Seal. This office eventually attained great importance, since it became gradually established that the chancellor could not affix the great seal to any document, except under the authority of the privy seal, and therefore with the cognizance of the officer who had the custody of it. To this authority that of the royal signet was at one time added, in order to insure that the proceeding took place with the king's knowledge and under his sanction. For the sovereign was no longer an habitual attendant at the deliberations of the council. He had originally been always present at its meetings, and all its determinations had been in fact his own, arrived at with the assistance of his councillors. But from the close of the fourteenth century the ordinary debates of the council, when there was no special business of importance to be transacted, were carried on in his absence, and his consent to their decisions was given by means of the royal seals. The power of the council was, of course, considerably enhanced by this change; and under the Lancastrian kings it was further expressly extended by regulations passed in Parliament, and by a royal ordinance, which required that the consent of the council should be given to all grants made by royal writ or letter. Besides its judicial functions noticed in the preceding chapter, it had the direction of the finances, of trade both domestic and foreign, of the fortifications of the realm, of the preservation of the peace, and of the relations between the Church and the State, and generally regulated the administration of public affairs.

Privy Council.—From the reign of Hen. 6 the

right of taking part in the deliberations of the Council, and of exercising its powers, was withdrawn from the whole body of persons composing the Ordinary Council, and became confined to the small number amongst them who attended regularly, and who acquired the name of the Privy Council, and absolute secrecy was enjoined upon these as to what passed at their council board. As late as Hen. 8's reign, we find ordinary councillors as distinguished from privy councillors, and though the distinction of name was subsequently abandoned, and all were in later times termed privy councillors, the real difference was, as we shall see, revived after the Restoration in another form; and at the present day the fact of being appointed a privy councillor confers no right on a person to take part in the proceedings of the council, or any of its committees, without a summons to do so.

Growing Power of Commoners.—Another important alteration in the balance of the executive power was at the same time in progress, being nothing less than the admission of commoners to a share—and eventually a preponderating share—in the exercise of it. Their only avenue to power had originally been through holy orders, by elevation to an ecclesiastical peerage. But the gradual introduction of lay commoners into the king's council has been already noticed (pp. 177, 8); and, though they naturally at first held a subordinate position in it, their power speedily increased, either through their own superior abilities, or through a preference on the part of the king to entrust authority to a man of humble extraction without influence or property, who would be entirely dependent on his favour, and towards whom he could have no cause for jealousy, rather than to a powerful and independent noble. Moreover the diminution in the numbers and power of the nobility during the wars of the Roses no doubt contributed to this result. It is to be noticed that this growth of the commoners' influence in the executive was marked, not by their promotion to higher offices, but by the elevation in point of importance and authority of the offices which they originally filled. Thus the secretary (for there was at first only one officer of that name) was in old times merely the king's clerk, possessing no political influence unless he chanced to be one of the council. After a time two were appointed, and the dignity of the office increased. Beckington, secretary under Henry VI., was a diplomatist of considerable reputation. In the following reign many bills and warrants were made to pass through the secretary's hands. Dr Fox, one of Henry VII.'s secretaries, became Bishop of Exeter, and to his successor in the secretariate was entrusted the duty of signing a treaty with Portugal. In Hen. 8's reign the office was held by Cromwell, before he was advanced to be Lord Privy Seal; and the chief secretary became *ex officio* a member of the Privy Council, and ranked as a baron of the realm, taking precedence, if he was himself a baron or bishop, of the other peers of the same rank.

4. Ecclesiastical Supremacy.—The kings of England, with few exceptions, had, in every age, more or less successfully asserted the independence of this country and its Church as against the see of Rome. But the final acquisition by them of that control over English ecclesiastical affairs, for which the Papal Court had long struggled, took place at the Reformation. The assumption of ecclesiastical supremacy by Henry VIII. involved the recognition of the sovereign as head of the Church, not only in matters of legislation and judicature (see pp. 191, 214), but also in reference to the appointment of Church

officers, and the exercise of administrative functions by them. The nomination of the bishops and deans of the English Church has, since 1533, except during Mary's reign, rested exclusively with the sovereign; but, when once appointed, the sacred character of their office preserves them from being removed, like the holders of state offices, at the will of the sovereign. The ecclesiastical supremacy of the Crown was at one time delegated by Henry VIII. to Cromwell, whom he appointed his vicegerent to administer all matters connected with the church. The supremacy was entirely renounced by Mary, but was resumed by Elizabeth upon her accession. The Crown does not in general interfere in the administration of Church affairs; but the sovereign in council has the power, which is exercised on extraordinary occasions, of prescribing the observance of days of national fasting and thanksgiving, the use of special forms of prayer, and other matters of ecclesiastical detail; and the whole of the episcopal, cathedral, and other landed property of the Church is now vested in a body of ecclesiastical commissioners constituted in 1836, and consisting of the archbishops and bishops, and certain ministers of state and judges (provided they belong to the Church of England), as *ex officio* members, and other persons from time to time nominated by the Crown. These commissioners dispense the revenues of the property entrusted to them under the sanction and control of the queen in council.

Power of the Crown in Civil Matters.—In state affairs the Tudor and Stuart monarchs recovered and retained in their own hands much of that administrative and executive authority which the Council had wrested from their predecessors. The sovereign resumed his place at the meetings of the council, and James I. even assisted at the exercise of its judicial functions in its Court of

Star Chamber. The name of the council was still associated with that of the king in the government of the State; but, instead of this being carried on almost entirely by that body as a whole, the various branches of it were for the most part directed by the king himself through his ministers—the members of the council holding offices of state—each of whom thenceforth was occupied with his own department, and interfered comparatively little with those of his colleagues. In Edw. 6's time the council was divided into five committees, to which separate functions were assigned; and Elizabeth carried on the government mainly through her secretaries, or *Secretaries of State*, as they were now called in reference to the increased importance of their office.

Control of Parliament.—The struggle between the first two Stuarts and the Parliament, which was for a long time mainly confined to the regions of legislation, judicature, and taxation, was ultimately extended to the domain of the executive, and the determination of Parliament to obtain the control of the militia was the immediate cause of the civil war. Previously to this, however, the power of the Crown to grant monopolies had been restrained (see p. 33), its right to billet soldiers on the people, and to inflict arbitrary imprisonment, had been repudiated, and Parliament had begun to exercise an indirect but effectual control over the general government of the country, by refusing or stinting the supplies so long as measures which it disapproved were persisted in. After the Restoration, the right of the Crown to have the command of the militia, and of the other naval and military forces, and the fortresses of the kingdom, was reaffirmed (see p. 37), and the executive power of the sovereign was in other respects reinstated. Parliament remained, as it had been before the commencement of the contest, destitute of any direct control over a single department of the state. The two Houses might pass resolutions and present addresses to the Crown, expressive of their opinion upon matters of administration, and the risk of impeachment was incurred by an officer of the Crown who acted in those matters in such a manner as to call for the condemnation of Parliament; but this body continued unable to give an order or direction to the very lowest of the executive officers of the kingdom in reference to the discharge of his duties.

Cabinet Council.—A considerable change in the method of our administration does, however, date from soon after the Restoration; but it was initiated by the king himself. The abolition of the Court of Star Chamber had destroyed the overweening judicial power of the Privy Council, and Charles II., while he increased its members, at the same time virtually deprived it of its political power. Notwithstanding the separation of the affairs of state into different departments as already noticed, many matters had still been brought before the whole body; but Charles, from his personal dislike of long debates, and from the feeling that the deliberations of a large body were not conducive to secrecy or despatch, abstained more and more from calling it together, and acted with the advice of a smaller number of counsellors instead. The previous existence of committees of the council for various branches of administration (see p. 178) constituted a precedent for the formation of this select body, though not for the transfer to it of all the functions of the council. It received the title of Cabinet Council, a designation not entirely unknown in Cha. 1's reign; and though, when composed of the five unprincipled politicians,[2] from the initials of whose names it was

[2] Clifford, Ashley, Buckingham, Arlington, and Lauderdale.

called the Cabal,* it fell into disrepute, and an attempt was made to reinstate the whole Privy Council in its former position, yet this attempt proved a failure, and the Cabinet has ever since directed the government of the country.

Political Parties.—While the instrument for the future administration of affairs was being thus fashioned, the two political parties, through the conflict of which Parliament was destined to exercise a control over the executive, were also gradually assuming shape. The germs of party first appeared in the reign of Eliz., when the Puritan members of the Lower House began to array themselves in opposition to the exercise of the queen's prerogatives in ecclesiastical and civil matters. In the reigns of Ja. 1 and Cha. 1 this opposition assumed a more definite shape—the members who took part in it being called the country party, as opposed to the court party. The former party, after triumphing during the Commonwealth, was almost annihilated at the Restoration; but it revived again in the contest upon the Exclusion Bill in 1679–80 (see p. 133), a contest which gave rise to the abiding names of Whig and Tory. The supporters of the Duke of York were called Tories, after a gang of Irish Roman Catholic freebooters, while the country party obtained the soubriquet of Whigs, either from a Scotch word denoting sour whey, or from the name applied to the Scottish Covenanters who made a raid upon Edinburgh in 1648.

5. The Ministry.—The two reigns which immediately followed the Revolution witnessed the amalgamation of the members of the Cabinet and the subordinate officers who wielded the executive power into a ministry,

* The word *cabal*, however, with the meaning of "club" or "coalition," had already existed in the English language.

united among themselves, and responsible to Parliament.
The formation of such a ministry was the natural, though
not the immediate result of the division of the country
and Parliament into the two political parties of Whigs and
Tories. Up to the year 1693, William III., from a desire
to conciliate both these parties, distributed the principal offices of state with tolerable equality between them.
Hence there was, of course, no unity of opinion or of
purpose among the holders of these offices. Each discharged his own duties independently of and often in
opposition to his colleagues. The king and Parliament
were alike distracted by the cross-counsels and cross-
action of those who constitutionally represented the
Crown, and were responsible for its proceedings. The
only remedy for this state of things evidently lay in
committing all the offices of government to men of the
same general politics, who would act harmoniously together in all important matters. Accordingly, between
1693 and 1696 the offices held by Tories were almost all
transferred to Whigs. At the same time the Whig
leaders were united together in a manner so unusual at
that period, as to acquire for them the nickname of "The
Junto," and the party followed their guidance in a
manner which was then equally unprecedented. Moreover the election of 1695 put this party in a decided
majority in the House of Commons. Again, the death
of Mary in the same year necessitated the appointment,
during William's subsequent foreign expeditions, of a
Council of Regency, under the name of Lords Justices,
and, with the exception of the Archbishop of Canterbury,
composed entirely of officers of state, who were thus
directly led to act in concert. These various accidental
rather than premeditated causes combined to bring about
during the years 1695-1698 something of the modern

ministerial form of government. But the system was as yet by no means thoroughly settled. Thus the ministry continued in office notwithstanding that the election of 1698 destroyed their majority in the Lower House, and that Montague, who was their chief representative in that House, and, according to modern ideas, would have been styled and considered leader of the House, thenceforth completely lost control over it. The old state of things consequently returned, and lasted till 1705, when a Whig Parliament was again elected. Moreover William III., who was the ablest statesman of his day, was his own minister for foreign affairs, and in person conducted negotiations with other nations as well as commanded armies in the field. And clauses were even inserted in the Act of Settlement of 1700 (12 & 13 Will. 3, c. 2), providing that, after the accession of the house of Brunswick, all matters relating to the Government, which were cognisable in the Privy Council, should be transacted there, and that no person holding an office or place of profit under the king, or receiving a pension from the Crown, should sit in the House of Commons. These clauses were calculated to destroy the institution of the Cabinet and ministry, and completely to sever the connection between Parliament and the executive; but they were repealed in Anne's reign before they came into operation.

After the death of William there followed a succession of three sovereigns, who, while endowed with only moderate capacities themselves—the last two being, moreover, imperfectly acquainted with the English constitution, manners, and language—were at the same time served by ministers of remarkable ability. During their reigns the ministerial system was gradually developed, and the real government of the country became finally entrusted to the body of state officials with whom it now rests, but who, as a body, have no legally recognised position in our institutions. Under the system thus established, ministers are equally responsible to the Crown and to the country.⁴ If their policy in either domestic or foreign affairs is persistently opposed by the king, they must abandon it or throw up their seals of office. They are equally bound to resign if their action in any important particular is condemned by the voice of the country as uttered in Parliament. It is unnecessary to specify any of the numerous cases in which a change of ministry has occurred from the latter cause. As an instance of the retirement of a minister owing to a want of harmony with the sovereign, may be mentioned that of Mr Pitt in 1801, after holding office for seventeen years, in consequence of the irreconcileable opposition of George III. to the admission of Roman Catholics to Parliament,

⁴ The English ministry is thus described by Macaulay (Hist. of Engl. ch. xx.):—"The ministry is, in fact, a committee of leading members of the two Houses. It is nominated by the Crown, but it consists exclusively of statesmen whose opinions on the pressing questions of the time agree, in the main, with the opinions of the majority of the House of Commons. Among the members of this committee are distributed the great departments of the administration. Each minister conducts the ordinary business of his own office without reference to his colleagues. But the most important business of every office, and especially such business as is likely to be the subject of discussion in Parliament, is brought under the consideration of the whole ministry. In Parliament the ministers are bound to act as one man on all questions relating to the executive government. If one of them dissents from the rest on a question too important to admit of compromise, it is his duty to retire. While the ministers retain the confidence of the Parliamentary majority, that majority supports them against opposition, and rejects every motion which reflects on them, or is likely to embarrass them. If they forfeit that confidence, if the Parliamentary majority is dissatisfied with the way in which patronage is distributed, with the way in which the prerogative of mercy is used, with the conduct of foreign affairs, with the conduct of a war, the remedy is simple. . . . . They have merely to declare that they have ceased to trust the ministry, and to ask for a ministry which they can trust."

and removal from them of other disabilities, which he was desirous to effect. Theoretically this double responsibility of the ministry might lead to a dead lock in Government, if king and people stubbornly adhered to opposite views upon an important question, as the existence of a ministry would then become impossible; but this flaw in the system—a flaw which must at some point or other exist in all forms of limited monarchy—has practically never caused serious inconvenience; for upon all such questions, when the desire of the people has been unequivocally and persistently expressed, the sovereign has ultimately given way, content, perhaps, with exercising, unknown to the public, a predominant influence over the counsels of the Cabinet on matters about which the country at large has felt no interest, or has not pronounced a distinct opinion. Meanwhile this state of things has materially increased the safety both of the Crown and of its ministers. It had always been a maxim of our constitution that "the king can do no wrong," and that his advisers are answerable for illegal or improper acts on the part of the Crown. Yet before the institution of ministerial responsibility, not only was Strafford beheaded, Clarendon banished, and Danby and other ministers disgraced, imprisoned, and attainted, but even Charles I. lost his head and James II. his throne. Now, however, when the conduct of the executive is in conflict with the will of the nation, a change of dynasty is unnecessary, for harmony is restored by a change of ministry instead; and since ministers are supported while in office by the majority of the representatives of the nation, and cease to hold office directly they lose that confidence, their policy is in some sort the policy of the nation at large, which the latter can scarcely repudiate to such an extent as to visit with punishment those who

have carried it out. Hence, since the establishment of
the ministerial system, there has been only one instance
of the impeachment of a minister, namely, that of Lord
Melville in 1805, and even this was for offences not
connected with his political duties as a minister.

Control of Parliament.—Besides the indirect control which Parliament has obtained over the executive
by means of the ministerial system, there are other not
less effectual means of securing that government shall
be carried on in accordance with the wishes of the
country. Foremost among these is the absolute dependence of the executive from year to year on the vote
of Parliament for obtaining the supplies of money necessary for conducting the administration of affairs. This
dependence became more absolute after the Revolution of
1688, in proportion as the expenses of government grew
more heavy, (see ch. x. p. 282), while the Crown was in
a less advantageous position to meet them from its own
resources, owing to the extent to which William III.
impoverished it by granting away the Crown lands to
favoured subjects. Another check on the executive is
the right acquired by Parliament, as will be noticed in
the next chapter (p. 278), of directing the objects to
which the supplies voted by it shall be applied. Again,
it was laid down by the Bill of Rights, that "the raising
or keeping a standing army within the kingdome in time of
peace, unlesse it be with consent of Parlyament, is against
law;" and the power of the Crown to maintain a standing army at home and abroad depends on an Act called
the Mutiny Act, which has been passed annually since
the Revolution, and which enables the Crown to maintain martial law and discipline in its land forces during
the ensuing year. And though Parliament remained
unable to dictate as to the administration of affairs pro-

spectively, it asserted the right of instituting retrospective inquiries into that administration. Previously to the Revolution the only mode of conducting such inquiries had been by the impeachment of the minister, but it was now done by committees appointed by the two Houses for the purpose—a proceeding which, when recognised as lawful, necessarily carried with it a right to examine witnesses, records, and papers. Two proposals were made soon after the Revolution with a view to a more direct parliamentary control over the executive: the one in 1692, for a committee of both Houses to consider the state of the nation, and advise the king respecting it; and the other, for the nomination by Parliament of a Council of Trade. But neither of them was ever carried into effect.

Increased Power of Executive.—The various means which Parliament, and through it the nation, thus possessed of regulating the course of government, enabled large additions to be made to the power of the executive, without any danger to the liberties of the country. The first two Georges, being themselves foreigners, and having their interest centered in the affairs of Hanover, exercised little personal influence in English politics; and during their reigns the Whig party, which was then in the ascendancy, fostered the consolidation and growth of the authority of the Crown, wielded, as that authority then was, by ministers who were supplied from its own ranks, and who, not trusting for support solely to their political principles and the merits of their measures, largely resorted to bribes from the public money for the purpose of retaining for themselves the approval of the House of Commons. Greatly increased powers were given to the executive in the matter of taxation, especially in the department of excise. The revenue officers were

entrusted with a large and arbitrary authority as to
collecting the duties and searching for evasions of them,
and difficulties were thrown in the way of obtaining
redress in case of an illegal stretch of their authority;
while, on the other hand, persons accused by them of
breaches of the revenue laws were placed under a disadvantage, by the fact that such accusations were made
cognisable by commissioners or magistrates, instead of by
a jury, and that less accurate proof of their guilt was
required than in ordinary criminal or penal proceedings.
Another important measure for strengthening the executive was the Riot Act (1 Geo. 1, st. 2, c. 5) which
imposed the penalty of death, without benefit of clergy,
on any persons who, to the number of twelve or more,
continued together in an unlawful and tumultuous manner
for one hour after being required to disperse by proclamation made in the king's name by a sheriff, mayor,
justice, or other officer. Moreover, in 1718, a power to
inflict death on members of the regular forces for mutiny
or desertion was inserted in the Mutiny Act, and has
been since annually renewed. Another clause repeated
every year in that Act has effected the suspension of
what was considered in Cha. 1.'s time as one of the
fundamental liberties of Englishmen, their exemption
from having soldiers billeted upon them against their
will, and authorises the billeting of soldiers on innkeepers
and victuallers.

Personal influence of the Sovereign.—The personal influence of the sovereign over the administration
of affairs was considerably weakened at the Revolution,
and, as has been already remarked, was little exercised
by the first two Georges. At the commencement of
Geo. 1.'s reign, owing to that king's ignorance of the
English language, the practice was begun, which has

prevailed ever since, of the Cabinet Councils being held, like the meetings of the Privy Council in old time (see p. 238), without the presence of the king. But though weakened, the sovereign's influence was yet far from annihilated. Even in Geo. 2's reign, it was manifested in the continued prosecution of the war of 1743 against the French by two rival ministries, and by the observance of a general line of policy for the benefit of Hanover; and George III., from the very outset of his reign, endeavoured to reassert it to the full extent which our constitution would at that time permit. He began by calling into his confidence an inner knot of counsellors with Lord Bute at their head, who held their position independently of the approval of Parliament or the country, and supplanted the Cabinet in its relations with the Crown. Perhaps nothing has more strongly shown the practical excellence of our system of ministerial government, than the fact that it was found impossible long to maintain this irregular state of things. Its immediate result was the overthrow of the existing ministry, and the substitution of the king's real advisers in their place, thus restoring the constitutional order of things. But inasmuch as Lord Bute's ministry was not acceptable to the country, he found the difficulties of his position so great that he was obliged to resign office within a twelvemonth; and though he attempted to resume his unconstitutional position of secret adviser, his entire dismissal from court was in a short time forced upon the king by the very minister who had been appointed at his instance, and was expected to submit to his control. The inability of the king at this time permanently to commit the government to men of his own mind who lacked the support of the country, is shown by the fact that he was reduced, in 1765, to the necessity of accepting as premier the Marquis of Rockingham, whom he had a short time before removed from the lord-lieutenancy of a county, and, as a secretary of state and leader of the ministry in the Lower House, General Conway, whom he had once deprived of all civil and military appointments. But George III. attempted to carry out his own personal views of government in another manner. Being unable to dissuade his ministry from proposing the repeal of the Stamp Act, which they thought necessary for the conciliation of the colonies, and not venturing to dismiss them from his counsels, he brought his influence to bear against them by causing his private opinions on the measure to be made known to members of the House of Commons, who were holding office under the Crown, and whom he could trust. Hence was presented the singular spectacle of office-holders under the Crown voting against its own ministers. This proceeding led to a resolution of the House of Commons, affirming that "to report any opinion, or pretended opinion, of his Majesty, upon any bill or other proceeding depending in either House of Parliament, with a view to influence the votes of members, is a high crime and misdemeanour, derogatory to the honour of the Crown, a breach of the fundamental privileges of Parliament, and subversive of the constitution." George III., in fact, keenly watched the debates in Parliament, commented on the silence of those whom he had expected to speak, and marked his displeasure at the conduct of members in a debate by his behaviour to them at his drawing-rooms and levées, and in the case of one or two officers, even by passing them over in the order of promotion in the army. George III.'s personal influence in the management of public affairs attained its climax during Lord North's administration (1770-1782). That minister suffered himself to be directed, both in his general policy and

in the details of his administration, by his royal master. During the last five years of his tenure of office he was personally averse to the continuance of the war in America, but surrendered his own judgment to that of the king. The king prescribed for his minister the mode in which the debates should be managed and measures carried in Parliament. He appointed to parliamentary, judicial, and military offices, and granted honours and pensions at his own discretion, and interfered in the affairs of the army to such an extent as even, on one occasion, himself to order the marching of troops. In short, there was at this time too much truth in the complaints of the opposition, that "his Majesty was his own unadvised minister." He on more than one occasion threatened to abdicate, or appeal to the sword, rather than yield his convictions, or accept a minister whom he disliked. With respect to his right of veto, he wrote, in 1774, as follows:—
"I hope the Crown will always be able, in either House of Parliament, to throw out a Bill; but I shall never consent to use any expression which tends to establish that at no time the right of the Crown to dissent is to be used."

But the will of Parliament was destined at length to prevail. In 1780 the House of Commons passed resolutions, affirming that the influence of the Crown had increased, was increasing, and ought to be diminished, and that the House of Commons had a right to correct abuses in the civil list expenditure and every other branch of the public revenue. Two years later Lord North was forced to resign office, and the American war was brought to a close in spite of the wishes of the king; and the civil list was dealt with in a manner which will be noticed in ch. x. (p. 283).

The accession to office of Mr Pitt, in December 1783,

was the occasion of another struggle between George III. and the House of Commons. The latter at once, and before any trial had been made of the policy of the new ministers, endeavoured, by votes of want of confidence and by withholding the supplies, to make their position untenable in the existing Parliament, and at the same time to prevent an appeal to the country by a dissolution. The opposition, which commenced the struggle with an overwhelming majority, was vanquished by the courage, abilities, and perseverance of Mr Pitt. Within four months after the contest had commenced with a majority of nearly two to one against ministers, that majority dwindled down to one. The defeat of the opposition was then complete; the supplies were voted, and Parliament was dissolved. Mr Fox's India Bill was considered by the country as an audacious attempt to interfere with the prerogatives of the Crown; and its verdict gave Mr Pitt an overwhelming majority, which he retained for seventeen years, and, at the end of that time, went out of office on a misunderstanding, not with the House of Commons, but with the king (see p. 247). From the date of Mr Pitt's triumph, the Crown, for nearly fifty years, continued to prevail over every other power in the state. The king, however, was no longer his own minister; for though he continued his application to public affairs, and every act and appointment was submitted to him for his approval, Mr Pitt was not the man to subject his will to that of another. And during this period we find the breaking out of hostilities, and the opening of negotiations for peace, communicated by the Crown to Parliament, and frequent motions made in both Houses in favour of overtures for peace, which were successfully rejected by ministers, but were not objected to on constitutional grounds. We find also clauses inserted in the Militia Acts, providing that, whenever the king calls out the militia, Parliament shall, if not sitting, be promptly assembled.

Regencies.—No definite arrangement exists in our constitution as to the exercise of the executive power when the king is a minor, or afflicted with mental incapacity; and the prospect or actual occurrence of such an emergency has, on each occasion, been specially provided for at the time. Thus, after the death of Frederick Prince of Wales, the Regency Act of 1751 directed that, in the event of the death of George II. during the minority of the next heir to the throne, the widowed princess should be regent, with a council of regency, in part named in the Act, and in part left for nomination by the king, by an instrument not to be opened till after his death. Again, the Regency Act of 1765 empowered George III. to nominate, by instruments to be kept sealed during his life, one of the royal family to be the guardian of his successor while under eighteen, and to exercise royal power as regent during the same period. It also appointed a council of regency, and authorised the king to nominate a substitute in the place of any of its members who might predecease him, or be appointed the regent. Neither of these Acts, in the event, came into operation; but in 1788 it became again necessary to consider the question of a regency, owing to the king's mental derangement. On this occasion Parliament was obliged to assume some of the royal functions. The king had become ill during the summer recess, and it was necessary to dispense with the royal summons for the meeting of Parliament for dispatch of business on the day to which it had been prorogued, and also with the royal license to the Commons to elect a new speaker in the place of the speaker who had died during the crisis, and with the king's approval of their choice. Moreover, as Parliament was not yet formally opened, the two Houses voted that the great seal should be affixed to a commission for opening it—a proceeding which, properly speaking, required the direction and signature of the king. It had been intended to get over by a similar formality the impossibility of duly obtaining the royal assent to a bill for the appointment of a regency; but owing to the disputes between ministers on the one hand and the Prince of Wales (the intended regent) and the opposition on the other, as to the limits to be imposed on the regent's power, the Bill was still under discussion when the king recovered. The delegation of the royal authority was, however, only postponed for a time. In 1810 the king became permanently deranged in mind, and, as on the previous occasion, a commission under the great seal for opening Parliament was issued by authority of the two Houses. By the same authority letters-patent under the great seal were issued for giving the royal assent to a Regency Bill, which vested the royal authority in the Prince of Wales, subject to certain restrictions as to his power of granting peerages, offices, and pensions. Before this Bill was passed, the exigencies of the public service required the two houses to assume another executive function, and to order the officers of the Exchequer to pay out certain sums which had been appropriated for the army and navy, but for the issue of which a warrant by authority of the king under the privy seal was legally requisite.

Another Regency Act, to provide for the event of a minority, was passed soon after the accession of William IV., and a third in Queen Victoria's reign, after her Majesty's marriage. Before that event, the fact that the king of Hanover was hair-presumptive to the throne led to an Act providing for the administration of the government by Lords Justices until the arrival of the queen's successor, in case he should be out of the realm at the time of her decease. All these Acts happily proved unnecessary.

Substitution for Royal Sign-Manual.—In the last year of Geo. 4's reign there occurred a delegation of royal power of a more restricted and less important kind than those which had been necessary in the preceding reign. Owing to the difficulty and pain which the king experienced in affixing his signature to documents for which it was required, an Act was passed empowering him, during the current session, to appoint one or more persons to affix in his presence, and under his oral direction, the royal signature by means of a stamp. This proceeding had been occasionally adopted by former kings of their own accord, as, for instance, by Henry VIII. and the two succeeding sovereigns; and William III. on his deathbed affixed a stamp to a commission for signifying the royal assent to certain Bills. But a Bill for the attainder of the Duke of Norfolk, having received the royal assent under a commission to which Henry VIII.'s signature was given by a stamp affixed, not by himself, but by a clerk, was on that account declared invalid by Parliament. And when the occasion for using a stamp arose in Geo. 4's reign, it was considered that such a course would be illegal unless expressly sanctioned by the Legislature.

6. Personal Influence of the Sovereign.—The sovereigns who have reigned since George III. have not, as a rule, openly taken the same prominent part in the executive administration which he did. But apart from the general personal influence, which they have exercised in their conferences with their ministers on the various affairs of state, and the extent of which can, of course, be known only to the ministers themselves, instances have not been wanting in which their personal attitude has avowedly affected the government of the country. In 1834, William IV., of his own motion, dismissed the Whig ministry of Lord Melbourne, which at that time enjoyed the confidence of the House of Commons, and took Sir Robert Peel into his counsels. The king was, however, only able for a few months to maintain his own inclinations in opposition to the will of the nation; for Sir Robert Peel, after in vain appealing to the country for support by a dissolution and general election, found it impossible to retain office in the face of a hostile House of Commons, and William was obliged to recall his former ministers. The personal influence of the sovereign, which had been favourable to Sir Robert Peel on that occasion, became at the commencement of Queen Victoria's reign the cause of his exclusion from office for two years. Owing to Lord Melbourne having been in office at the accession of Her Majesty, nearly all the ladies of the royal household were closely related to his ministers and chief political supporters. When his ministry, whose unpopularity had been growing since 1835, felt it expedient to resign in 1839, Sir Robert Peel, to whom the formation of a new ministry was entrusted, represented to the queen that he could not undertake the task unless he was permitted to make some changes in the royal household, by which her Majesty would cease to be surrounded by ladies intimately connected with his political opponents. As this was not accorded to him he declined to accept office, and Lord Melbourne's administration was reinstated, until being, in 1841, in a minority in the House of Commons and in the constituencies, they again resigned. On this occasion Sir Robert Peel, in arranging the new ministry, was allowed to make the necessary changes in the royal household; and the removal from it, on a change of ministry, of those ladies who are connected with the outgoing ministers, has ever since been the established practice. The importance which Sir Robert Peel attached to this matter is an indication of the extent to which he was sensible that the personal inclinations of the sovereign influence the course of public affairs, so that he felt it impossible to hold office while those inclinations were liable to be biassed by others in a direction adverse to his own policy.

A memorandum given by the queen to Lord Palmerston when secretary of state for foreign affairs in 1850, indicates the personal share which the sovereign takes in that branch of the public business. It required him to state distinctly what he proposed in a given case, in order that the queen might know to what she was giving her sanction. Any alteration of a measure after that sanction was given would be a breach of sincerity to the Crown, and be justly visited by the exercise of the sovereign's constitutional right of dismissal. The queen was to be informed of communications between him and foreign ministers; was to receive the despatches in good time, and be furnished with the drafts for her approval in sufficient time to make herself acquainted with their contents before they were sent off.[5]

Ministers.—The constitutional right of the Crown to dismiss its ministers, referred to in the queen's memorandum, enables the prime minister and the Cabinet as a whole to exercise, through the Crown, a check upon and control over each individual minister in the department of which he is the special head. Thus, in the very year after the memorandum was written, Lord Palmerston was removed from his office in Lord John Russell's government, owing to his having adopted a tone towards the

[5] See Hansard's Parliamentary Debates, 3d series, vol. cxix. p. 90.

French Government which the prime minister considered
to be inconsistent with the policy determined upon by
the Cabinet.

The composition of the Cabinet has slightly varied
from time to time, both before and since 1832; for since,
as has been observed, the body has no legal existence, its
constitution depends on the will of the Crown, that is,
practically, of the prime minister. It has been the invariable practice that the following ministers should be
members of it:—The Prime Minister, as First Lord of the
Treasury, the Lord Chancellor, Lord President of the
Council, Lord Privy Seal, and Chancellor of the Exchequer; and the Secretaries of State—of whom there are
now five—for the Home Department, Foreign Affairs,
War, Colonies, and India. In addition to these, from
five to eight of the other ministers are usually admitted
into it. In 1872 the following six had seats in it—the
First Lord of the Admiralty, President of the Board of
Trade, Chief-Secretary for Ireland, Vice-President of the
Committee of Council on Education, President of the
Local Government Board, and Chancellor of the Duchy
of Lancaster. The ministry in that year comprised, in
addition to the members of the Cabinet, the First Commissioner of Works and Public Buildings, the Postmaster-
General, Attorney-General, and Solicitor-General, two
junior Lords and two Secretaries of the Treasury, and
two junior Lords and one Secretary of the Admiralty;
also the Lord Steward, Lord Chamberlain, Earl Marshal,
Master of the Horse, and Commander-in-Chief, the last of
whom holds office permanently, and is independent of
changes in the ministry; besides under-secretaries of the
different departments, and special officials for Scotland
and Ireland.

The ministers are, as a rule, all of them members of

one House of Parliament or the other, though, of course,
there is no legal necessity for their being so. On the
other hand, certain restrictions exist as to the proportion
of the ministry who can sit in the Lower House. Certain
of the offices—those designated with the prefix "Lord,"
except the Lords of the Treasury and Admiralty—are
always held by peers; and though, as has been already
mentioned (see p. 246), the exclusion of the whole ministry from the Lower House, which was once contemplated,
was never carried into effect, yet until 1855 only two of
the principal Secretaries of State, and two of the Under
Secretaries could sit in it. In that year the number of
each who were permitted to do so was increased to three;
and three years later, when the Indian department was
added to the Government, it was changed to four. But
one principal secretary and one under secretary are still
inadmissible, and are, therefore, always chosen from the
peerage.

Growth of Executive Power.—Complaint has
sometimes been made that the gain which the country
received from the Reform Act of 1832 in a more
adequate representation of the people, has been acquired
at a loss of firmness and stability in the executive
power, owing to the frequent changes of ministry which
have since taken place. It is no doubt true that
the average duration of the Liberal and Conservative
ministries during the forty years since 1832 has been considerably shorter than that of the Whig and Tory admi-
nistrations in the century preceding that year. But
whether the power of the executive has since 1832 been
feebly wielded or not, the gradual augmentation of that
power, which was noticed as in progress from the Revolution onwards (p. 250), has continued to be uninterruptedly
maintained to the present time. The establishment of

the Police and of the central Poor Law and Local Government systems, and of the Educational Department, have been already mentioned in ch. iii. Besides these, various powers of control over inland and marine commerce, railways and other public modes of locomotion, merchant shipping, and navigation in general, have been from time to time, and are still continually, given to the Committee of the Privy Council known as the Board of Trade, while other administrative powers are nominally entrusted to the Privy Council as a whole.[6] The police are under the control of the Secretary of State for the Home Department; and the Local Government Board, Education Department, and Board of Trade, are largely composed of and are presided over by cabinet ministers, and therefore reflect the policy of the ministry; while to the meetings of the Council as a whole, only those Privy Councillors are summoned who are members of or are in accord with the ministry for the time being in office. It is beyond the scope of the present work to do more than allude to the increase of the executive power which resulted from the transfer of the government of India from the East India Company to the Crown in 1858, previously to which year the only means of interference on the part of the home government with the administration of Indian affairs had been through the Board of Control for India, established by Pitt in 1784, and remodelled in 1793.

Military Forces.—Nor is it in civil matters alone that the power of the central executive has been consolidated and strengthened. In 1871, after a bill had been introduced for suppressing the purchase of commissions in the army, but had been thrown out by the House of Lords, a royal warrant was issued, by the advice of the

[6] See, for instances of this, p. 195.

ministry, abolishing the practice; and the crown thus obtained complete control over the appointment of officers in the army. This warrant was followed by an Act which transferred to the sovereign, to be exercised through the Secretary of State for War and officers appointed with his advice, all the jurisdiction and command over the militia, yeomanry, and volunteers, which had been previously vested in the lord-lieutenants of counties; so that the whole of these forces are now placed under the direct control of the War Office, and can be arranged and worked in connection with the regular army.

CHAPTER X.

TAXATION.

1. Early English Finance.—Before the Conquest the ordinary public expenditure was met, in the first place, by the rents of the folc-land, and the liability to which its holders were subject of assisting in public works, and providing sustenance for the king and high public officials during their progresses through the country—a liability which was ultimately commuted for a fixed money payment; and in the second place, by the obligation called the *trinoda necessitas*, which lay on the holders of all lands in the kingdom, except some church lands, and which consisted of *burhbot*, *brigbot*, and *fyrd*, or the repair of fortresses and of bridges, and military service. The hostilities with the Danes occasionally rendered necessary the further imposition of the *Danegeld*, for the purpose of buying off their incursions or maintaining a fleet to resist them. It was levied in the form of a tax of 2s. on every *hyde* of land, or of a contribution from

each shire of a fully equipped ship, and was always
imposed by the authority of the Witenagemot. That
body had also originally a voice in the disposition and
management of the folc-land, but this appears in the
eleventh century to have fallen almost completely under
the control of the king. The king had, besides, an
immemorial right to duties on exports and imports; but
these duties were at that time of a very trifling amount.

2. Feudal Sources of Revenue.—At the Conquest
none of the old forms of taxation were at once abolished.
The Danegeld, for instance, was occasionally levied down
to 20 Hen. 2. But they were gradually supplanted by
the feudal impositions established by their side, consisting
of the aids and reliefs from barons and military tenants
in capite, as well as an annual tax payable by them, under
the name of *scutage* or *escuage*, as a commutation for the
forty days' personal service in the field, which they were
feudally bound to render to the king every year; and the
annual taxes called *hydage* and talliage—taxes which
correspond to scutage, but were exacted from the socage
tenants of the king's demesne lands and from the inhabitants of the royal boroughs. These payments by the
tenants of Crown lands took the place of the old burdens
imposed on the holders of folc-land, which, according to
feudal principles, had become the property of the Crown.
The customs duties on exports and imports gradually
assumed a more prominent place in the revenue, under
the names of tonnage and poundage, and prisage, the latter
term being specially applied to the duty on imported
wines. These duties were, in fact, only part of a
general system, which at this time prevailed, of imposing
tolls or taxes on various transactions of trade; the right
to levy them being in many places enjoyed by the lord

of the manor or district, while in others it belonged to
the king, as was, of course, the case in all the royal
boroughs, lordships, and demesne lands.

The prerogative of the king to avail himself of the
property and labour of private individuals for public
purposes, and his right to purveyance, have been already
noticed (ch. ii.).

Crown Lands.—In the confiscations and redistribution
of the soil of the kingdom, which followed the Conquest,
the amount of land reserved in the hands of the king as
royal demesne, popularly known as Crown land, was very
large, and was subject to continual increase through forfeitures and escheats. On the other hand, grants and
alienations of it were made on the most liberal scale by
all the early kings, some of whom were so prodigal that
they themselves, or their successors, were obliged arbitrarily to resume what they had improvidently parted
with. This policy of abandonment by the Crown of its
landed possessions (which was perpetually persisted in,
and, as we shall see, demanded eventually the restraint
of Parliament) prevented the king from supporting himself
in independence, as he might otherwise have done, upon
the revenues of the Crown lands, and necessitated his appeal
for pecuniary assistance to the people—a result of incalcul-
able constitutional importance to the country, as the needs
of the sovereign were taken advantage of to wring from
him securities for good government and for the liberty of
the subject, to which in many cases he would not have
consented, had not the grant to him of the requisite supply
been made conditional upon his concession of them.

Imposition and Collection of Taxes.—As a
matter of policy, the early Norman kings usually consulted their council of barons on the imposition of any
extraordinary aid or tax; but the reference to them was

little more than a form, for no instance is recorded in which the demand of the king was refused, or even questioned. The collection of the revenues was distributed throughout the shires, the sheriff of each shire being accountable for the amount due from it. The assessment of this amount, and of the proportions in which it was chargeable on the different lands, was sometimes ascertained by the sheriff in the county court, and sometimes by royal officers sent on circuit through the country under the direction of the chief justiciary. These fiscal circuits preceded the circuits for judicial purposes, for which they no doubt paved the way. They subsequently became united with the latter, and were ultimately superseded by them. In addition to circuits, the collection of the revenue led to the adoption of another institution, which has become one of the fundamental elements of our judicial system—that of trial by jury. In investigating the liability of the various lands and inhabitants of the county, the sheriff, or itinerant officers, as the case might be, were assisted by chosen men of the neighbourhood sworn to certify according to the truth. In the reigns of Hen. 2 and his sons the levying of taxes became more heavy, and at the same time more arbitrary. The scutage seems to have been first levied as a regular tax in 5 Hen. 2, to defray the cost of the expedition to Toulouse. The scutage, proving insufficient for the royal needs, was supplemented by a tax on all the movables or personal effects in the kingdom. This tax at first amounted to one-tenth of the value of the movables, and, being raised to support the crusade against Saladin, was called the Saladin tithe. It subsequently became a very usual mode of raising money, and varied in amount between one-tenth and one-fifteenth of the value of the chattels, the latter being the more common proportion. In Ric. 1's reign, when the expenses of the crusades, and of providing the king's ransom, required to be met by extraordinary contributions, a new tax was levied on the land under the name of *carucage*, being so much for each *caruca* or plough.

Magna Carta.—Both in Ric. 1's reign and at the commencement of the following reign, some feeble opposition was shown to the increasing exactions to which the people were subjected; but it was in Magna Carta that the first determined effort was made to restrain extortions in taxation, and place it under the control of those who contributed to it. A clause was inserted in that instrument, by which the king bound himself not to impose, except through the General Council of the realm, any scutage or aid other than the three recognised feudal aids —(1), for ransoming the lord's person; (2), for making his eldest son a knight; and, (3), for providing once a suitable marriage for his daughter; and these aids were not to be of an unreasonable amount. Care was taken to prescribe how the council for purposes of taxation should be constituted; namely, that the archbishops, bishops, abbots, counts, and greater barons should be summoned individually, and a general summons be sent, through the sheriffs and king's bailiffs, to all the king's tenants *in capite*. These clauses were not, however, confirmed by Henry III., nor do they appear in subsequent confirmations of the Charter.

Control of the Great Council.—Yet the principle thus affirmed was, partly no doubt from motives of evident policy, or even necessity, in many cases observed, especially in the levying of carucage and the tax on movables, which were almost invariably voted by the Great Council. The primary object of summoning the

commons and clergy to this council was to obtain their
consent to taxation—a subject on which, as we saw in
ch. v., they were consulted long before they took
part in legislation. And the right of self-taxation was
recognised to the extent of each class of the community
determining independently of the rest what amount it
would contribute. The lords made a separate grant, the
knights voted their own quota, and the burgesses theirs,
while the clergy decided for themselves the amount of
their taxation. Hence it often happened that the rate of
contribution varied very considerably in the different
classes.

A tax of a fifteenth on movables was frequently obtained by the king in exchange for a confirmation of the
Great Charter and Charter of the Forests, with, from time
to time, certain further concessions. This was the case
in 1297 (25 Edw. 1) when the confirmation of the charters
contained a promise by the king, for himself and his heirs,
that thenceforth no aids, tasks, or prises, beyond the
ancient customary aids and prises, should be taken except
by the common assent of the whole realm, and for the
common profit thereof. In the same year the energy of
Humfrey Bohun, Earl of Hereford and Essex and Constable of England, and Roger Bigot, Earl of Norfolk and
Suffolk and Marshal of England, also obtained the assent
of the king to the Statute of Tallage, which enacted that
no tallings or aid should be imposed or levied in the realm
without the will and assent of the archbishops, bishops,
earls, barons, knights, burgesses, and other freemen of
the land; that no king's officer should take the corn,
leather, cattle, or any other goods of a man without his
will and assent; and that nothing should thenceforth
be taken from sacks of wool under the pretext of *maletolte*.

3. **Control of Parliament.**—In the reign of Edw. 3 the drain on the exchequer caused by the wars in France rendered necessary the imposition of frequent and heavy taxes. In 8 Edw. 3 an assessment was made of all the cities, boroughs, and towns of England, and the value of the tax of the fifteenth on the movables was permanently fixed according to this assessment; so that from that time forward, whenever fifteenths were voted, as they continued to be until the end of the sixteenth century, a definite fixed sum was meant, being the fifteenth of the value assessed in that year. In 14 Edw. 3 the Lords and Commons, meaning by the latter the freeholders of the counties, granted to the king the ninth lamb, the ninth fleece, and the ninth sheaf for two years. The citizens and burgesses, at the same time, granted the ninth part of their goods, and the foreign merchants the fifteenth part of their goods. But it was expressly stipulated that these grants should not be taken as a precedent, and that the king's subjects should not thenceforth be charged to make any aid, or sustain any burden, except by the common assent of the prelates, earls, barons, and other great men, and commons of the realm, and that in Parliament; and that all the profits arising out of the grant then made, and from wards and marriages, customs and escheats, and other profits rising of the said realm of England, should be put and spent upon the maintenance and the safeguard of the said realm, and of the wars in Scotland, France, and Gascony, and in no places elsewhere during those wars (14 Edw. 3, st. 2, c. 1). This is the first instance of Parliament assuming any control over the expenditure of the revenues. A few years later we find another instance of this, and also of a grant being made for a longer period than one year. In 18 Edw. 3 the Commons alone granted two-fifteenths of the goods of

the commonalty, and two-tenths of those of cities and boroughs, to be paid in two years, "so that the money levied of the same be dispended on the business shewed to them in this Parliament by the advice of the great men thereto assigned; and that the aids beyond Trent be put in defence of the North" (18 Edw. 3, st. 2, c. 1). Eighteen years later the grant of a subsidy on wools, leather, and wool-fells, or woollen cloths, for the unusual period of three years, was made the occasion of passing an Act of Parliament to the effect, that after that time nothing should be taken or demanded of the Commons, except the ancient custom of half a mark; and that no subsidy, or other charge, should thenceforth be granted or imposed upon wools by merchants or others, without the assent of Parliament. One instance of the appropriation of the supplies by Parliament occurs in the following reign, when it was enacted that a subsidy granted on wool should be wholly applied upon the defence of the realm of England, and the keeping and governance of the king's towns and fortresses beyond the sea, after the good advice of the lords of the realm, and other wise men of the king's council (5 Ric. 2, st. 2, c. 2).

Taxation of the Clergy.—After the cessation of the clergy to attend Parliament in Edw. 3's reign, they continued to tax themselves in Convocation, voting subsidies at the rate of 4s. in the pound, according to the valuation of their livings in the king's books. The subsidies so voted were, however, considered to require the confirmation of Parliament.

Relative Power of the two Houses.—After the withdrawal of the clergy from Parliament, the knights and burgesses were speedily amalgamated, and voted together on all questions, including taxation. And after the middle of Edw. 3's reign, the two Houses acted together in the matter, sometimes after joint deliberation. Thus, in 43 Edw. 3, it is stated that the Lords, with one assent, and afterwards the Commons, granted a subsidy on exported wool. In the two following reigns we find recitals that the Commons grant, with the assent of the Lords. As late, however, as Edw. 4's reign, the Court of King's Bench laid down that a money grant by the Commons would be binding on commoners without the assent of the Lords. The grants were originally made in the shape, not of bills, but of written indentures, tendered to the king and entered on the Roll of Parliament. Unless accompanied by some condition or relief of grievances having the effect of a new law, they do not appear as statutes till the time of Hen. 8. In the early part of his reign they are said to be enacted by Parliament alone, but latterly the king's name is introduced. The preamble, however, has continued to the present day to be in the form of an address to the sovereign. With a view to securing the independence of the two Houses in respect of the grants solicited from them by the Crown, a promise was obtained from Henry IV., and recorded on the Rolls of Parliament, to the effect that no report should be made to the king of any grant made by the Commons and assented to by the Lords, or any communications which passed in reference to such grant, until the Lords and Commons had come to an agreement about it.

Subsidies.—About the time of Ric. 2 and Hen. 4, the scutage, hydage, and talliage gradually fell into disuse, being replaced by subsidies, which were a tax imposed upon persons in respect of their reputed estates, after the nominal rate of 4s. in the pound for lands, and £2 8s. in the pound for goods—the goods of aliens being liable to twice that amount.

Increase of Taxation.—About the same time we

find a growing liberality on the part of the Lower House
in the grant of supplies to the Crown. This liberality,
however, was not always responded to by the people at
large, as is shown by the insurrection under Wat Tyler,
occasioned by the extraordinary imposition of the poll
tax in 1381, the rebellion in Yorkshire in 1489, and the
revolt in 1525. In 1397 a subsidy on wools, leather, and
wool-fells, was granted to Richard II. *for his life.* The
practice of making a grant for the life of the sovereign, of
which this was the first instance, soon became common.
A similar grant was made to Henry V. in 1415, after the
taking of Harfleur. And from the time of that monarch
till the accession of Charles I., a grant of tonnage and
poundage for the king's life was made in the first Parliament of every reign.

Loans and Benevolences.—The revenues of the
Crown from the recognised sources not being sufficient to
meet its requirements, other means of raising money were
resorted to by our sovereigns. Richard II. frequently extorted forced loans from his subjects, and Edward IV. did
the same thing under a different form, by taking what were
nominally benevolences or voluntary gifts instead. These
were abrogated by Parliament in Ric. 3's reign, but were
renewed by Henry VII., in whose reign they received the
sanction of the Legislature.

4. Reigns of Elizabeth and James I.—Until
towards the end of Eliz.'s reign the supply voted for
any one year by the Commons never exceeded one subsidy on lands and two fifteenths on goods, while that
granted by the clergy was limited to one subsidy. The
fifteenth had, as we have seen, been a stereotyped sum
since 8 Edw. 3, and the value of the subsidy had also
become fixed; so that while money was depreciated, and

land and other property rose in pecuniary value, the yield of the lay subsidy remained at £70,000, and that of the clerical subsidy at £20,000. These sums became under the altered circumstances inadequate to meet the public expenditure; and in 1588, on the occasion of the Spanish Armada, the Commons for the first time voted two subsidies and four fifteenths. From that time onwards the number of subsidies and fifteenths voted became larger. The amount which they produced was, however, still insufficient to meet the necessities of the Crown, and throughout Eliz.'s reign the practice of raising loans by circular letters or privy seals was resorted to, but they were always punctually repaid. James I. had recourse, for the purpose of replenishing his exchequer, to the sale of peerages and the new order of baronetcies, and also of monopolies and exemptions from penalties, until these were declared illegal in 1624. He also, of his own authority, imposed arbitrary duties on articles of commerce, and his right to do so, being called in question, was upheld in courts of law.

Post-Office.—The establishment of the post office dates from Jn. 1's reign; but a regular postal service was first set up under the Commonwealth, and was perpetuated after the Restoration, with the addition from time to time of various improvements and rearrangements.

Reign of Charles I.—Charles I., on succeeding to the throne, laid before his first Parliament an estimate of £300,000 as the probable cost of preparing a fleet for the war with Spain; but the Commons declined to vote him half that amount. They at the same time further showed their determination to keep a check upon the king's revenue, by passing a Bill which granted tonnage and poundage for two years only, instead of for the king's life, as was customary. The Bill was in consequence thrown out by the Lords. After the dissolution of Parliament, which immediately followed on these proceedings, Charles, being in urgent want of money for the expenses of the war, issued commissions for compulsory loans, and levied the tonnage and poundage as if it had been voted, as well as other heavy duties on merchandise. And when his second Parliament was dissolved without having voted any supplies, he proceeded to issue privy seals for the loan of money from private persons. Moreover, the impost called ship-money, for which a precedent was found in the reign of Eliz., was levied upon all seaports without distinction for the equipment of a fleet. He went further; for a proposal having been made in the late Parliament for a vote of four subsidies, which, however, had never been seriously entertained, much less voted, Charles caused them to be levied as if they had been voted. The disastrous expedition to the Isle of Rhé absorbed the sums thus raised, and in 1628 the king was forced to summon his third Parliament. This Parliament presented to the king the famous Petition of Right, in which it was provided that no man should thereafter be compelled to make or yield any gift, loan, benevolence, tax, or such like charge, without common consent by Act of Parliament. The assent of Charles to this petition obtained for him a vote of the then unprecedently large amount of five subsidies; but as even this proved inadequate for his wants, the levy of tonnage and poundage, which remained unvoted, was continued in defiance of the petition. And, after the dissolution of Parliament in 1629, all persons possessed of landed property to the amount of £40 per annum were required to accept the honour of knighthood, which involved heavy fees to the Crown, or pay a fine. Moreover, monopolies were revived in every department of trade, and were thrown into the hands, not of individuals, but of companies. Dispensations from the penal laws were also again freely sold, and forced loans were extracted from the occupiers of Crown lands, for which they were compensated by a confirmation and extension of their tenure of the land.

Charles at the same time issued a proclamation for the levying of ship-money, not only on the coast towns, but throughout the whole of England. This unparalleled imposition on the inhabitants of the inland counties was resisted by Hampden, who, on being tried for his refusal to pay, was condemned by seven out of the twelve common law judges. The levy of the impost was in consequence continued, and a general forced loan was added to it. By means of the revenues thus illegally raised Charles was able to carry on the government for eleven years without summoning Parliament; but they were at length exhausted by the Scotch insurrection, and a Parliament was convened in the summer of 1640. It was, however, almost immediately dismissed; and, aided by the £200,000, for the raising of which he induced his Council of Peers at York to tax themselves (see p. 143), Charles struggled on until November in that year, but was then obliged to convene the Parliament, which proved his last, and is known as the Long Parliament.

From the day of the meeting of this Parliament Charles was powerless to impose any further illegal taxation upon the people. By one of its first measures it was declared and enacted that it was and had been the ancient right of the subjects of the realm, that no subsidy, custom, impost, or other charge whatsoever, ought to or might be laid or imposed upon any merchandise exported or imported by subjects, denizens, or aliens, without common consent in Parliament (16 Cha. 1, c. 8).

Reign of Charles II.—The acquisition by the Commons of complete control over taxation has from the first produced an effect quite the reverse of diminishing its amount. During the Commonwealth the Parliament imposed heavy and, in some respects, novel burdens on the people. Shortly after the Restoration, when all the oppressive feudal tenures with their incidents, and also the rights of purveyance and pre-emption, were abolished, the Commons granted to the king, as a compensation for the loss of his feudal revenues, an hereditary excise on beer and some other liquors, after a precedent set in the time of the Commonwealth, when an excise duty of double the amount had been levied on the same articles by ordinance of Parliament. Other excise and customs duties were added during the king's life, and these duties, together with the tax of 2s. on every house, called hearth money, and a few other trifling taxes, and the hereditary revenues from the post-office, the Crown lands, and some other small sources, gave to Charles II. an income of £1,200,000; being a considerable improvement upon that which had been enjoyed by his father, and which, during the years 1637-41 had not averaged more than £900,000. The king was at this time obliged to provide out of the royal revenues not only for his own personal expenses, but also for the cost of government and the defence of the realm. The various indirect modes of taxation, of which mention has just been made, took the place of subsidies, which were discontinued in 1665. Two years previously the hearth money, which had at first been imposed annually, was made perpetual, thus furnishing the first instance of a permanent tax in this country.

Control of the Commons.—But while the Commons dealt thus liberally with the king, they, during this reign, successfully asserted their exclusive right to determine "as to the matter, the measure, and the time" of every tax imposed on the people. Since the first Parliament of Charles I. the Commons had omitted the name of the Lords from the preamble of all money Bills, reciting the grant as if wholly their own, though of course in the enacting part mention of the sovereign and Lords was introduced as in other bills. In the convention Parliament, and for ten years after the Restoration, the Lords made several alterations in money Bills, which were acquiesced in by the Commons. But in 1661, the introduction in the Upper House of a Bill for paving the streets of Westminster gave rise to a question whether the Lords could initiate a Bill laying a charge upon the people. And in 1671 their right to make amendments in money Bills was successfully disputed by the Commons. Since that year, whenever the Lords have suggested amendments in a money Bill which the Lower House has been disposed to accept, it has invariably thrown out the amended Bill, and introduced a fresh Bill embodying the amendments. Nor did the king find the Commons uniformly compliant in meeting his pecuniary needs. In 1675 they refused a supply to discharge the anticipations on his revenue, and in 1677 they declined a further supply till his Majesty's alliances were made known. In the next year also they refused the king an additional revenue. In the same reign they began to scrutinize the public expenditure, and introduced the salutary plan of appropriating their grants to particular purposes.

The latter practice dates from 1665, when a proviso was introduced in an Act for granting £1,250,000 to the king (17 Cha. 2, c. 1), that the money raised by virtue of that Act should be applicable only to the purposes of the war. Two years later was passed an Act which appointed commissioners, with extensive powers as to auditing the public accounts, and as to investigating frauds in the expenditure of public money.

Taxation of the Clergy.—The clergy continued to tax themselves, by voting subsidies in Convocation, until 1664, when the practice was discontinued by a verbal agreement between Archbishop Sheldon and Lord Chancellor Clarendon, with the tacit consent of the clergy, who esteemed it as a boon. In the following year the clergy were for the first time charged with a tax in common with the laity, and were expressly exempted from liability to vote subsidies in Convocation. Their right to tax themselves was, however, reserved; but since the discontinuance of subsidies it has never been exercised.

National Debt.—The reign of Cha. 2 is also remarkable, from a fiscal point of view, as being the period of the commencement of a national debt. The profession of banking had sprung up during the troubles of the civil war, when large sums of money were deposited for safe custody in the hands of rich and trustworthy goldsmiths. This practice was continued after the Restoration; and though in 1665 the bankers did not consist of more than five or six persons, they speedily became of sufficient importance to have extensive monetary dealings with the exchequer. At the outbreak of the Dutch war in 1672, after the bankers had advanced a sum of £664,263 to the nation, payment at the exchequer was stopped; and instead of repayment of the loan, they were promised interest upon it at the rate of 6 per cent. per annum. This interest was paid down to the year 1683, when it was suspended until Christmas 1705; from which time, by an Act of 1699, the excise was charged with 3 per cent. interest on the principal sum of £1,328,526, redeemable on payment of a moiety; but no compensation was given for the loss of arrears of interest.

Reign of James II.—James II., on coming to the throne, issued a proclamation for the payment of customs, which had expired at the death of his predecessor—an illegal proceeding, which was, however, acquiesced in by the Parliament of 1685. The revenue of this king, from the same sources as those appointed for that of Charles II., amounted on the average to £1,500,964. His demand of £1,400,000 from the Commons in 1685, was met by a grant of half that sum only; but they imposed certain additional duties for a period of eight years, which added annually to the royal revenue a sum of £400,000. The annual expenses of the Crown were at this time, upon an average, £1,700,000.

5. **Control of Commons.**—The imitation by James II. of his father's practice of raising money without the authority of Parliament led to the insertion in the Bill of Rights of a clause which once more, and for the last time, laid down the principle "that levying money for or to the use of the Crowne by pretence of prerogative without grant of Parlyament for longer time, or in other manner than the same is or shall be granted, is illegall." Not a single attempt has since been made to infringe this principle, but instances have occasionally occurred of an interference by the Lords in taxation. In 1701 they passed a resolution, that whatever ill consequences might arise from the supplies for the year being so long deferred, were to be attributed to unnecessary delays of the House of Commons. In 1763 they opposed the third reading of the Wines and Cider Duties Bill, and it was observed that this was the first occasion on which they had been known to divide upon a money Bill. Moreover they occasionally, without incurring the animadversion of the Lower House, rejected or postponed Bills embracing other subjects

incidentally affecting supply and taxation. But when, in 1790, they amended a Bill for regulating Warwick Gaol, which had been sent up to them from the Lower House, by shifting the proposed rate from the owners to the occupiers of the land, the Commons in consequence threw out the Bill.

Upon the whole, however, the exclusive right of the Commons to grant taxes has been admitted since the Revolution, as existing in the terms in which it has been defined by Lord Chatham, when he says, "Taxation is no part of the governing or legislative power. The taxes are a voluntary gift and grant of the Commons alone. In legislation the three estates of the realm[2] are alike concerned; but the concurrence of the peers and the Crown to a tax is only necessary to clothe it with the form of a law. The gift and grant is of the Commons alone."

The grants of the Commons since the Revolution have been founded on annual estimates laid before them on the responsibility of ministers, and strictly appropriated to the service of the year. This control over the public expenditure, while it has given to the Commons a preponderating power in the state, has made them ever ready to vote the sums which the Crown through its ministers has demanded from them. Their conduct in this respect has furnished a striking contrast to the behaviour of the House before the Revolution. It is true that, while prepared to vote the amount required of them, they have sometimes refused to sanction the precise mode in which the ministers of the Crown have proposed that it should be raised. But the temporary delays in 1701, which have been already noticed, and the attempt to embarrass Mr Pitt's ministry in 1784, by stopping the supplies, a course in which they found themselves unable to persist,

[2] He should have said "estates of Parliament," see p. 138, note 1.

constitute the nearest approaches on record since the
Revolution to a refusal by the Commons to meet the
pecuniary requirements of the executive. The subsequent
enormous increase of the annual expenditure and the
creation of a vast national debt bear witness alike
to the magnitude of the demands made upon them, and
to the readiness with which those demands have been
acceded to.

Public Revenue.—The annual revenue of the Crown
in time of peace was fixed after the Revolution at
£1,200,000, of which one-half was devoted to the maintenance of the king's government and the royal family,
or what was afterwards called the civil list, and the other
half to the public expenses and contingent outgoings.
But, in 1697, the Commons resolved that, in acknowledg-
ment of the services done by William to the country, a
sum not exceeding £700,000 should be granted to him
for life for the support of the civil list. The supplies
annually voted during the war which began in 1689 were
about five millions, or more than double the revenue of
James II. From that time the rate of the annual expenditure continued gradually to advance, but the periods of
its chief increase were the American war of independence,
and the great French war.

Civil List.—While the necessities of the country thus
occasioned an augmentation of the national expenditure
for public purposes, the royal civil list was maintained at
£700,000 till the accession of George II.; but in each of
the two preceding reigns debts of a million were incurred
upon it, which were discharged by Parliament by loans
charged on the list itself. When George II. came to the
throne, it was arranged that if the hereditary revenues did
not make up the civil list to £800,000 a year, Parliament
should supply the deficiency, and this it was in fact

called upon to do. At the commencement of the following reign Parliament obtained a still further control over the appropriation of the revenues, by the agreement of George III. to accept £800,000, which was afterwards raised to £900,000, as the amount of his civil list, and to surrender for his life the hereditary revenues, with the benefit of any surplus which might arise from them, to be dealt with by Parliament for public purposes. The nation profited considerably by this arrangement, notwithstanding that various public expenses, having no connection with the king's personal establishment, were from time to time withdrawn from the civil list and charged on the general revenues instead, and that the gain to the nation was to a certain extent diminished by the necessity of periodically defraying debts incurred by the king, which he was unable to meet out of the appointed civil list. On one of these occasions in 1782, the expenditure of the civil list was regulated and considerably curtailed by Parliament. After surrendering the hereditary revenues, George III. and his successor still continued to enjoy a considerable income arising from Admiralty and other sources, which was wholly beyond the interference of Parliament. William IV. and Queen Victoria, however, surrendered not only the hereditary revenues, but also all these other sources of income; so that Parliament has now control over all the public revenues of the Crown, except (if this can be properly termed part of the public revenues) the income derived from the estates of the Duchies of Lancaster and Cornwall, which belong to the sovereign and the Prince of Wales respectively.

Crown Lands.—Having considered the vast increase which took place in the public expenditure after the Revolution, it remains to inquire how this expenditure was met. Very little towards it was contributed by the

Crown lands. The mode in which successive sovereigns squandered away the landed property of the Crown has been already mentioned. A large portion of that which had been sold by Charles I. to meet his necessities was recovered at the Revolution by annulling the sales, but only to be again diminished by the prodigal grants of the last two Stuarts. William III. in this respect showed no improvement upon his predecessors, and some of the grants which he made were recalled by the authority of Parliament.

At length, at the commencement of Anne's reign, the small remnants of the landed possessions of the Crown were effectually preserved for the future by an Act which prohibited any absolute grants of them, and even prescribed the limits as to length of time, and other conditions, under which they might be let on lease. Since then the Crown lands have received some additions from the forfeitures after the rebellions in 1715, and 1745, and have gradually improved in value with the rest of the land of the country.

Duties.—During the two reigns which immediately followed the Revolution, permanent duties were granted on salt, paper, and coffee, and stamp duties on various documents were also imposed. Excise duties, other than the hereditary duties, were granted during the lives of William and Mary, while the customs duties were limited to four years. From this time onwards there was a gradual multiplication of the customs, excise, and stamp duties and licenses. While they were all imposed mainly with a view to meet the expenses of our wars, the customs duties were also considered to serve the additional purpose of *protecting* home manufactures, by laying foreign goods under a disadvantage in competing with them, and by checking the withdrawal of raw material out of the country.

As a further artificial stimulus to the industry of the country, manufactured articles, which, if consumed or used at home, were subjected to excise duty, were, if exported, allowed a bounty or a drawback of that duty. Some idea of the number and complication of these duties previously to 1787 may be gathered from the fact that Mr Pitt, in consolidating them during that year, moved no less than 2537 resolutions on the subject. The increase of the duties, in addition to its inherent evils, gave rise to a gigantic system of smuggling, which it required a heavy expenditure to keep in check. Mr Pitt exerted himself to regulate the duties during the first half of his administration, but the outbreak of the great French war required their reimposition with double intensity, and no decided attempt to reduce them was made until the reign of Queen Victoria.

Direct Taxation.—Soon after the Revolution, a considerable falling off in the customs and excise duties led, in 1690, to a kind of revival of the old subsidies, in the imposition of an aid or a land-tax of 3s. in the pound, which was afterwards annually granted together with a poundage on personal property and on pensions and official salaries, and was usually at the rate of 4s. in the pound, until in 1798 it was made perpetual. Provision was at the same time made for its redemption by landowners by payment at once of a lump sum by way of composition. This arrangement was probably adopted under the expectation that all owners of land would hasten to avail themselves of it, and that so the whole land of the country would in a short time be entirely freed from the old tax, and be available for the imposition of a new tax. This expectation was, however, disappointed; a large portion of the land-tax of 1798 remains unredeemed, and is annually paid to this day; and it has therefore never been possible to re-tax those lands which have been relieved of it. In addition to the land-tax, a permanent tax on houses was imposed in Will. 3's reign, assessed according to the number of windows in each house, and this was followed by other assessed taxes levied on objects or articles of domestic use, such as servants, horses, dogs, and carriages.

Legacy Duty.—Previously to 1796 a small revenue had been derived from successions to personal property, owing to the requirement that stamps should be affixed to probates of wills, letters of administration, and receipts for legacies; but in that year Mr Pitt proposed a percentage tax on successions to both landed and personal property. The opposition to the former was so great that he was obliged to divide the measure into two bills; and while he carried the legacy duty or tax on personal successions, he failed to carry the proposed impost on successions to landed property.

Income Tax.—In 1797, the financial depression of the country led to the substitution of a paper currency for cash payments, which an Act of that year prohibited the bank from making, except in case of sums below twenty shillings, and which were not resumed until 1819. To meet the financial embarrassments, Pitt tripled the assessed taxes, and in the following year imposed, for the first time, a uniform tax on all incomes except those under £200, those below that amount being either subjected to a smaller tax or exempted altogether, according as they nearly approached that figure or fell far short of it. The first imposition of the tax was signalised by voluntary contributions in aid of it by public men beyond what was legally required them. Thus Pitt, Dundas, the Speaker, and the two chief justices, subscribed £2000 each during their continuance in office, and the king added his name to the subscription list for £20,000 a year. The income tax was removed in 1802, after the peace of Amiens, but was again imposed under the name of the property tax in 1803, from which time it remained in force until 1816.

Penal Taxation.—In addition to the modes of raising money already enumerated, with which we are familiar at the present day, other expedients were adopted which would not now be countenanced. In the early part of the 18th century the penal laws against Roman Catholics were made use of for fiscal purposes. It had been the practice to insert in the Land Tax Acts a clause rendering Popish recusants liable to pay at a double rate. But, in addition to this, it was arranged in 1715 that the two-thirds of the income of their lands, which were by law forfeitable to the Crown, should be applied towards the expenses of suppressing the rebellion of that year; and in 1722, a direct tax was levied upon all Papists above the age of 18 possessed of any property, the payment of which was to secure exemption from all other forfeitures and penalties. This tax was not, however, repeated in subsequent years.

Lotteries.—The evil effects of lotteries on public morality were recognised in an act of 1699, which prohibited them under a heavy penalty, designating them as public nuisances, and declaring that any licence to carry them on should be void. But notwithstanding this enactment, which was enforced by many subsequent statutes, it was considered expedient to make an exception for the public service; and acts authorising the Treasury to raise specified sums by means of lotteries were passed year after year until 1823, after which the practice was discontinued.

National Debt.—But besides the various forms of

taxation imposed to meet the current expenditure, it appeared expedient that, when this was increased by a costly war, some portion of it should be spread over a series of years by contracting a public loan. A precedent for this had, as has been mentioned (p. 279), been furnished before the Revolution, and in 1694 the national debt was commenced in its present form by the raising of a loan of £1,200,000, at 8 per cent., the subscribers to which were incorporated, with special privileges, as "The Governor and Company of the Bank of England." The practice thus begun was in itself by no means unreasonable; for if the interests of the nation imperatively required a special outlay at a particular crisis, it was fair that the prosperity of future years should be called upon to bear some portion of the outlay, to which it in part might be said to owe its existence. It was, however, by no means easy to fix the proportion which in any given case might thus be fairly charged on posterity; and, the precedent having been once set, statesmen were under a great temptation unduly to defray the expenses of government by the pleasant device of a loan, instead of by imposing an adequate amount of taxation. In the case of the debt of 1694, Parliament reserved the right to redeem it at any time after 1705 upon a year's notice; and upon this being done, the Bank Corporation was to be dissolved. Instead, however, of this taking place, additional money was from time to time procured in the same manner, and the debt which, at the close of William's reign, amounted to upwards of £16,000,000, was raised in the following reign to £54,000,000. The unfunded debt, or that which was borrowed on exchequer bills and bonds for merely temporary purposes, was always paid off within a limited time; and the funded debt was slightly reduced in Geo. 2's reign, and during one or two intervals afterwards. But, upon the whole, after the accession of Geo. 3, it was rapidly augmented, £121,000,000 being added to it during the American War of Independence, and £601,000,000 during the great French war; at the close of which it stood at its highest figure, £840,850,491—involving an annual charge to the nation of £32,000,000 for interest and management. Since then it has been gradually reduced, so that in 1872 it amounted to about £736,000,000.

With a view to a systematic reduction of it, a permanent sinking fund of a million a-year was set on foot by Mr Pitt in 1786, and was for many years adhered to, even when it was necessary to borrow the million thus set aside, and many millions besides. But the futility of borrowing for the purpose of paying off was recognised in 1829, and the practice was accordingly abandoned. Since that year the reductions in the debt have been effected exclusively out of the excess of revenue over expenditure.

6. **House of Lords.**—The last instance of the interference of the Lords in matters of taxation occurred in 1860, when they rejected a bill for the repeal of the duties on paper, after bills for the increase of the income tax and stamp duties, to make up the deficiency which the repeal would occasion, had actually received the royal assent. They were fortified in this course by the fact that the bill had only been carried in the Commons by a majority of 9, and the Lower House contented itself with passing resolutions affirming its exclusive right of granting aids and supplies to the Crown, and its power to maintain that right inviolate. The proposed repeal was postponed till the following session, when, in order to preclude the possibility of a second interference of the Upper House, the clauses for effecting it were inserted in

a bill by which customs and excise duties were granted for the year.

Civil List.—The annual sum to be paid to Queen Victoria out of the consolidated fund of the United Kingdom for the civil list, or, as it was expressed, "for the support of her Majesty's household, and of the honour and dignity of the Crown," was fixed at the commencement of her reign at £385,000, at which figure it has ever since remained. Independent annuities have, however, from time to time been settled upon the Queen's children as they have attained full age or have married. The Queen and Prince of Wales have likewise derived a benefit from the general rise of the value of land, in an increase of the income which they have respectively received from the possessions of the Duchy of Lancaster and Duchy of Cornwall. The annual revenues of the former amounted in 1872 to about £52,000, giving a net income of £32,000 after deducting the expenses of management; while those of the Duchy of Cornwall were at the same time about £91,000, which yielded to the Prince £65,000, after a similar deduction.

Public Expenditure.—Notwithstanding the almost uninterrupted peace which the country has enjoyed since 1832, the public expenditure has latterly increased with the wealth of the nation and the abundance of money. Its average annual amount in Geo. 4's reign was about 55 millions, and during Will. 4's reign it was more than once reduced below 50 millions. But the increase which took place in it during the Crimean War (1854-56), has been very nearly maintained ever since; the expenditure, which was 75½ millions in 1855-6, having been only one million less in 1868-9, when it was swelled by the cost of the Abyssinian expedition, and five millions less in 1872-3, when there was no special cause for outlay.

Sources of Revenue. — From the Crown lands the country at present derives a net annual revenue of £375,000. The adoption during the last thirty years of the policy of free trade, instead of that of protection, has led to the repeal of almost all the customs duties, and a great reduction in the rate of the remainder. The repeal of the import duties on corn was vehemently opposed as prejudicial to the agricultural interests of the country, but was after a considerable struggle effected by Sir Robert Peel in 1847. And in 1849 the machinery for collecting the excise and stamp duties was simplified by the amalgamation of the Commissioners of Excise and Commissioners of Stamps and Taxes into one Board of Commissioners of Inland Revenue. Such has been the enormous development of our commerce that the few articles—such as wines, spirits, sugar, tea, and coffee—upon the importation of which duties on a small scale are still charged, now yield about £20,000,000, or nearly as large a revenue as was derived from the 1100 articles charged with duty in 1842. The number and scale of the excise duties has also been considerably diminished; yet in 1872-3, they produced a revenue of about £26,000,000,[1] or nearly double that which they produced thirty years ago. In like manner, since the introduction of the penny post in 1839, at the instance of Mr Rowland Hill, the net revenue of the Post Office has considerably increased, being now over 4½ millions, instead of under 2½ millions, notwithstanding that in 1870 the rates of postage were further lowered. Attached to the Post Office, the Government has now under its control the entire telegraphic system of the country, the purchase of which from the various telegraph companies was sanc-

[1] This sum, however, includes the imposts transferred to the excise in 1869 (see p. 292).

tioned by Parliament in 1868. The financial gain to the country from the working of the telegraphs is not at present large; but the receipt of revenue, both from them and from the Post Office, is only a secondary consideration, and is subordinated to their main object of providing the public with the cheapest, and at the same time most efficient means of inter-communication which can be established.

The income tax, which had been discontinued in 1816, was reimposed by Sir Robert Peel in 1842, at the rate of 7d. in the pound for a period of three years, on the understanding that it was to be remitted at the end of that period. But it has ever since been continued, though its amount has varied between 16d. (during the Crimean war) and 3d., according to the exigencies of the public service.

In 1853 Mr Gladstone, as Chancellor of the Exchequer, succeeded in passing the measure, which Mr Pitt had failed to carry in 1796, for imposing a tax on successions to real property, which became thenceforth liable to duty on the same scale as that which had been paid since Mr Pitt's time on successions to personal property, under the name of legacy duty.

Down to 1851 the injurious practice of assessing houses according to the number of windows or lights had offered a direct encouragement to bad lighting and bad ventilation, but it was then abandoned, and the rational method adopted of taxing houses in proportion to their rental, those whose rental was below £20 being entirely exempt.

In 1869 Mr Lowe made an important change in the mode of collecting the imposts in respect of male servants, carriages, horses, and armorial bearings; repealing the assessed taxes previously payable upon them, and requiring that excise licences should, at the commencement of every year, be taken out for the use of them instead.

The present immense material prosperity of the country is evidenced by the fact that the revenue from the various sources above enumerated amounted, during the twelve months ending March 31st, 1873, to £76,608,700, or five millions more than its amount had been estimated at in the budget of 1872.

CHRONOLOGICAL TABLE

SHOWING AT INTERVALS THE DATES OF THE SESSIONS OF PARLIAMENT ACCORDING TO THE CORRESPONDING YEARS OF THE CHRISTIAN ERA, AND OF THE REIGNS OF THE ENGLISH SOVEREIGNS, AND THE DATES OF THE COMMENCEMENT OF THE REIGNS FROM A.D. 1216.

A.D.		
1216, Oct. 28,	.	HENRY III.
1235–6,	. . .	20 Hen. 3.
1267,	. . . .	52 Hen. 3.
1272, Nov. 20,	.	EDWARD I.
1285,	. . . .	13 Edw. 1.
1295,	. . . .	23 Edw. 1.
1297,	. . . .	25 Edw. 1.
1300,	. . . .	28 Edw. 1.
1307, July 8,	. .	EDWARD II.
1315–6,	. . . .	9 Edw. 2.
1326 (7),* Jan. 25,	EDWARD III.
1335,	. . . .	9 Edw. 3.
1344,	. . . .	18 Edw. 3.
1357,	. . . .	31 Edw. 3.
1363–4,	. . . .	38 Edw. 3.
1370–1,	. . .	45 Edw. 3.
1377, June 22,	.	RICHARD II.
1381,	. . . .	5 Ric. 2.
1388,	. . . .	12 Ric. 2.
1399, Sept. 30,	.	HENRY IV.
1400–1,	. . .	2 Hen. 4.
1405–6,	. . .	7 Hen. 4.
1412 (3),* Mar. 21,	HENRY V.
1420,	. . . .	8 Hen. 5.
1422, Sept. 1,	. .	HENRY VI.
1429,	. . . .	8 Hen. 6.
1435,	. . . .	14 Hen. 6.
1444–5,	. . . .	23 Hen. 6.
1460 (1),* Mar. 4,	EDWARD IV.
1472,	. . . .	12 Edw. 4.
1483, Apr. 9,	. .	EDWARD V.
1483, June 26,	RICHARD III.
1485, Aug. 22,	HENRY VII.
1495,	. . . .	11 Hen. 7.
1509, Apr. 22,	HENRY VIII.
1512,	. . . .	4 Hen. 8.
1523,	. .	14 & 15 Hen. 8.
1533–4,	. . .	25 Hen. 8.
1541,	. . .	32 Hen. 8.
1546 (7),* Jan. 28,	EDWARD VI.
1551–2,	. .	5 & 6 Edw. 6.
1553, July 6,	. .	MARY.
1554–5,	. .	1 & 2 Ph. & Mar.
1558, Nov. 17,	ELIZABETH.
1562–3,	. . . .	5 Eliz.
1580–1,	. . .	23 Eliz.
1592–3,	. . .	35 Eliz.
1601,	. . . .	43 Eliz.
1602 (3),* Mar. 24,	JAMES I.
1605–6,	. . . .	3 Ja. 1.
1609–10,	. . .	7 Ja. 1.
1623–4,	. . . .	21 Ja. 1.
1625, Mar. 27,	CHARLES I.
1627,	. . . .	3 Cha. 1.
1640,	. . . .	16 Cha. 1.
1660,	. . . .	12 Cha. 2.
1665,	. . . .	17 Cha. 2.
1670,	. . . .	22 Cha. 2.
1679,	. . . .	31 Cha. 2.
1684 (5,* Feb. 6,	JAMES II.
1688 (9),* Feb. 13,	WILLIAM & MARY.
1694,	6 & 7 Will. & Mar.
1695–6,	. . .	7 & 8 Will. 3.
1700–1,	. .	12 & 13 Will. 3.
1701 (2)* Mar. 8,	.	ANNE.
1706–7,	. . . .	6 Ann.
1714, Aug. 1,	. .	GEORGE I.
1719–20,	. . .	6 Geo. 1.
1727, June 11,	.	GEORGE II.

* It must be borne in mind that under the old style until 1751 inclusive, the year was reckoned as beginning on the 25th of March. (See 24 Geo. 2, c. 23.)

Chronological Table

A.D.				A.D.			
1729-30,	.	.	3 Geo. 2.	1825,	. . .		6 Geo. 4.
1739-40,	.	.	13 Geo. 2.	1829,	. . .		10 Geo. 4.
1749-50,	.	.	23 Geo. 2.	1830, June 26,			WILLIAM IV.
1760, Oct. 25,		.	GEORGE III.	1832,	. . .		2 & 3 Will. 4.
1770,	.	.	10 Geo. 3.	1835,	. . .		5 & 6 Will. 4.
1779-80,	.	.	20 Geo. 3.	1837, June 20,			VICTORIA.
1790,	.	.	30 Geo. 3.	1840,	. . .		3 & 4 Vict.
1801,	.	.	41 Geo. 3.	1850,	. . .		13 & 14 Vict.
1810,	.	.	50 Geo. 3.	1860,	. . .		23 & 24 Vict.
1820, Jan. 29,		.	GEORGE IV	1870,	. . .		33 & 34 Vict.

INDEX AND GLOSSARY

[In the case of words which have been explained in the body of the work, the explanation is not repeated in the index.]

Abbots 6, 13, 16
Acts of Parliament 185, 194, 196
Admiralty Court 211, 213, 220, 227, 230
Afforest [turn into forest] 19
Aid [contribution from a tenant to his feudal lord] 8, 17, 27, 265, 268-9
Aliens 12, 19, 23, 36, 54-6, 65-7
Appropriation of revenues 249, 270-1, 278, 281
Army (*See also* Military Service) 37, 56-9, 242, 263
Array, Commissions of 24, 37
Ashby v. *White* . . . 225
Assize [trial] 204
,, grand 207
[The word also means a law, and an assessment.]
Attainder 9
,, Bills of . . . 220
Attaint [proceeding involving attainder] . . 204
,, writ of 214
Audit of public accounts . 279

Bailiffs 78, 84
Ballot 123-4, 174-5
Bank of England . . . 288
Bankruptcy (*See also* Debtors) . . 153, 167, 230
Baptists 80
Barons [men, the king's men or vassals] (*See also* Lords) 8, 31
Baronets 26, 274
Battel (*See* Wager).

Benevolences (*See* Loans).
Bill of Rights 46, 57, 147, 167, 192, 222, 249, 280
Bills (*See also* Money Bills) 185, 180
Billeting . . . 26-7, 251
Bishops 5, 6, 13, 16, 76, 137, 234, 241
Boc-land 4
Body-guard . . . 7, 24, 87
Boroughs 8, 75, 83-5, 88, 101, 109
Borsholder [surety-holder] (*See* Tithingman).
Bribery of members . 165-6
,, of voters 161, 167, 174
Bridges, repair of 82, 90, 95, 204
Brig-bot [bridge-tribute] . 264
Burgage-tenure [socage-tenure in an ancient borough] 150
Burh-bot [fortress-tribute] 264

Cabinet (*See* Council).
Carucage [plough money] 268
Central Criminal Court . 228
Ceorls 4-6
Chancery, Court of 211, 213, 218, 230-1
Chancellor 154, 175, 202, 211, 231, 235-6
Charter, Forest . . . 19, 82
,, Great 16-19, 80-2, 139, 202, 204, 207-8, 236, 268
Chartists 84
Chief Justiciary, chief justice 201, 203-4, 223, 235

298   Index and Glossary

Cinque Ports 85
Circuits, fiscal and judicial 79-80,
  203-4, 230, 267
Civil List . . 262-3, 290
Clarendon, constitutions of 15,
  205
Clergy 6, 8, 15, 140, 271, 279
Comes (See Count).
Commendams 221
Common Law 209
Common Pleas . 200, 202, 219
Commons, House of (See
  also Parliament) 159-175, 192,
  194, 209, 226, 277, 280-1
Compurgation . . 199, 208
Concilium ordinarium (See
  Council, ordinary).
Conscience, Courts of (See
  Small Debts).
Constable [comes stabuli,
  stable or stall attendant] 175,
  203, 212
„ high 83, 94, 106-7
„ parish or petty 86,
  94, 106-8
„ police . 103, 106-8
Contempt of Court 45, 229-30
Conventicles 30
Convocation . 191-2, 271, 279
Copyhold . . 12, 27, 116
Corn-laws 63
Coroners 52
Coronation . . 126, 129-30
„ oath 197
Corporation Act . . . 30, 42
Corsned bread [execration
  bread] 199
Council, cabinet, and ministry 179, 243-9, 260-2
„ Great 137-9, 176, 200,
  210, 235-6, 268
„ ordinary and privy 32,
  175-80, 182, 185, 195,
  201-2, 210, 217, 227,
  231, 235, 237-9, 242-3,
  253
„ Judicial Committee
  of . . 180, 228, 231
„ of Peers . . . 143, 276

Council of Wales and of the
  North 216
Count [comes, attendant] 3, 13,
  71, 137
County [Lat. comitatus,
  district presided over by
  a count] (See Shire).
County courts (See also
  Shire-moot) . . . 104-6
Counties Palatine . 78-9, 94,
  103-4, 186
„ courts of . 216, 230
Courts-leet 74, 76, 80, 94, 107
Crown, lands 236, 249, 266,
  283-4, 290-1
„ pleas of the . . 30, 200
Cumulative voting . . . 129
Curia Regia (See also Council;
  King's Bench) 176, 201-2, 234
Customs (See Duties).
Custodes regni . 235, 237
Custos rotulorum . . . 88

Danegeld [Dane-money] 84, 264-5
Divorce Court . . . 229-30
Debtors 44-5, 60-1
Declaration of Rights (See Bill of
  Rights).
Delegates, Court of 214-5, 227
Demesne 11, 64
Denization [making a denizen, ex donatione regis]
  (See Aliens).
Dissenters (See Religious
  disabilities).
Disseise [deprive of the
  seisin or possession of
  land] 18, 22
Duke [Lat. dux, leader or
  general] 20
Durham (See also Counties
  Palatine) 163
Duties, customs 265, 284-5, 291-2
„ excise 44, 250-1, 277,
  284-5, 291-2
„ newspaper . . 50, 64
„ paper . . 64, 264, 289

Ealdormen [aldermen,
  elders] 5, 7, 36, 70-1, 75, 234

Index and Glossary 299

Earls 13, 75, 234
Ecclesiastical, commissioners 241
  ,, courts 76, 205, 214–5,
              227, 228, 231
  ,, legislation 181, 186–7,
                  191-2
  ,, supremacy . . 240–1
Education . . 63, 121–4, 180
Elections, Parliamentary
(*See also* Ballot) 50, 81, 161,
                167, 225
Ely 79, 104
Earls 4, 5, 75, 234
Escheat 9
Escuage or Scutage [shield-
money] . . 27, 265, 267
Exchequer Court 201–2, 210
  ,, Chamber 210, 220
Excise (*See* Duties).
Exclusion Bill . . 133, 244
Expenditure, public 282, 290

Fealty [fidelity] 8
Felony 9, 13
  ,, appeal of . . . 208
Feudalism . 3, 7–10, 20, 25–7
Fifteenths . . 267–70, 273–4
Five Mile Act 31
Folc-gemot, folk-mote (*See
also* Shire-moot) . . . 84
Folc-land [public land] 4, 234,
                264–5
Forest laws and customs
(*See also* Charter) 14-5, 19,
          26, 76–7, 82
Franchise . 73, 79, 87, 106
Frankpledge (*See* Frithborga).
Freemen 8
  ,, of boroughs 101, 170
Frithborga [peace-pledge,
association for keeping
the peace] . . . 72, 74, 78
Fyrd [service in the field] 73,
                  264

Gaols 87, 95–6
Gemot or moot [assembly] 70
Gerefa or reeve [chief officer] 70
Gilds 72

Great Charter (*See* Charter).
Great Council (*See* Council).

Habeas Corpus [a writ for
bringing the body or per-
son of an Individual before
the Court] 32–3
  ,, suspension of Act 43, 191
Halimote or hallmoot . . 77
Headborough (*See* Tithing-
man).
Health, public . . . 115–8
Hearth-money 277
Heresy 22, 27-8, 184
Heretoga [Germ. *herzog*,
leader] 70
High Commission, Court of 215,
                  222
Highways . . 91, 97, 114–5
Hlaford, hlaefdige . . 5, 71
Homage [acknowledging
oneself the *homo* or vassal
of another] 8
House tax . . 277, 286, 292
Hue and Cry 209
Hundred . 2, 74, 85, 106, 209
  Court of 74, 78, 106
Huscarls [house-troops] (*See
Bodyguard*).
Husting [court or assembly
held in a house, a bor-
ough court] 84
Hustings 175
Hydage [tax on hydes of
land] 265, 272
Hyde [120 acres] . . 6, 264

Impeachment, 211, 226–7, 243,
                249
Impressment (*See* Navy).
Income Tax 286, 292
Indemnity Acts . . 39, 63
Indulgence, Declarations of 31,
                189
Insolvency (*See* Bank-
ruptcy; Debtors).

Jews, . . . 12, 30, 39, 55, 61
Judges . . 164, 220–4, 231

Index and Glossary

Jury 205, 207-9, 212-4, 221-2, 224.
Justices, in eyre [*in itinere*, itinerating] 203-4
,, of the peace 86, 90, 108-9
Justices, writ of 81

King 2, 125-135
,, suspending and dispensing powers of 186, 188, 192
,, judicial power of 197-8
,, executive power of 232, 234, 241-2, 251-6, 258-60
King's Bench, Court of 202, 204, 212
Knighthood . . . 26, 275
Knight's service (*See* Tenant in chivalry).

Labourers, statutes of . 21, 87
Land-tax 285
Legacy-duty 286
Letters, opening of (*See* Post-Office).
Libel 50-54, 64
Licensing Act . . 35, 50-1
Life peerages 158
Livery [delivery of possession of land] . . 2, 21, 27
Loans and benevolences 221-6
Local Government Board 118-20, 130
London . . . 103, 104, 120
Lord-Lieutenant . 36, 94, 264
Lords, House of . . . 153-9
,, jurisdiction of 210, 219-20, 231
,, power of, as to money bills (*See also* Parliament) 278, 280, 289
Lotteries . . . 165-6, 287
Lordship or manor 6, 7, 10, 71-9, 77, 79, 106, 264
Lunatic asylums . . 96, 169

Mægth [kindred] . . 70-2, 80
Magna Carta (*See* Charter, Great).

Magnum concilium (*See* Council, Great).
Male-tolte [sack-toll, on wool] 269
Manor (*See* Lordship).
Mark 71
Marquess [warder of a *march* or frontier] . . 20
Marriage. 39, 61
Marshal [horse-servant] 202, 212
Master of the Rolls 164, 231
Meetings, seditious . . 48-9
Mesne [intermediate] Process, arrest on [arrest by a writ after the commencement and before the end of a suit] 45
Metropolis . . 103, 106, 120
Michel-gemot [great or general assembly] . . 126
Military service 7, 16, 22, 24-5, 56-7
Militia 37, 59, 67-8, 256, 264
Reserve 67
Ministry (*See* Council, cabinet).
Money Bills 192-3, 272, 278, 280, 289
Monopolies . . . 33, 274-5
Moot, mote (*See* Gemot).
Mortmain, statutes of . 18
Municipal government 8, 75, 83-5, 88, 101, 109-11
Murder, compensation for (*See* Weregild) ; conspiracy to 66
Mutiny Act 57-8, 147, 249, 251

National debt . . 279, 287-9
Naturalisation (*See* Aliens).
Navy . . . 37, 57, 68-9, 242
,, impressment for 24, 57, 69
Newspapers 34-5, 50, 64-5
Nisi Prius 205
Nonconformists (*See* Religious Disabilities).

Oaths of Allegiance and Supremacy, 29, 36, 38, 55, 61-3
Ordeal 199, 208

Index and Glossary

Ouster-le-main [delivery of a ward's land out of the guardian's hands] . . 9–27

Parish 71–3
Parliament 136–175, 224–5, 220, 237, 242, 270
,, Convention . . 144
,, Long . . 35, 162, 276
,, privilege of 142, 144–5, 148–9, 151, 153, 225–6
Paper (*See* Duties).
Papists (*See* Religious Disabilities).
Parties 244
Patents 33–4, 228
Peace, preservation of the 102
Peers (*See also* Lords) 13, 20, 40, 208
Petition of Right 26, 32, 217, 275
Petitions . . . 40, 63–4, 184
Pillory 216, 220
Pleadings 209
Police (*See* Constable).
Pone, writ of 100
Poor law . . . 91, 97, 111–4
,, Board . . 112, 119
Post-Office 36, 54, 65, 274, 277, 291
Poundage (*See* Tonnage).
Præmunientes clause . . 141
Præmunire facias, 135. [A writ under which penalties were inflicted by Acts of Edw. 3 and Ric. 2, for acting in obedience to the Court of Rome in defiance of the law or the king's authority. The like penalties were afterwards imposed for other offences.]
Pre-emption (*See* Purveyance).
Press . . 23, 34–5, 49, 64–5
Primer Seisin . . . 9, 27
Prince of Wales . . 14, 290
Printing (*See* Press).
Prisage, prises . . 265, 269
Privilege (*See* Parliament).

Probate Court . . . 229–30
Protection . . . 234, 291
Purveyance and Pre-emption 14, 22, 27, 277

Quakers 39, 61
Quia Emptores, statute of 183
Quorum, Justices of the 87

Rates (*See* Poor Law; Taxation, local).
Recognition 207
Record, Courts of . . 106
(So called from the enrolment of their proceedings on parchment.)
Recordari, writ of . . . 100
Recorders 111
Reeve (*See* Gerefa).
Reform Acts . 49, 63, 168–173
Regarder 77
Regency . 235–6, 245, 256–8
Relief 9
Religious Disabilities 22, 27–31, 38–42, 61–3, 287
Request, Courts of (*See* Small Debts).
Reserve forces 67–9
Revenues, royal and public, 277, 280, 282, 291–3
Riding [trithing or third] 74
Right (*See* Bill of Rights; Petition of Right).
Riot 41, 47, 161
,, Act 251
Roman Catholics (*See* Religious Disabilities).
Rome, See and Court of . 240
Royal assent . . . 191, 193
,, withholding of 147, 165

Saladin tithe 267
Sanitary laws(*See* Health, Public).
Scandalum Magnatum [scandal of nobles] . . 13
School Boards 122–4
Scot and lot [*Scot* or *shot*, tax; *lot*, share. The payment of an assessed share of a general impost] 84, 169

Index and Glossary

Scutage (*See* Escuage).
Seal, Great . . . 202, 237-8
,, Privy . . . 237-8
Secretary of State, 240, 242, 261
Sedition 48-9
Seisin (*See* Disseise) . . 9
Sessions, petty and special 91, 99
,, quarter . . 87, 99
Settlement, Acts of 134-5, 223
Settlement of pauper . . 93
Sewers 90, 118, 121
Sheriff [scir-gerefa, shire-reeve] 70-1, 75, 78, 80-1, 83, 85-6, 236
Ship-money . . . 265, 275-6
Shire [scir, division], or county (*See also* County Palatine) 70
Shire-moot [scir-gemot] or County Court 70-1, 74-6, 80-1, 100, 104, 160, 204
Sign Manual, Royal . . 258
Signet, royal 238
Sithcsocna (franchise of a gesith or comes) . . 73
Sithcundman [man of noble or gentle birth] . . . 5
Six Acts . . . 49, 50, 53
Slaves, slavery 2, 6, 24-5, 38, 60
Slave Trade . . . 38, 47-8
Small Debts Courts 100, 106
Socage 10, 27
Stannaries 85, 231
Star Chamber 32, 34-5, 51, 212, 216-7, 222-3
Statute duty . . . 91, 97, 115
Stockdale v. *Hansard* 152, 229
Subinfeudation . . . 8, 10
Subsidies . 271-4, 276-7, 279
Succession-duty . . 286, 202
Supremacy (*See* Ecclesiastical; Oath).
Supreme Court of Judicature 230-2
Swein-mote [assembly of sweins or freemen] . . 77
Syxhyndman 5

Talliage . . . 265, 269, 272

Taxation 264, 293
,, local . 90, 95-6, 109
Telegraphs 291
Tenants *in capite* . 8, 13, 137
,, in chivalry 8-10, 26-27
,, in socage . . . 10, 27
Test Act 31, 42
,, Universities . . 63
Thegns . . . 5-6, 175, 192
Theows *or* thralls . . . 6
Tithing 72
Tithing-man . . 72, 94, 108
Toleration Act (*See also* Religious Disabilities) 38
Tonnage and Poundage 265, 274-5
Torture 216
Tourn (*See* Courts-leet).
Township 71-3
Trade, Board of . 180, 195-6
Treason 10, 224
Trinoda necessitas [threefold obligation] . . 82, 264
Tun-gemot [town-moot] . 71
Twelfhyndman . . . 5
Twyhyndman . . . 4

Uniformity, Acts of 29, 30, 192
Unitarians 39
Verderor [warder of the vert, *i.e.*, sward and timber] 77, 81
Verge [compass of the Royal Court] . . . 203
Vestries . . . 95, 101-2, 120
Veto (*See* Royal Assent).
Vice-comes (*See* Sheriff; Viscount).
Vill 71
Villeins, villenage 6, 11-2, 21, 24, 38, 78
Viscount [vice-comes] . . 20
Volunteers 24, 59, 60, 68-9, 264
Wager of battel : 84, 208
,, of law . . . 199, 208
Wapentake 74
[So called from the inhabitants touching each other's weapons at stated meetings in token of fidelity.]

Ward-mote [assembly of a borough ward] . . . 84	Weregild [murder-money] 4, 7, 81
Wards and Liveries, Court of 21, 27	Witan, witenagemot [assembly of the witan or wise men] 127-8, 136-7, 181, 198, 203-4, 263
Warrants, general . 43-4, 51	
,, search . . 35, 51	
Watchmen 103	Woodmote 77
Welshman [foreigner, man not of Teutonic birth] . 6	Yeomanry . . . 59, 68, 204

PRINTED BY
NEILL AND COMPANY,
EDINBURGH.

3, WATERLOO PLACE, PALL MALL,
October, 1873.

Books for Schools and Colleges

PUBLISHED BY

Messrs. RIVINGTON

HISTORY

An English History for the Use of Public Schools.

With special reference to the most important Epochs of Social and Constitutional Change.

By the Rev. J. FRANCK BRIGHT, M.A., *late Master of the Modern School at Marlborough College.*

[*In the Press.*

A Sketch of Grecian and Roman History.

By A. H. BEESLY, M.A., *Assistant-Master at Marlborough College.* With Maps. Small 8vo. 2s. 6d.

History of the Church under the Roman Empire, A.D. 30–476.

By the Rev. A. D. CRAKE, B.A., *Chaplain of All Saints' School, Bloxham.*
Crown 8vo. [*Just Ready.*

A History of England for Children.

By GEORGE DAVYS, D.D., *formerly Bishop of Peterborough.*
New Edition. 18mo. 1s. 6d.
With twelve Coloured Illustrations. Square cr. 8vo. 3s. 6d.

LONDON, OXFORD, AND CAMBRIDGE.

In the Press

HISTORICAL HANDBOOKS
FOR USE IN SCHOOLS.
Edited by
OSCAR BROWNING, M.A.,
FELLOW OF KING'S COLLEGE, CAMBRIDGE; ASSISTANT-MASTER AT ETON COLLEGE.

Each Book will consist of 250 to 300 pages, small 8vo, will treat of a distinct Period of History, and will be complete in itself. The Series will include Handbooks of the History of Literature, and of the Constitution and Laws.

HISTORY OF FRENCH LITERATURE.
 Adapted from the French of M. Demogeot by CHRISTIANA BRIDGE.

HISTORY OF THE ENGLISH INSTITUTIONS.
 By PHILIP V. SMITH, M.A., *Barrister-at-Law; Fellow of King's College, Cambridge.*

HISTORY OF MODERN ENGLISH LAW.
 By ROLAND KNYVET WILSON, M.A., *Barrister-at-Law; late Fellow of King's College, Cambridge.*

THE SUPREMACY OF ATHENS.
 By R. C. JEBB, M.A., *Fellow and Tutor of Trinity College, Cambridge, and Public Orator of the University.*

THE ROMAN REVOLUTION. From B.C. 133 to the Battle of Actium.
 By H. F. PELHAM, M.A., *Fellow and Lecturer of Exeter College, Oxford.*

THE ROMAN EMPIRE. From A.D. 400 to 800.
 By A. M. CURTEIS, M.A., *late Fellow of Trinity College, Oxford, and Assistant-Master at Sherborne School.*

ENGLISH HISTORY IN THE XIVTH CENTURY.
 By CHARLES H. PEARSON, M.A., *Fellow of Oriel College, Oxford.*

HISTORY OF THE FRENCH REVOLUTION.
 By the Rev. J. FRANCK BRIGHT, M.A., *late Master of the Modern School at Marlborough College.*

THE REIGN OF GEORGE III.
 By Sir W. R. ANSON, Bart., M.A., *Fellow of All Souls' College, Oxford.*

THE GREAT REBELLION.
 By the EDITOR.

THE REIGN OF LOUIS XI.
 By F. WILLERT, M.A., *Fellow of Exeter College, Oxford, and Assistant-Master at Eton College.*

ENGLISH

In the Press

ENGLISH SCHOOL CLASSICS

Edited by

FRANCIS STORR, B.A.,

ASSISTANT-MASTER AT MARLBOROUGH COLLEGE, LATE SCHOLAR OF TRINITY COLLEGE, CAMBRIDGE, AND BELL UNIVERSITY SCHOLAR.

The object of these Volumes is to supply preparatory Schools, and the fourth or fifth forms of larger Schools, with cheap Annotated Text-Books for English reading. It is intended that each Volume should contain enough for one term's work.

The Series will include the following:—

THOMSON'S SEASONS. BACON'S ESSAYS AND NEW ATLANTIS. COWPER'S TASK. GRAY'S POEMS. WORDSWORTH'S EXCURSION. GOLDSMITH'S DESERTED VILLAGE. MILTON'S PARADISE LOST AND AREOPAGITICA. SCOTT'S MARMION, ROKEBY, LORD OF THE ISLES, LADY OF THE LAKE, AND LAY OF THE LAST MINSTREL. SWIFT'S GULLIVER. BYRON'S CHILDE HAROLD AND THE CORSAIR. POPE'S ESSAYS. ADDISON'S SPECTATOR. CHAUCER'S PROLOGUE TO THE CANTERBURY TALES. DEFOE'S CAVALIER AND ROBINSON CRUSOE. BURKE ON THE FRENCH REVOLUTION. DRYDEN'S POEMS. BROWNE'S RELIGIO MEDICI. LOCKE ON THE HUMAN UNDERSTANDING. WASHINGTON IRVING'S SKETCH BOOK.

SELECT PLAYS OF SHAKSPERE
RUGBY EDITION.
With an Introduction and Notes to each Play. Small 8vo.

AS YOU LIKE IT. 2s.; paper cover, 1s. 6d.

Edited by the Rev. CHARLES E. MOBERLY, M.A., Assistant-Master in Rugby School, and formerly Scholar of Balliol College, Oxford.

"This is a handy, clearly printed school edition of Shakspere's bright play. The notes are sensible, and not overdone, and the Introduction is helpful."—*Athenæum.*

"The Notes are clear, to the point, and brief, and for the most part excellent."—*Standard.*

MACBETH. 2s.; paper cover, 1s. 6d.

Edited by the SAME.

"A very excellent text, very ably annotated."—*Standard.*

"The plan of giving a brief sketch of each character in the play lends additional interest to it for the young learner. The notes are mainly explanatory, and serve the same useful purpose of clearing away difficulties from the path of the young reader. Of all school Shaksperes, this seems to us considerably the best."—*Educational Times.*

"'Macbeth' is now added to these handy, neatly printed, and well-annotated editions of Shakspere's Plays. Mr. Moberly's historical and critical remarks in the Introduction will be of great value to the student."—*Record.*

CORIOLANUS. 2s. 6d.; paper cover, 2s.

Edited by ROBERT WHITELAW, M.A., Assistant-Master in Rugby School, formerly Fellow of Trinity College, Cambridge.

"The way in which the play is edited displays careful scholarship, and the whole edition is extremely well adapted for school use."—*Educational Times.*

"This number of the Rugby Edition of Select Plays of Shakspere we think the best of the series. There is more effort than before to bring out the characteristics of the central figure of the play, the Notes are fuller, and the glossary too."—*Athenæum.*

HAMLET. 2s. 6d.; paper cover, 2s.

Edited by the Rev. CHARLES E. MOBERLY, M.A.

"Surely these are good times for students of our literature. The number of scholarly, well-edited handbooks, and annotated editions of masterpieces, both in prose and poetry, is continually augmenting. The introductions in this edition are particularly good, rising above the dull level of antiquarianism into a region of intelligent and sympathetic comment and analysis not often reached in school-books. We know by experience that Shakspere may be so read in schools as to combine a considerable amount of philological and grammatical teaching with a cultivation of the imagination and taste, perhaps more serviceable still. The Rugby Edition will do well either for school or home reading."—*London Quarterly Review.*

LONDON, OXFORD, AND CAMBRIDGE.

SELECT PLAYS OF SHAKSPERE—continued.

THE TEMPEST.
  Edited by J. SURTEES PHILLPOTTS, M.A., *Assistant-Master in Rugby School, formerly Fellow of New College, Oxford.*
  [*In the Press.*

MUCH ADO ABOUT NOTHING.
  Edited by the SAME. [*In the Press.*
  (*See Specimen Page, No. 1.*)

A Practical Introduction to English Prose Composition.

An English Grammar for Classical Schools, with Questions, and a Course of Exercises.

By THOMAS KERCHEVER ARNOLD, M.A.
  Ninth Edition. 12mo. 4*s.* 6*d.*

LONDON, OXFORD, AND CAMBRIDGE.

MATHEMATICS
Rivingtons' Mathematical Series

The following Schools, amongst many others, use this Series:—Eton: Harrow: Winchester: Charterhouse: Marlborough: Shrewsbury: Cheltenham: Clifton College: City of London School: Haileybury: Tonbridge: Durham: Fettes College, Edinburgh: Owen's College, Manchester: H.M.'s Dockyard School, Sheerness: The College, Hurstpierpoint: King William's College, Isle of Man: St. Peter's, Clifton, York: Birmingham: Bedford: Felsted: Christ's College, Finchley: Liverpool College: Windermere College: Eastbourne College: Brentwood; Perse School, Cambridge. Also in use in Canada, the other Colonies, and some of the Government Schools in India.

OPINIONS OF TUTORS AND SCHOOLMASTERS.

"I have great pleasure in expressing my opinion of your Mathematical books. We have for some time used them in our Lecture Room, and find them well arranged, and well calculated to clear up the difficulties of the subjects. The examples also are numerous and well-selected."—*N. M. Ferrers, M.A., Fellow and Tutor of Gonville and Caius College, Cambridge.*

"I have used in my Lecture Room Mr. Hamblin Smith's text-books on Algebra, Trigonometry, Mechanics, and Hydrostatics with very great advantage. I consider them admirably adapted for preparing students for the general examination for B.A. degrees, and for the extra subjects required in the previous examination from candidates for honours. They are distinguished by great clearness of explanation and arrangement, and at the same time by great scientific accuracy."—*James Porter, M.A., Fellow and Tutor of St. Peter's College, Cambridge.*

"Many students who attend my classes have used with great benefit to themselves Mr. Hamblin Smith's books, especially his Algebra and Arithmetic. Mr. Smith's great experience enables him to see the difficulties which trouble beginners, and he knows how to remove those difficulties. The examples are well arranged. For beginners there could be no better books, as I have found when examining different schools."—*A. W. W. Steel, M.A., Fellow and Assistant-Tutor of Gonville and Caius College, Cambridge.*

"I consider Mr. Hamblin Smith's Mathematical Works to be a very valuable series for beginners. His Algebra in particular seems to me to be marked by a singular clearness in the explanations, and by great judgement in the selection and arrangement of the exercises; and after my experience of it in the Lecture Room, I think it is the best book of its kind for schools and for the ordinary course at Cambridge."—*F. Patrick, M.A., Fellow and Tutor of Magdalen College, Cambridge.*

"I beg to state that I have used Mr. Hamblin Smith's various mathematical works extensively in my Lecture Room in this College, and have found them admirably adapted for class teaching. A person who carefully studies these books will have a thorough and accurate knowledge of the subjects on which they treat."—*H. A. Morgan, M.A., Tutor of Jesus College, Cambridge.*

"I can say with pleasure that I have used your books extensively in my work at Haileybury, and have found them on the whole well adapted for boys."—*Thomas Pitts, M.A., Assistant Mathematical Master at Haileybury College.*

"Your Arithmetic, Algebra, Euclid, and Trigonometry have been used here for several years. I have great pleasure in saying that I consider them most excellent school-books. The Algebra is certainly the best book published of its kind. I can strongly recommend them all."—*W. Henry, M.A., Sub-Warden, Trinity College, Glenalmond.*

"I have used all Mr. Hamblin Smith's Mathematical Works with my pupils, and have invariably found that greater progress

LONDON, OXFORD, AND CAMBRIDGE.

MATHEMATICS.] *EDUCATIONAL LIST.* 7

RIVINGTONS' MATHEMATICAL SERIES—continued.

has been made than when using other works on the same subjects. I believe the mathematical student, in the earlier part of his reading, cannot do better than confine his attention to these works. The investigations are simple and straightforward, while the arrangements of the text and the printing are admirable. The chapters are not too long, and they all contain numerous Examples worked out, with others, for exercise. His edition of Euclid cannot be too highly commended. Here the pupil will always find the figure facing the text, and, I may add, I have never seen a work on Geometry in which the figures of the XIth Book so forcibly strike the eye with their meaning. Mr. Smith has eliminated the so-called Rule of Three from his Arithmetic, and substituted the more rational method of First Principles. Both the Algebra and Trigonometry are well suited for Schools. Numerous Illustrative examples worked out with well-chosen collections for practice will be found in his Statics and Hydrostatics. In all cases the answers are given at the end of each work. I consider Mr. Smith has supplied a great want, and cannot but think that his works must command extensive use in good schools."—*J. Henry, B.A., Head-Master, H.M. Dockyard School, Sheerness, and Instructor of Engineers, R.N.*

"I shall certainly be delighted to have an opportunity of bearing testimony to the value of your work on Statics as a school text-book. I have used it from the time it first appeared, and find it preferable on many grounds to any other text-book of a similar nature with which I am acquainted. I gave it to two of my pupils to read at Christmas, and found they had gained a very fair knowledge of the subject without assistance; that is I think in itself a fair test of the clearness of the book. I shall be very happy if this expression of my opinion will be of any service to you in any way."—*C. W. Bourne, M.A., Assistant-Master at Marlborough College.*

"We have used your Algebra and Trigonometry extensively at this School from the time they were first published, and I thoroughly agree with every mathematical teacher I have met, that, as school text-books, they have no equals. The care you have taken to make clear every step, and especially those points which always used to baffle the boy-intellect, has rendered these subjects capable of being read, *both* in the time it usually took to read *one*.

The ample supply of easy problems at the end of each chapter enables the student to acquire confidence in his own powers, and taste for his work—qualities, as every teacher knows, indispensable to success. We are introducing your Euclid gradually into the School."—*Rev. B. Edwardes, sen., Mathematical Master at the College, Hurstpierpoint, Sussex.*

"I have much pleasure in stating that we have for some time used your Algebra and Trigonometry, and found them admirably adapted for the purposes of elementary instruction. I consider them to be the best books of their kind on the subject which I have yet seen."—*Joshua Jones, D.C.L., Head-Master, King William's College, Isle of Man.*

"The Algebra is the gem of the series, especially as compared with other works on the subject—no point is left unexplained, and all is made perfectly clear. The series is a model of clearness and insight into possible difficulties; by the aid of these works a student has only his own inattention to thank if he fails to make himself master of the elements of the various subjects."—*Rev. J. F. Blake, St. Peter's College, Clifton, York.*

"Your works on elementary Mathematics have been in constant use in this School for the last two or three years, and I for one have to thank you very much for elucidating many points which have always, in my experience, formed great stumbling-blocks to pupils. I have no doubt the better these works are known, the more generally will they be adopted in Schools."—*A. L. Taylor, M.A., Head-Master of the Ruabon Grammar School.*

"I have very great pleasure in expressing an opinion as to the value of these books. I have used them under very different circumstances, and have always been satisfied with the results obtained. The Algebra and Geometry I have used with science classes, with students preparing for various competitive examinations, with private pupils, and have seen them adopted and used in ordinary school-work, and always with success. The Trigonometry and Hydrostatics I have used almost as extensively and still with complete satisfaction. In most books one can generally point out particular chapters which seem more satisfactory than the rest; but in attempting to do this with the Algebra, I find myself desirous of noticing almost all the principal chapters."—*C. H. W. Biggs, Mathematical Editor of the English Mechanic.*

LONDON, OXFORD, AND CAMBRIDGE.

RIVINGTONS' MATHEMATICAL SERIES—continued.

ELEMENTARY ALGEBRA.

By J. HAMBLIN SMITH, M.A., *of Gonville and Caius College, and late Lecturer at St. Peter's College, Cambridge.*

12mo. 3s. Without Answers, 2s. 6d.

"It is evident that Mr. Hamblin Smith is a teacher, and has written to meet the special wants of students. He does not carry the student out of his depth by sudden plunges, but leads him gradually onward, never beyond his depth from any desire to hurry forward. The examples appear to be particularly well arranged, so as to afford a means of steady progress. With such books the judicious teacher will have abundant supply of examples and problems for those who need to have each step ensured by familiarity, and he will be able to allow the more rapid learner to travel onward with ease and swiftness. We can confidently recommend Mr. Hamblin Smith's books. Candidates preparing for Civil Service examinations under the new system of open competition will find these works to be of great value."—*Civil Service Gazette.*

"There are many valuable and characteristic features in Mr. Smith's works which will meet with the approval of teachers, and taught wherever they are used. The steps by which he leads the pupil are gradual but effectual, the examples are copious and well selected, the explanatory portions of the works are simple and concise, the whole forming an admirable example of the best means of writing scientific treatises. A real teacher, knowing a teacher's difficulties, and meeting them in the best possible manner, is what has long been wanted, and is what we have now obtained."—*Quarterly Journal of Education.*

(*See Specimen Page, No.* 6.)

A KEY, for the use of Tutors only.

Crown 8vo. [*In the Press.*

ALGEBRA. Part II.

By E. J. GROSS, M.A., *Fellow of Gonville and Caius College, Cambridge.*

Crown 8vo. [*In the Press.*

EXERCISES ON ALGEBRA.

By J. HAMBLIN SMITH, M.A.

12mo. 2s. 6d.

Copies may be had without the Answers.

"The exercises are arranged on the following plan:—Part I. conducts the student by gradual steps as far as Geometrical Progression, each exercise having the limit of its extent specified in the heading by a reference to the chapters of my Elementary Algebra. Part II. contains papers of greater length and somewhat more difficulty than those in Part I. No question in these papers implies a knowledge of any part of Algebra beyond Geometrical Progression, but at the end of each exercise one piece of bookwork is given. Part III. takes in the whole of the subject, so far as I have written on it in my treatise, especial prominence being given to that portion of the work which follows the chapter on Geometrical Progression. The questions in bookwork in Parts II. and III. follow the order in which the matters to which they refer are given in my treatise."—*From the Preface.*

[MATHEMATICS.] *EDUCATIONAL LIST.* 9

RIVINGTONS' MATHEMATICAL SERIES—continued.

A Treatise on Arithmetic.
By J. Hamblin Smith, M.A.
Second Edition, revised. 12mo. 3s. 6d.
(*See Specimen Page, No.* 4.) [*Just Published.*

Elements of Geometry.
By J. Hamblin Smith, M.A.
12mo. 3s. 6d.

Containing Books 1 to 6, and portions of Books 11 and 12, of Euclid, with Exercises and Notes, arranged with the Abbreviations admitted in the Cambridge Examinations.

Part I., containing Books 1 and 2 of Euclid, limp cloth, 1s. 6d., may be had separately.

"To preserve Euclid's order, to supply omissions, to remove defects, to give brief notes of explanation and simpler methods of proof in cases of acknowledged difficulty—such are the main objects of this edition of the Elements. The work is based on the Greek text, as it is given in the editions of August and Peyrard. To the suggestions of the late Professor De Morgan, published in the Companion to the British Almanack for 1849, I have paid constant deference. A limited use of symbolic representation, wherein the symbols stand for words and not for operations, is generally regarded as desirable, and the symbols employed in this book are admissible in the Examinations at Oxford and Cambridge. I have generally followed Euclid's method of proof, but not to the exclusion of other methods recommended by their simplicity, such as the demonstrations by which I propose to replace the difficult Theorems 5 and 7 in the First Book. I have also attempted to render many of the proofs, as, for instance, those of Propositions 2, 13, and 35 in Book I., and those of 7, 8, and 13 in Book II., less confusing to the learner. In Propositions 4–8 of Book II. I have made an important change, by omitting the diagonals from the diagrams, and the gnomons from the text. In Book III. I have given new proofs of the Propositions relating to the Contact of Circles, and made use of Superposition to prove Propositions 26–28. My treatment of the Fifth Book is based on the method of notation proposed by Professor De Morgan. The diagrams of Book XI. have been carefully drawn, and the Exercises, many of which are attached as Riders to the Propositions, are progressive and easy. A complete series of the Euclid Papers set in the Cambridge Mathematical Tripos from 1848 to 1872 is given."—*From the Preface.*

"Our space permits us to say but few words. The departure from the Euclidean form is not great, but it is a step in the right direction; it is another addition to the chronicle of progress, and we are promised that the third book, now in preparation, 'will deviate with even greater boldness from the precise line of Euclid's method.' This is as it should be; there must be no haste, but a quiet, continued amendment upon previous methods, or we shall be plunged into greater difficulties than even Euclid presents. Throughout the work, those abbreviations allowed at the Cambridge Examinations are used, thus, ∠ for angle, △ for triangle, ∵ for because, ∴ for therefore, = for equals, and so on, enabling the proposition to be printed in much less space. We thus bring Mr. Smith's works before the notice of our readers, confidently recommending them as being excellent treatises upon the various subjects of which they profess to treat. It is, however, our intention to return to the 'Geometry' at another opportunity."—*Quarterly Journal of Education.*

(*See Specimen Page, No.* 3.)

Geometrical Conic Sections.
By G. Richardson, M.A., *Assistant-Master at Winchester College, and late Fellow of St. John's College, Cambridge.*
Crown 8vo. 4s. 6d.

LONDON, OXFORD, AND CAMBRIDGE.

Trigonometry.

By J. Hamblin Smith, M.A.
12mo. 4s. 6d.

"The method of explanation is similar to that adopted in my Elementary Algebra. The examples, progressive and easy, have been selected chiefly from College and University Examination Papers; but I am indebted for many to the works of several German writers, especially those of Dienger, Meyer, Weiss, and Weigand. I have carried on the subject somewhat beyond the limits set by the Regulations for the Examination of Candidates for Honours in the Previous Examination, for two reasons; first, because I hope to see those limits extended; secondly, that my work may be more useful to those who are reading the subject in schools, and to candidates in the Local Examinations."—*From the Preface.*

"The arrangement of Trigonometry is excellent."—*Quarterly Journal of Education.*

(*See Specimen Page, No. 5.*)

Elementary Statics.

By J. Hamblin Smith, M.A.
12mo. 3s.

"This book is now published in such a form that it may meet the requirements of Students in Schools, especially those who are preparing for the Local Examinations. . . . . . The Examples have been selected from Papers set in Cambridge University Examinations. The propositions requiring a knowledge of Trigonometry are marked with *Roman* numerals."—*From the Preface.*

Elementary Hydrostatics.

By J. Hamblin Smith, M.A.
12mo. 3s.

"The elements of Hydrostatics seem capable of being presented in a simpler form than that in which they appear in all the works on the subject with which I am acquainted. I have therefore attempted to give a simple explanation of the Mathematical Theory of Hydrostatics and the practical application of it."—*From the Preface.*

Arithmetic, Theoretical and Practical.

By W. H. GIRDLESTONE, M.A., *of Christ's College, Cambridge, Principal of the Theological College, Gloucester.*
New Edition. Crown 8vo. 6s. 6d.
Also a School Edition. Small 8vo. 3s. 6d.

Arithmetic for the Use of Schools.

With a numerous Collection of Examples.
By R. D. BEASLEY, M.A., *Head-Master of Grantham Grammar School.*
12mo. 3s.
The Examples separately:—Part I. 8d. Part II. 1s. 6d.

LONDON, OXFORD, AND CAMBRIDGE.

… SCIENCE.]   EDUCATIONAL LIST.   11

SCIENCE

Preparing for Publication,

SCIENCE CLASS-BOOKS
Edited by
The Rev. ARTHUR RIGG, M.A.,
LATE PRINCIPAL OF THE COLLEGE, CHESTER.

These Volumes are designed expressly for School use, and by their especial reference to the requirements of a School Class-Book, aim at making Science-teaching a subject for regular and methodical study in Public and Private Schools.

AN ELEMENTARY CLASS-BOOK ON SOUND.
  By GEORGE CAREY FOSTER, B.A., F.R.S., *Fellow of, and Professor of Physics in, University College, London.*

AN ELEMENTARY CLASS-BOOK ON ELECTRICITY.
  By GEORGE CAREY FOSTER, B.A., F.R.S., *Fellow of, and Professor of Physics in, University College, London.*

BOTANY FOR CLASS-TEACHING.
  With Exercises for Private Work.
  By F. E. KITCHENER, M.A., F.L.S., *Assistant-Master at Rugby School, and late Fellow of Trinity College, Cambridge.*

Other Works are in preparation.

An Easy Introduction to Chemistry.
For the use of those who wish to acquire an elementary knowledge of the subject, and for Families and Schools.
  Edited by the Rev. ARTHUR RIGG, M.A., *late Principal of The College, Chester.*
  With Illustrations. Crown 8vo. 3s. 6d.
  (*See Specimen Page, No. 2.*)

A Year's Botany.
Adapted to Home Reading.
By FRANCES ANNA KITCHENER.
  With Illustrations. Crown 8vo.   [*In the Press.*

LONDON, OXFORD, AND CAMBRIDGE.

LATIN

Easy Exercises in Latin Prose.
With Notes.
By CHARLES BIGG, M.A., *Principal of Brighton College.*
Small 8vo. 1s. 4d.; sewed, 9d.

"This little book is intended for use in Lower Forms—for boys who have just emerged from the Subsidia. Too much time is spent as a rule over exercises upon idiomatic sentences. The first object should be to teach a boy to construct a period and give him some command of language. Not till these two steps have been taken can he really appropriate those more difficult phrases and constructions which have little or no analogy in English, and are comparatively rarely met with in reading Latin. I have given a few Notes by way of Introduction. Their object is not so much to instruct as to warn. It is a more important thing to make a boy feel a difficulty than to show him how to avoid it. I would suggest that, in the case of Exercises 1–21, the passages in Livy should be carefully read and explained in form. Then the English should be turned into Latin, and the Latin carefully corrected. Then a week or a fortnight afterwards, the Exercise should be done over again orally and from memory."—*From the Preface.*

Latin Prose Exercises.
For Beginners, and Junior Forms of Schools.
By R. PROWDE SMITH, B.A., *Assistant-Master at Cheltenham College.*
[This Book can be used with or without the PUBLIC SCHOOL LATIN PRIMER.]
Second Edition. Crown 8vo. 2s. 6d.

"The object of this book is to teach Latin composition and English Grammar simultaneously, and it is believed that the beginner will find the acquisition of the former much easier, when he finds he is approaching it through routes, which turn out on inspection to be already familiar to him. This system has been tested for several years, and has always been found to work successfully."—*From the Preface.*

"This is certainly an improvement on the grammar-school method, and may be a step in the way of teaching English before Latin."—*Examiner.*

"The plan upon which these exercises are founded is decidedly a good one, and none the less so that it is a very simple one."—*Educational Times.*

"This book differs from others of the same class in containing lessons in English to assist beginners in doing the Latin exercises. We quite agree with Mr. Smith as to the necessity of some knowledge of English and the principles of Grammar, as a qualification for writing Latin Prose correctly. His explanation of the more difficult constructions and idioms is very distinct, and altogether the book is highly satisfactory."—*Athenæum.*

"We have turned at random to various pages, and in each one have found the method the author has laid down for himself in the Preface well carried out. The examples on the dative are done with special care and judgment."—*John Bull.*

LONDON, OXFORD, AND CAMBRIDGE.

Henry's First Latin Book.
By THOMAS KERCHEVER ARNOLD, M.A.
Twenty-first Edition. 12mo. 3s. Tutor's Key, 1s.

A Practical Introduction to Latin Prose Composition.
By THOMAS KERCHEVER ARNOLD, M.A.
Sixteenth Edition. 8vo. 6s. 6d. Tutor's Key, 1s. 6d.

Cornelius Nepos.
With Critical Questions and Answers, and an Imitative Exercise on each Chapter.
By THOMAS KERCHEVER ARNOLD, M.A.
Fifth Edition. 12mo. 4s.

A First Verse Book.
Being an Easy Introduction to the Mechanism of the Latin Hexameter and Pentameter.
By THOMAS KERCHEVER ARNOLD, M.A.
Ninth Edition. 12mo. 2s. Tutor's Key, 1s.

Progressive Exercises in Latin Elegiac Verse.
By C. G. GEPP, B.A., *late Junior Student of Christ Church, Oxford; Head-Master of the College, Stratford-on-Avon.*
Second Edition. Crown 8vo. 3s. 6d. Tutor's Key, 5s.

"The selection is well made, and the Notes appear to be judicious."—*Examiner.*

"A very carefully prepared book, and will be useful to those who still find that time devoted to the making of Latin Verse is not time wasted."—*Standard.*

"Now that the absurdity of making all boys, however unfitted by nature, write Latin Verse is universally admitted, there is a danger of falling into the opposite error of supposing that the exercise can be of no use to any. The comparatively few who, besides being able to read Latin poetry intelligently, have a taste for versification, may derive both advantage and pleasure from it, and could not have a better guide to direct them than Mr. Gepp, who cautions them against the faults to which they are liable, and furnishes them with such aids as will prevent them from being baffled by the difficulties of the task, without, however, relieving them from the necessity of mental exertion."—*Athenæum.*

"A well-planned and skilfully worked-out little book."—*Daily Telegraph.*

"There would probably be a less fierce set against a study, which is simply delightful to those who have mastered it, had reformers and reviewers had so pleasant a manual as Mr. Gepp's to begin with.... We shall be glad if our brief notice of this book leads to its introduction into Preparatory Schools."—*Illustrated Review.*

LONDON, OXFORD, AND CAMBRIDGE.

Materials and Models for Greek and Latin Prose Composition.

Selected and arranged by J. Y. SARGENT, M.A., *Tutor, late Fellow, of Magdalen College, Oxford;* and T. F. DALLIN, M.A., *Fellow and Tutor of Queen's College, Oxford.*

Crown 8vo. 7s. 6d.

Latin Version of (60) Selected Pieces from Materials and Models.

By J. Y. SARGENT, M.A.

Crown 8vo. 5s.

May be had by Tutors only, by direct application to the Publishers.

Classical Examination Papers.

Edited, *with Notes and References,* by P. J. F. GANTILLON, M.A., *sometime Scholar of St. John's College, Cambridge; Classical Master in Cheltenham College.*

Crown 8vo. 7s. 6d.

Or interleaved with writing-paper, half-bound, 10s. 6d.

Eclogæ Ovidianæ.

From the Elegiac Poems. With English Notes.

By THOMAS KERCHEVER ARNOLD, M.A.

Twelfth Edition. 12mo. 2s. 6d.

Cicero.

With English Notes.

Edited by THOMAS KERCHEVER ARNOLD, M.A.

12mo.

SELECTED ORATIONS. Third Edition. 4s.

SELECTED EPISTLES. 5s.

THE TUSCULAN DISPUTATIONS. Second Edition. 5s. 6d.

DE FINIBUS MALORUM ET BONORUM. 5s. 6d.

CATO MAJOR, SIVE DE SENECTUTE DIALOGUS. 2s. 6d.

LONDON, OXFORD, AND CAMBRIDGE.

Terenti Comoediae.

Edited by T. L. PAPILLON, M.A., *Fellow of New College, and late Fellow of Merton, Oxford.*
ANDRIA ET EUNUCHUS.
Crown 8vo. 4s. 6d.
Forming a Part of the "Catena Classicorum."

Juvenalis Satirae.

Edited by G. A. SIMCOX, M.A., *Fellow and Classical Lecturer of Queen's College, Oxford.*
THIRTEEN SATIRES.
Second Edition, enlarged and revised. Crown 8vo. 5s.
Forming a Part of the "Catena Classicorum."
(*See Specimen Page, No. 7.*)

Persii Satirae.

Edited by A. PRETOR, M.A., *of Trinity College, Cambridge, Classical Lecturer of Trinity Hall, Composition Lecturer of the Perse Grammar School, Cambridge.*
Crown 8vo. 3s. 6d.
Forming a Part of the "Catena Classicorum."

A Copious and Critical English-Latin Lexicon.

By T. K. ARNOLD, M.A., *and* J. E. RIDDLE, M.A.
New Edition. 8vo. 21s.

GREEK

A Table of Irregular Greek Verbs.
Classified according to the arrangement of Curtius's Greek Grammar.
By FRANCIS STORR, B.A., *Assistant-Master in Marlborough College, late Scholar of Trinity College, Cambridge, and Bell University Scholar.*

On a Card. 1s.

A Greek Grammar.
By EVELYN ABBOTT, *Lecturer in Balliol College, Oxford, and late Assistant-Master in Clifton College.*

Crown 8vo. Part I. [*In the Press.*

Selections from Lucian.
With English Notes.
By EVELYN ABBOTT, *Lecturer in Balliol College, Oxford, and late Assistant-Master in Clifton College.*

Small 8vo. 3s. 6d.

"It is by far the best school edition we have seen."—*Standard.*

"Mr. Abbott has done wisely in publishing a selection from Lucian, an author, part of whose writings are just suited to boys who know enough Greek to read an easy prose author. His references to the English poets and the exercises for re-translation are good points in his book."—*Athenæum.*

"Lucian is certainly an author who deserves to be more read than he is. His style is easy enough, and his matter by no means uninteresting. Perhaps these selections may do something towards popularizing him. They seem well-chosen and the notes are ample. . . . The introduction, giving a sketch of Lucian and his works, is very well and pleasantly written."—*Educational Times.*

"We are predisposed to welcome Mr. Abbott's selections from a favourite author, more producible and easier to master than Aristophanes, and yet little, if at all, less entertaining. . . . . . We have found the critical and explanatory notes sound and serviceable. . . . The dialogues, of which Mr. Abbott supplies such excellent samples, will be excellent and delightful reading."—*Saturday Review.*

Extracts from Herodotus.
The Tales of Rhampsinitus and Polycrates. In Attic Greek.

Edited, with English Notes for use in Schools, by J. SURTEES PHILL-POTTS, M.A., *Assistant-Master in Rugby School; formerly Fellow of New College, Oxford.*

In Wrapper. Crown 8vo. 9d.

LONDON, OXFORD, AND CAMBRIDGE.

Iophon: an Introduction to the Art of Writing Greek Iambic Verses.

By the WRITER of "*Nuces*" and "*Lucretilis.*"

Crown 8vo. 2s.

"This book contains a number of easy exercises, to be turned into Iambics. There are also some instructions for beginners in Greek verse-making, which are clearly put, and, we think, likely to be very useful to the class for whom they are designed."—*Educational Times.*

(*See Specimen Page, No.* 9.)

The First Greek Book.
On the plan of "Henry's First Latin Book."

By THOMAS KERCHEVER ARNOLD, M.A.

Sixth Edition. 12mo. 5s. Tutor's Key, 1s. 6d.

A Practical Introduction to Greek Accidence.

By THOMAS KERCHEVER ARNOLD, M.A.

Eighth Edition. 8vo. 5s. 6d.

A Practical Introduction to Greek Prose Composition.

By THOMAS KERCHEVER ARNOLD, M.A.

Eleventh Edition. 8vo. 5s. 6d. Tutor's Key, 1s. 6d.

Madvig's Syntax of the Greek Language, especially of the Attic Dialect.
For the use of Schools.

Edited by THOMAS KERCHEVER ARNOLD, M.A.

New Edition, imperial 16mo. 8s. 6d.

LONDON, OXFORD, AND CAMBRIDGE.

SCENES FROM GREEK PLAYS
RUGBY EDITION

Abridged and adapted for the use of Schools, by

ARTHUR SIDGWICK, M.A.,
ASSISTANT-MASTER AT RUGBY SCHOOL, AND FORMERLY FELLOW OF
TRINITY COLLEGE, CAMBRIDGE.

Small 8vo. 1s. 6d. each; or, in paper cover, 1s.

ARISTOPHANES.
THE CLOUDS. THE FROGS. THE KNIGHTS. PLUTUS.

EURIPIDES.
IPHIGENIA IN TAURIS. THE CYCLOPS. ION. ELECTRA.

"Mr. Sidgwick has put on the title-pages of these modest little volumes the words 'Rugby Edition,' but we shall be much mistaken if they do not find a far wider circulation. The prefaces or introductions which Mr. Sidgwick has prefixed to his 'Scenes' tell the youthful student all that he need know about the play that he is taking in hand, and the parts chosen are those which give the general scope and drift of the action of the play."—*School Board Chronicle.*

"Each play is printed separately, on good paper, and in a neat and handy form. The difficult passages are explained by the notes appended, which are of a particularly useful and intelligible kind. In all respects this edition presents a very pleasing contrast to the German editions hitherto in general use, with their Latin explanatory notes—themselves often requiring explanation. A new feature in this edition, which deserves mention, is the insertion in English of the stage directions. By means of these and the argument prefixed, the study of the play is much simplified."—*Scotsman.*

"A short preface explains the action of the play in each case, and there are a few notes at the end which will clear up most of the difficulties likely to be met with by the young student."—*Educational Times.*

"Just the book to be put into the hands of boys who are reading Greek plays. They are carefully and judiciously edited, and form the most valuable aid to the study of the elements of Greek that we have seen for many a day. The Grammatical Indices are especially to be commended."—*Athenæum.*

"These editions afford exactly the kind of help that school-boys require, and are really excellent class-books. The notes, though very brief, are of much use and always to the point, and the arguments and arrangement of the text are equally good in their way."—*Standard.*

"Not professing to give whole dramas, with their customary admixture of iambics, trochaics, and choral odes, as pabulum for learners who can barely digest the level speeches and dialogues commonly confined to the first-named metre, he has arranged extracted scenes with much tact and skill, and set them before the pupil with all needful information in the shape of notes at the end of the book; besides which he has added a somewhat novel, but highly commendable and valuable feature—namely, appropriate headings to the commencement of each scene, and appropriate stage directions during its progress."—*Saturday Review.*

"These are attractive little books, novel in design and admirable in execution..... It would hardly be possible to find a better introduction to Aristophanes for a young student than these little books afford."—*London Quarterly Review.*

(*See Specimen Page, No.* 8.)

Homer for Beginners.
ILIAD, Books I.—III. With English Notes.
By THOMAS KERCHEVER ARNOLD, M.A.
Third Edition. 12mo. 3s. 6d.

The Iliad of Homer.
From the Text of Dindorf. With Preface and Notes.
By S. H. REYNOLDS, M.A., *Fellow and Tutor of Brasenose College, Oxford.*
Crown 8vo.
Books I.—XII. 6s.
Forming a Part of the " Catena Classicorum."

The Iliad of Homer.
With English Notes and Grammatical References.
By THOMAS KERCHEVER ARNOLD, M.A.
Fourth Edition. 12mo. Half-bound, 12s.

A Complete Greek and English Lexicon for the Poems of Homer and the Homeridæ.
By G. CH. CRUSIUS. *Translated from the German.* Edited by T. K. ARNOLD, M.A.
New Edition. 12mo. 9s.

Materials and Models for Greek and Latin Prose Composition.
Selected and arranged by J. Y. SARGENT, M.A., *Tutor, late Fellow of Magdalen College, Oxford; and* T. F. DALLIN, M.A., *Fellow and Tutor of Queen's College, Oxford.*
Crown 8vo. 7s. 6d.

LONDON, OXFORD, AND CAMBRIDGE.

Classical Examination Papers.

Edited, with Notes and References, by P. J. F. GANTILLON, M.A., sometime Scholar of St. John's College, Cambridge; Classical Master at Cheltenham College.
Crown 8vo. 7s. 6d.
Or interleaved with writing-paper for Notes, half-bound, 10s. 6d.

Demosthenes.

Edited, with English Notes and Grammatical References, by THOMAS KERCHEVER ARNOLD, M.A.
12mo.
OLYNTHIAC ORATIONS. Third Edition. 3s.
PHILIPPIC ORATIONS. Third Edition. 4s.
ORATION ON THE CROWN. Second Edition. 4s. 6d.

Demosthenis Orationes Privatae.

Edited by ARTHUR HOLMES, M.A., Senior Fellow and Dean of Clare College, Cambridge, and late Preacher at the Chapel Royal, Whitehall.
Crown 8vo.
DE CORONA. 5s.
Forming a Part of the "Catena Classicorum."

Demosthenis Orationes Publicae.

Edited by G. H. HESLOP, M.A., late Fellow and Assistant-Tutor of Queen's College, Oxford; Head-Master of St. Bees.
Crown 8vo.
OLYNTHIACS, 2s. 6d. } or, in One Volume, 4s. 6d.
PHILIPPICS, 3s.
DE FALSA LEGATIONE, 6s.
Forming Parts of the "Catena Classicorum."

Isocratis Orationes.

Edited by JOHN EDWIN SANDYS, M.A., Fellow and Tutor of St. John's College, Cambridge.
Crown 8vo.
AD DEMONICUM ET PANEGYRICUS. 4s. 6d.
Forming a Part of the "Catena Classicorum."

The Greek Testament.

With a Critically Revised Text; a Digest of Various Readings; Marginal References to Verbal and Idiomatic Usage; Prolegomena; and a Critical and Exegetical Commentary. For the use of Theological Students and Ministers.

By HENRY ALFORD, D.D., *late Dean of Canterbury*.

New Edition. 4 vols. 8vo. 102*s*.

The Volumes are sold separately, as follows:
Vol. I.—The Four Gospels. 28*s*.
Vol. II.—Acts to II. Corinthians. 24*s*.
Vol. III.—Galatians to Philemon. 18*s*.
Vol. IV.—Hebrews to Revelation. 32*s*.

The Greek Testament.

With Notes, Introductions, and Index.

By CHR. WORDSWORTH, D.D., *Bishop of Lincoln; formerly Canon of Westminster, and Archdeacon*.

New and cheaper Edition. 2 vols. Impl. 8vo. 60*s*.

The Parts may be had separately, as follows:—
The Gospels. 16*s*.
The Acts. 8*s*.
St. Paul's Epistles. 23*s*.
General Epistles, Revelation, and Index. 16*s*.

An Introduction to Aristotle's Ethics.

Books I.—IV. (Book X., c. vi.—ix. in an Appendix). With a Continuous Analysis and Notes. Intended for the use of Beginners and Junior Students.

By the Rev. EDWARD MOORE, B.D., *Principal of S. Edmund Hall, and late Fellow and Tutor of Queen's College, Oxford*.

Crown 8vo. 10*s*. 6*d*.

Aristotelis Ethica Nicomachea.

Edidit, emendavit, crebrisque locis parallelis e libro ipso, aliisque ejusdem Auctoris scriptis, illustravit JACOBUS E. T. ROGERS, A.M. Small 8vo. 4*s*. 6*d*. Interleaved with writing-paper, half-bound. 6*s*.

LONDON, OXFORD, AND CAMBRIDGE.

Sophocles.

With English Notes from SCHNEIDEWIN.
Edited by T. K. ARNOLD, M.A., ARCHDEACON PAUL, *and* HENRY BROWNE, M.A.

12mo.

AJAX. 3s. PHILOCTETES. 3s. ŒDIPUS TYRANNUS. 4s. ŒDIPUS COLONEUS. 4s. ANTIGONE. 4s.

Sophoclis Tragoediae.

Edited by R. C. JEBB, M.A., *Fellow and Assistant-Tutor of Trinity College, Cambridge, and Public Orator of the University.*

Crown 8vo.

ELECTRA. Second Edition, revised. 3s. 6d.
AJAX. 3s. 6d.

Forming Parts of the "Catena Classicorum."

Aristophanis Comoediae.

Edited by W. C. GREEN, M.A., *late Fellow of King's College, Cambridge; Assistant-Master at Rugby School.*

Crown 8vo.

THE ACHARNIANS and THE KNIGHTS. 4s.
THE CLOUDS. 3s. 6d.
THE WASPS. 3s. 6d.

An Edition of "THE ACHARNIANS and THE KNIGHTS," revised and especially prepared for Schools. 4s.

Forming Parts of the "Catena Classicorum."

Herodoti Historia.

Edited by H. G. WOODS, M.A., *Fellow and Tutor of Trinity College, Oxford.*

Crown 8vo.

BOOK I. 6s. BOOK II. 5s.

Forming Parts of the "Catena Classicorum."

LONDON, OXFORD, AND CAMBRIDGE.

A Copious Phraseological English-Greek Lexicon.

Founded on a work prepared by J. W. FRÄDERSDORFF, Ph.D., late Professor of Modern Languages, Queen's College, Belfast.

Revised, Enlarged, and Improved by the late THOMAS KERCHEVER ARNOLD, M.A., and HENRY BROWNE, M.A.

Fourth Edition. 8vo. 21s.

Thucydidis Historia.

Edited by CHARLES BIGG, M.A., late Senior Student and Tutor of Christ Church, Oxford; Principal of Brighton College.

Crown 8vo.

BOOKS I. AND II. 6s. BOOKS III. AND IV. *in the Press.*

Forming Parts of the "Catena Classicorum."

DIVINITY

Handbooks of Religious Instruction for Pupil Teachers.

By JOHN PILKINGTON NORRIS, M.A., *Canon of Bristol, Church Inspector of Training Colleges.*

The Old Testament.
The New Testament.
The Prayer Book.

Each Book in Three Parts. Small 8vo. 1s. each Part.

A Companion to the Old Testament.

Being a plain Commentary on Scripture History down to the Birth of our Lord.

Small 8vo. 3s. 6d.

[Especially adapted for use in Training Colleges and Schools.]

"A very compact summary of the Old Testament narrative, put together so as to explain the connection and bearing of its contents, and written in a very good tone; with a final chapter on the history of the Jews between the Old and New Testaments. It will be found very useful for its purpose. It does not confine itself to merely chronological difficulties, but comments freely upon the religious bearing of the text also."—*Guardian.*

"A most admirable *Companion to the Old Testament*, being far the most concise yet complete commentary on Old Testament history with which we have met. Here are combined orthodoxy and learning, an intelligent and at the same time interesting summary of the leading facts of the sacred story. It should be a text-book in every school, and its value is immensely enhanced by the copious and complete index."—*John Bull.*

"This will be found a sufficient text-book for teaching Old Testament history. There are no lengthy comments and the plan of the work excludes arguments; but the historical narratives are well condensed and the explanatory notes are scholarly and clear. The tone of the book is thoroughly reverent and Christian."—*London Quarterly Review.*

(*See Specimen Page, No.* 10.)

A Companion to the New Testament.

[*In preparation.*]

LONDON, OXFORD, AND CAMBRIDGE.

The Young Churchman's Companion to the Prayer-Book.

Part I.—Morning and Evening Prayer and Litany.

By the Rev. J. W. GEDGE, M.A., *Diocesan Inspector of Schools for the Archdeaconry of Surrey.*

Recommended by the LORD BISHOP OF WINCHESTER.

18mo. 1s.

History of the Church under the Roman Empire, A.D. 30-476.

By the Rev. A. D. CRAKE, B.A., *Chaplain of All Saints' School, Bloxham.*

Crown 8vo. [*Just Ready.*

A Manual of Confirmation.

With a Pastoral Letter instructing Catechumens how to prepare themselves for their First Communion.

By EDWARD MEYRICK GOULBURN, D.D., *Dean of Norwich.*

Eighth Edition. Small 8vo. 1s. 6d.

The Way of Life.

A Book of Prayers and Instruction for the Young at School. With a Preparation for Holy Communion.

Compiled by a Priest. Edited by the Rev. T. T. CARTER, M.A., *Rector of Clewer, Berks.*

16mo, 1s. 6d.

The Lord's Supper.

By THOMAS WILSON, D.D., *late Lord Bishop of Sodor and Man.*

Complete Edition, with red borders, 16mo. 2s. 6d.

Also a Cheap Edition, without red borders, 1s.; or in paper cover, 6d.

Household Theology.

A Handbook of Religious Information respecting the Holy Bible, the Prayer-Book, the Church, the Ministry, Divine Worship, the Creeds, &c., &c.

By the Rev. JOHN HENRY BLUNT, M.A.

New Edition. Small 8vo. 3s. 6d.

LONDON, OXFORD, AND CAMBRIDGE.

KEYS TO CHRISTIAN KNOWLEDGE.

Small 8vo. 2s. 6d.

"Of cheap and reliable text-books of this nature there has hitherto been a great want. We are often asked to recommend books for use in Church Sunday-schools, and we therefore take this opportunity of saying that we know of none more likely to be of service both to teachers and scholars than these 'Keys.'"—*Churchman's Shilling Magazine.*

"Will be very useful for the higher classes in Sunday schools, or rather for the fuller instruction of the Sunday-school teachers themselves, where the parish Priest is wise enough to devote a certain time regularly to their preparation for their voluntary task."—*Union Review.*

A KEY TO THE KNOWLEDGE AND USE OF THE HOLY BIBLE.
  By *the* Rev. J. H. BLUNT, M.A. Editor of the 'Annotated Book of Common Prayer,' &c., &c.

A KEY TO THE KNOWLEDGE AND USE OF THE BOOK OF COMMON PRAYER.
  By *the* Rev. J. H. BLUNT, M.A.

A KEY TO THE KNOWLEDGE OF CHURCH HISTORY (ANCIENT).
  Edited by *the* Rev. J. H. BLUNT, M.A.

A KEY TO THE KNOWLEDGE OF CHURCH HISTORY (MODERN).
  Edited by *the* Rev. J. H. BLUNT, M.A.

A KEY TO CHRISTIAN DOCTRINE AND PRACTICE, FOUNDED ON THE CHURCH CATECHISM.
  By *the* Rev. J. H. BLUNT, M.A.

A KEY TO THE NARRATIVE OF THE FOUR GOSPELS.
  By *the* Rev. JOHN PILKINGTON NORRIS, M.A., *Canon of Bristol, Church Inspector of Training Colleges, and formerly one of Her Majesty's Inspectors of Schools.*

A KEY TO THE NARRATIVE OF THE ACTS OF THE APOSTLES.
  By *the* Rev. JOHN PILKINGTON NORRIS, M.A.

LONDON, OXFORD, AND CAMBRIDGE.

MISCELLANEOUS

The Campaigns of Napoleon.

The Text (in French) from M. THIERS' *"Histoire du Consulat et de l'Empire," and "Histoire de la Révolution Française." Edited with English Notes, for the use of Schools, by* EDWARD E. BOWEN, M.A., *Master of the Modern Side Harrow School, late Fellow of Trinity College, Cambridge.*

With Maps. Crown 8vo. 4s. 6d. each.

ARCOLA. [*Just Published.*
MARENGO. [*Just Published.*
JENA. [*In preparation.*
WATERLOO. [*In preparation.*

(*See Specimen Page, No.* 12.)

Selections from Modern French Authors.

Edited, with English Notes and Introductory Notice, by HENRI VAN LAUN, *formerly French Master at Cheltenham College, and now Master of the French Language and Literature at the Edinburgh Academy.*

Crown 8vo. 3s. 6d. each.

HONORÉ DE BALZAC. H. A. TAINE.

The First French Book.

On the plan of "Henry's First Latin Book."
By THOMAS KERCHEVER ARNOLD, M.A.
Sixth Edition. 12mo. 5s. 6d. Key, 2s. 6d.

The First German Book.

On the plan of "Henry's First Latin Book."
By THOMAS KERCHEVER ARNOLD, M.A., *and* J. W. FRÄDERSDORFF, Ph.D.
Sixth Edition. 12mo. 5s. 6d. Key, 2s. 6d.

The First Hebrew Book.

On the plan of "Henry's First Latin Book."
By THOMAS KERCHEVER ARNOLD, M.A.
Third Edition. 12mo. 7s. 6d. Key, 3s. 6d.

A Theory of Harmony.

Founded on the Tempered Scale. With Questions and Exercises for the Use of Students.

By JOHN STAINER, Mus. Doc., M.A., *Magd. Coll. Oxon, Organist to St. Paul's Cathedral.*

Second Edition. 8vo. 7s. 6d.

The Chorister's Guide.

By W. A. BARRETT, Mus. Bac., Oxon, *of St. Paul's Cathedral, Author of " Flowers and Festivals."*

Square 16mo. 2s. 6d.

(See Specimen Page, No. 11.)

" . . . One of the most useful books of instructions for choristers—and, we may add, choral singers generally—that has ever emanated from the musical press. The notion is a novel one; and, so far as we can recollect, has never been entertained before, and certainly has not been carried out in the able manner in which the 'Chorister's Guide' has been drawn up. It goes beyond elementary musical instruction, as for that purpose the world has been inundated with works; but Mr. Barrett has invented a code for choristers in the execution of rituals which has not existed before, and he has achieved this end by clear and simple directions, that he who runs may read. He indicates the character and meaning of a service; he points out how gesture should be reverential, how dignity and solemnity should be infused in notation.

. . . Mr. Barrett's teaching is not only conveyed to his readers with the consciousness of being master of his subject, but he employs words terse and clear, so that his meaning may be promptly caught by the neophyte. . . ."—*Athenæum.*

" . . . In a work of this kind careful and neat printing are very great advantages, and in these as in other respects the 'Chorister's Guide' is a highly satisfactory production."—*English Churchman.*

"A nicely graduated, clear, and excellent introduction to the duties of a chorister by a practical hand."—*Standard.*

"The 'Chorister's Guide' is written by Mr. Barrett, of St. Paul's Cathedral; it seems clear and precise enough to serve its end."—*Examiner.*

"By Mr. Barrett, of St. Paul's, who dedicates it to Dean Church; it seems to be a useful manual for giving boys such a practical and technical knowledge of music as shall enable them to sing both with confidence and precision."—*Church Herald.*

"In this little volume we have a manual long called for by the requirements of church music. In a series of thirty-two lessons it gives, with an admirable conciseness, and an equally observable completeness, all that is necessary a chorister should be taught out of a book, and a great deal calculated to have a value as bearing directly upon his actual practice in singing."—*Musical Standard.*

"We can highly recommend the present able manual."—*Educational Times.*

"A very useful manual, not only for choristers, or rather those who may aim at becoming choristers, but for others who wish to enter upon the study of music."—*Rock.*

LONDON, OXFORD, AND CAMBRIDGE.

CATENA CLASSICORUM

A SERIES OF

CLASSICAL AUTHORS,

Edited by Members of both Universities, under the direction of the Rev. ARTHUR HOLMES, M.A., *Senior Fellow and Dean of Clare College, Cambridge, and late Preacher at the Chapel Royal, Whitehall;*

and

The Rev. CHARLES BIGG, M.A., *late Senior Student and Tutor of Christ Church, Oxford; Principal of Brighton College.*

Crown 8vo.

SOPHOCLIS TRAGOEDIAE.

Edited by R. C. JEBB, M.A., *Fellow and Tutor of Trinity College, Cambridge, and Public Orator of the University.*

THE ELECTRA. 3*s*. 6*d.*   THE AJAX. 3*s*. 6*d.*

"We have no hesitation in saying that in style and manner Mr. Jebb's notes are admirably suited for their purpose. The explanations of grammatical points are singularly lucid, the parallel passages generally well chosen, the translations bright and graceful, the analysis of arguments terse and luminous. Mr. Jebb has clearly shown that he possesses some of the qualities most essential for a commentator."—*Spectator.*

"The Introduction proves that Mr. Jebb is something more than a mere scholar,—a man of real taste and feeling. His criticism upon Schlegel's remarks on the Electra are, we believe, new, and certainly just. As we have often had occasion to say in this Review, it is impossible to pass any reliable criticism upon school-books until they have been tested by experience. The notes, however, in this case appear to be clear and sensible, and direct attention to the points where attention is most needed."—*Westminster Review.*

"In a concise and succinct style of English annotation, forming the best substitute for the time-honoured Latin notes which had so much to do with making good scholars in days of yore, Mr. Jebb keeps a steady eye for all questions of grammar, construction, scholarship, and philology, and handles these as they arise with a helpful and sufficient precision. In matters of grammar and syntax, his practice for the most part is to refer his reader to the proper section of Madvig's 'Manual of Greek Syntax:' nor does he ever waste space and time in explaining a construction, unless it be such an one as is not satisfactorily dealt with in the grammars of Madvig or Jelf. Experience as a pupil and a teacher has probably taught him the value of the wholesome task of hunting out a grammar reference for one-self, instead of finding it handy for slurring over, amidst the hundred and one pieces of information in a voluminous footnote. But whenever there occurs any peculiarity of construction, which is hard to reconcile to the accepted usage, it is Mr. Jebb's general practice to be ready at hand with manful assistance."—*Contemporary Review.*

"Mr. Jebb has produced a work which will be read with interest and profit by the most advanced scholar, as it contains, in a compact form, not only a careful summary of the labours of preceding editors, but also many acute and ingenious original remarks. We do not know whether the matter or the manner of this excellent commentary is de-

LONDON, OXFORD, AND CAMBRIDGE.

CATENA CLASSICORUM—continued.

serving of the higher praise; the skill with which Mr. Jebb has avoided, on the one hand, the wearisome prolixity of the Germans, and on the other the jejune brevity of the Porsonian critics, or the versatility which has enabled him in turn to elucidate the plots, to explain the verbal difficulties, and to illustrate the idioms of his author. All this, by a studious economy of space and a remarkable precision of expression, he has done for the 'Ajax' in a volume of some 300 pages."—*Athenæum.*

"An accidental tardiness in noticing these instalments of a Sophocles which promises to be one of the ablest and most useful editions published in this country must not be construed into any lack of due appreciation of their value. It seemed best to wait till more than one play had issued from the press; but it is not too late to express the favourable impression which we have formed, from the two samples before us, of Mr. Jebb's eminent qualifications for the task of interpreting Sophocles. Eschewing the old fashion of furnishing merely a grammatical and textual commentary, he has concentrated very much of the interest of his edition in the excellent and exhaustive introductions which preface each play, and which, while excluding what is not strictly connected with the subject, discuss the real matter in hand with acuteness and tact, as well as originality and research."—*Saturday Review.*

JUVENALIS SATIRAE.

By G. A. SIMCOX, M.A., *Fellow and late Classical Lecturer of Queen's College, Oxford.*

New Edition, revised and enlarged, 5s.

"This is a very original and enjoyable Edition of one of our favourite classics."—*Spectator.*

"A very valuable and trustworthy school-book. The introduction, notes, and text are all marked with scholarly taste, and a real desire to place in the hands of the learner all that is most effective to throw light upon the author."—*Standard.*

THUCYDIDIS HISTORIA.

By CHARLES BIGG, M.A., *late Senior Student and Tutor of Christ Church, Oxford; Principal of Brighton College.*

Books I. and II. 6s.

"Mr. Bigg in his 'Thucydides' prefixes an analysis to each book, and an admirable introduction to the whole work, containing full information as to all that is known or related of Thucydides, and the date at which he wrote, followed by a very masterly critique on some of his characteristics as a writer."—*Athenæum.*

"While disclaiming absolute originality in his book, Mr. Bigg has so thoroughly digested the works of so many eminent predecessors in the same field, and is evidently on terms of such intimacy with his author as perforce to inspire confidence. A well-pondered and well-written introduction has formed a part of each link in the 'Catena' hitherto published, and Mr. Bigg, in addition to a general introduction, has given us an essay on 'Some Characteristics of Thucydides,' which no one can read without being impressed with the learning and judgment brought to bear on the subject."—*Standard.*

"We need hardly say that these books are carefully edited; the reputation of the editor is an assurance on this point. If the rest of the history is edited with equal care, it must become the standard book for school and college purposes."—*John Bull.*

"Mr. Bigg first discusses the facts of the life of Thucydides, then passes to an examination into the date at which Thucydides wrote; and in the third section expatiates on some characteristics of Thucydides. These essays are remarkably well written, are judicious in their opinions, and are calculated to give the student much insight into the work of Thucydides, and its relation to his own times, and to the works of subsequent historians."—*Museum.*

LONDON, OXFORD, AND CAMBRIDGE.

EDUCATIONAL LIST. 31

CATENA CLASSICORUM—continued.

DEMOSTHENIS ORATIONES PUBLICAE.

By G. H. HESLOP, M.A., *late Fellow and Assistant-Tutor of Queen's College, Oxford; Head-Master of St. Bees.*

THE OLYNTHIACS. 2s. 6d.
THE PHILIPPICS. 3s.   } or, in One Volume, 4s. 6d.
DE FALSA LEGATIONE. 6s.

THE OLYNTHIACS AND PHILIPPICS.

"The annotations are scarcely less to be commended for the exclusion of superfluous matter than for the excellence of what is supplied. Well-known works are not quoted, but simply referred to, and information which ought to have been previously acquired is omitted."—*Athenæum.*

"Mr. Heslop's critical scholarship is of an accurate and enlarged order. His reading of the chief authorities, historical, critical, explanatory, and technical, has been commendably thorough; and it would be impossible to go through either the Olynthiacs, or Philippics, with his aid, and not to have picked up many pieces of information to add to one's stock of knowledge of the Greek language and its use among the orators, who rendered its latter day famous. He is moreover an independent editor, and, we are glad to find, holds his own views as to readings and interpretations, undismayed by the formidable names that occasionally meet him in his way."—*Contemporary Review.*

DE FALSA LEGATIONE.

"The notes are full, the more difficult idioms being not only elucidated by references to grammars, but also illustrated by a wealth of apt and well-arranged quotations. Hence we imagine that the attentive reader will not be content with a single perusal of the commentary, but will find it worth while to have it by his side, when he is engaged upon other speeches of the Athenian orator. Mr. Heslop gives us an historical introduction as well as occasional summaries and historical notes, which seem to us just what they ought to be."—*Athenæum.*

"Deserves a welcome. There is abundant room for useful and handy editions of the chief orations of Demosthenes. Mr. Heslop has performed his editorial function faithfully and ably."—*Saturday Review.*

"The volume before us well maintains the high repute of the series in which it appears. A good text, well printed, with careful but not too elaborate notes, is the main characteristic of it, as of previous volumes. . . . An able introduction is prefixed to it, which the student will find useful; and altogether we cannot but feel how different the school-books of the present day are from those which we recollect."—*John Bull.*

"A well-written introduction, carefully edited text, ample and excellent footnotes—which include from time to time a short analysis of the text—and translations not less vigorous than accurate, make up a whole, which cannot fail to be equally acceptable to both masters and scholars."—*Standard.*

"Mr. Heslop has shown very great critical powers in the edition of the famous speech now before us, especially in his annotations. . . . Indeed, his array of authorities, grammatical, critical, technical, historical, and explanatory, is from first to last worthy of all praise; and nothing can exceed the clearness of the historical essay, which he has prefixed as an introduction to the work."—*School Board Chronicle.*

"In an elaborate introduction, the editor gives—what is eminently desirable for the student approaching such a speech—an account of the intricate complications of Athenian politics in the period when the State was struggling to maintain itself against the preponderating power of Macedonia. . . . In dealing with the text of his author, Mr. Heslop has exercised an independent judgment, while availing himself of the labours of other editors; and the grounds assigned for the course he has adopted will commend themselves to the attention of scholars. For the purposes of the student the commentary appended to the text affords all that is necessary in the way of judicious furtherance. Variations of reading are commented on, peculiarities of grammatical construction explained, and obscure allusions rendered intelligible by means of collateral information. An index affords the means of ready reference to the more important notes."—*Scotsman.*

LONDON, OXFORD, AND CAMBRIDGE.

CATENA CLASSICORUM—continued.

DEMOSTHENIS ORATIONES PRIVATAE.
By ARTHUR HOLMES, M.A., *Senior Fellow and Dean of Clare College, Cambridge, and late Preacher at the Chapel Royal, Whitehall.*
DE CORONA. 5s.

"We find a scholarship never at fault, an historical eye which sees over the whole field of the political area occupied by Philip of Macedonia and the great orator whose business in life was to combat and thwart him, and an acuteness of criticism sufficing to discriminate between the valuable and the worthless matter in the commentaries of previous editors. Of the speech itself and its famous *loci classici* of eloquence and invective it is scarcely necessary to speak. To do full justice to these the reader must go to the fountain-head; and he must have for commentator and guide one whose mind is clearly made up, so that there may be no doubt or hesitation as to the sense of the words and sentences which claim his admiration. In the grand outburst where Demosthenes assures his audience that his policy and teaching agree with their own hereditary instincts, and swears it by the memory of their forefathers' intrepidity, rather than their success against the Persians (§ 208-9, &c.), Mr. Holmes is careful to smooth every difficulty, and in the vivid picture of the excitement of Athens on the receipt of the news of Philip's occupation of Elatea (§ 169-70), he does good service in weighing the likeliest meaning of certain words which are important accessories of the picture. . . . In reading the speech a student seems to need the company of an exact annotator to assure him that his ears, or eyes, or powers of translation are not misleading him, when he finds an advocate letting loose upon another a flood of epithets so utterly beyond the widest license of modern political discussion. That Mr. Holmes supplies the want indicated we shall proceed to show in one or two examples of exact interpretation, having first glanced at the calm tenor of his judgment on one or two moot points connected with the speech itself."—*Saturday Review.*

"Mr. Holmes has compressed into a convenient shape the enormous mass of annotation which has been accumulated by critics, English and foreign, on Demosthenes' famous oration, and he has made no trifling contributions of his own. He appears to us to deal successfully with most of the difficulties which preceding commentators have failed to solve—difficulties, it may be observed, which are rather historical than critical, and which, for the most part, arise in the endeavour to reconcile the plain grammatical sense of the orator's words with known facts. . . . . In purely critical questions the notes show all the subtle scholarship which we should expect from so renowned a classic as Mr. Holmes. If we note any one peculiar excellence, it is the accuracy with which the shades of difference of meaning in the various uses of the tenses are noted, and nothing, as we need hardly say, could be more important in annotation on an oration which has for its subject-matter history partly contemporary, partly belonging to the recent past."—*Spectator.*

ARISTOPHANIS COMOEDIAE.
By W. C. GREEN, M.A., *late Fellow of King's College, Cambridge; Assistant-Master at Rugby School.*
THE ACHARNIANS AND THE KNIGHTS. 4s.
THE CLOUDS. 3s. 6d.   THE WASPS. 3s. 6d.

An Edition of THE ACHARNIANS AND THE KNIGHTS, revised and especially adapted for use in Schools. 4s.

"Mr. Green has discharged his part of the work with uncommon skill and ability. The notes show a thorough study of the two plays, an independent judgment in the interpretation of the poet, and a wealth of illustration, from which the editor draws whenever it is necessary."—*Museum.*

"Mr. Green's admirable introduction to 'The Clouds' of the celebrated comic poet deserves a careful perusal, as it contains an accurate analysis and many original comments on this remarkable play. The text is prefaced by a table of readings of Dindorf and Meineke, which will be of great service to students who wish to indulge in verbal criticism. The notes are copious and lucid, and the volume will be found useful for school and college purposes, and admirably adapted for private reading."—*Examiner.*

"Mr. Green furnishes an excellent introduction to 'The Clouds' of Aristophanes, explaining the circumstances under which it was produced, and ably discussing the probable object of the author in writing it."—*Athenæum.*

LONDON, OXFORD, AND CAMBRIDGE.

CATENA CLASSICORUM—continued.

ISOCRATIS ORATIONES.
By JOHN EDWIN SANDYS, M.A., *Fellow and Tutor of St. John's College, Classical Lecturer at Jesus College, Cambridge.*
AD DEMONICUM ET PANEGYRICUS. 4s. 6d.

"Isocrates has not received the attention to which the simplicity of his style and the purity of his Attic language entitle him as a means of education. Now that we have so admirable an edition of two of his Works best adapted for such a purpose, there will no longer be any excuse for this neglect. For carefulness and thoroughness of editing, it will bear comparison with the best, whether English or foreign. Besides an ample supply of exhaustive notes of rare excellence, we find in it valuable remarks on the style of Isocrates and the state of the text, a table of various readings, a list of editions, and a special introduction to each piece. As in other editions of this series, short summaries of the argument are inserted in suitable places, and will be found of great service to the student. The commentary embraces explanations of difficult passages, with instructive remarks on grammatical usages, and the derivation and meanings of words, illustrated by quotations and references. Occasionally the student's attention is called to the moral sentiment expressed or implied in the text. With all this abundance of annotation, founded on a diligent study of the best and latest authorities, there is no excess of matter and no waste of words. The elegance of the exterior is in harmony with the intrinsic worth of the volume."—*Athenæum.*

"By editing Isocrates Mr. Sandys does good service to students and teachers of Greek Prose. He places in our hands, in a convenient form, an author who will be found of great use in public schools, where he has been hitherto almost unknown."—*Cambridge University Gazette.*

"The feeling uppermost in our minds, after a careful and interesting study of this edition, is one of satisfaction and admiration; satisfaction that a somewhat unfamiliar author has been made so thoroughly readable, and admiration of the comparatively young scholar who has brought about this result by combining in the task such industry, research, and acumen, as are not always found united in editors who have had decades upon decades of mature experience."—*Saturday Review.*

"Mr. Sandys, of St. John's, has added to the 'Catena Classicorum' a very complete and interesting edition. The style of Isocrates is discussed in a separate essay remarkable for sense, clearness of expression, and aptness of illustration. In the introductions to the two orations, and in the notes, abundant attention is given to questions of authenticity and historical allusions."—*Pall Mall Gazette.*

PERSII SATIRAE.
By A. PRETOR, M.A., *Fellow of St. Catharine's College, Cambridge; Classical Lecturer of Trinity Hall.*
3s. 6d.

"This is one of the ablest editions published in the 'Catena Classicorum' under the superintendence of Mr. Holmes and Mr. Bigg. Mr. Pretor has adopted in his edition a plan which he defends on a general principle, but which has really its true defence in the special peculiarities of his author. Mr. Pretor has given his readers translations of almost all the difficult passages. We think he has done so wisely in this case; for the allusions and constructions are so obscure that help is absolutely necessary. He has also been particularly full in his notes, he has thought and written with great independence, he has used every means to get at the meaning of his author, he has gone to many sources for illustration, and altogether he has produced what we may fairly regard as the best edition of Persius in English."—*Museum.*

"Mr. Pretor has boldly grappled with a most difficult task. He has, however, performed it very well, because he has begun, as his Introduction shows, by making himself thoroughly acquainted with the mind and temper—a sufficiently cynical one—of the poet, and thus laying a good basis for his judgment on the conflicting opinions and varying interpretations of previous editors. It is a most useful book, and will be welcome in proportion as such an edition was really very much wanted. The good sense and sound judgment shown by the editor on controverted points, give promise of excellent literary work in future undertakings of the like kind."—*Cambridge University Gazette.*

34   MESSRS. RIVINGTON'S EDUCATIONAL LIST.

CATENA CLASSICORUM—continued.

HOMERI ILIAS.

By S. H. REYNOLDS, M.A., *late Fellow and Tutor of Brasenose College, Oxford.*

Books I. to XII. 6s.

"Adopting the usual plan of the series, and giving references to standard works, rather than extracts from them, Mr. Reynolds is able to find space for much comment that is purely Homeric, and to show that it is not only a theory but a working principle with him, to make Homer his own interpreter and Commentator. '*Ex ipso Homero Homerus optime intelligitur*,' is a dictum which no student of Homer would question for a moment; but to acknowledge its truth is one thing, and prove it in practice is another, and the manner in which Mr. Reynolds has effected this will go far to show his capacity for the difficult task he has executed. The notes are by no means overloaded, but seem to us to contain all that they should, in order to carry out the editor's purpose of assisting beginners, while there is much that will prove valuable to advanced students. We heartily commend the book to our readers' notice."—*Standard.*

"We have already more than once expressed a very high opinion of the reprints of classical authors under the title of 'Catena Classicorum' which Messrs. Holmes and Bigg are now issuing. Part I. of Homer's 'Iliad,' comprising the first twelve books, is now before us, and it is sufficient for us to say that it is a most scholar-like and excellent edition that is here presented. The notes are of medium length, neither too long to make the book inconveniently bulky, nor too brief to be useful. . . . Of Mr. Reynolds' Oxford reputation as a philosophical scholar it is needless to speak, and his name is a sufficient guarantee for the soundness and importance of this work."—*English Churchman.*

TERENTI COMOEDIAE.

By T. L. PAPILLON, M.A., *Fellow of New College, Oxford; late Fellow of Merton.*

ANDRIA ET EUNUCHUS. 4s. 6d.

"An excellent and supremely useful edition of the well-known plays of Terence. It makes no pretension to ordinary critical research, and yet perhaps, within the limits, it is all that could be desired. Its aim being merely 'to assist the ordinary students in the higher forms of schools and at the Universities,' numerous, and upon the whole very scholarly notes and references have been given at the bottom of each page of the text."—*Westminster Review.*

"Another volume of the 'Catena Classicorum,' containing the first portion of an edition of Terence, deserves a word of welcome; and though Mr. Papillon's labours cannot claim 'the merit of critical research, or independent collation of MSS.,' they exhibit a fair promise of usefulness as a school and college edition. The footnotes are, in the main, helpful and appropriate."—*Contemporary Review.*

"This first instalment of a school edition of Terence gives promise of a renewed vigour in the 'Catena Classicorum' series, to which it belongs. Mr. Papillon is a very competent Latin scholar, trained under Dr. Bradley at Marlborough, and young enough to know what schoolboys need; and we hail as a proof of this, his advice to the student of Terence to familiarize himself collaterally with such storehouses of Latin scholarship as Lachmann's or Munro's Lucretius, and Forbiger's or Conington's Virgil. He has himself made reference to these; and, as to grammatical references, limited himself mainly, as is the rule with editions in the Catena series, to the grammars of Madvig. There is a short but serviceable introduction, dealing with the life, style, and literary merits of Terence."—*English Churchman.*

"We have before us another link in that excellent chain of classical authors produced under the general superintendence of Mr. Holmes and Mr. Bigg. . . . Altogether we can pronounce this volume one admirably suited to the wants of students at school and college, and forming a useful introduction to the works of Terence."—*Examiner.*

HERODOTI HISTORIA.

By H. G. WOODS, M.A., *Fellow and Tutor of Trinity College, Oxford.*

Book I., 6s.   Book II., 5s.

Other Volumes are in preparation.

[*Specimen Page, No.* 1.]

Give every man thy ear, but few thy voice;
Take each man's censure, but reserve thy judgment.
Costly thy habit as thy purse can buy, 70
But not express'd in fancy; rich, not gaudy;
For the apparel oft proclaims the man;
And they in France of the best rank and station
Are of a most select and generous chief in that.
Neither a borrower nor a lender be;
For loan oft loses both itself and friend,
And borrowing dulls the edge of husbandry.
This above all: to thine ownself be true,

---

68 *Give every man thine ear.* For a good listener is generally thought by the willing speaker to be a man of sound judgment. "Mr. Canning," says Sir E. Bulwer, "would often make a kind of lounging tour of the House, listening to the tone of the observations which the previous debate had excited; so that at last, when he rose to speak, he seemed to a large part of his audience to be merely giving a more striking form to their own thoughts."

71 *Express'd in fancy.* Not marked or singular in device; but with a quiet costliness suggestive of habitual self-respect.

74 *A most select and generous chief.* Are of a most noble device in this—the 'chief' being the upper part of a heraldic shield. The passage is strangely misunderstood and even altered by Delius, Elze, and other editors. As regards the metre, the three first syllables of the line must be pronounced rapidly in the time of one, as in Macbeth, l. 5, we have:

"And take my milk for gall, you murdering ministers."

76 *Loses itself and friend.* Who ever loves the creditor whom he cannot pay?

77 *Dulls the edge of husbandry.* Takes the edge off economy. Money borrowed, whether by individuals or nations, represents no saving or self-denial, and is therefore lightly parted with.

78 *To thine ownself be true.* As you inwardly resolve, so do: then faithfulness to others as well as yourself becomes the habit of your soul. So Wordsworth (v. 49) speaks of the same steadfastness in—

"The generous spirit who when brought
Amongst the tasks of real life, has wrought
Upon the plan that pleased his childish thought."

And, in an equally noble style, an Eastern sage has said, "There is one way to gladden those whom you love: if one is not upright when retired into himself, never will he bring rejoicing to those who are near him."

[Specimen Page, No. 3.]
BOOK I. PROP. B.   17

PROPOSITION B. THEOREM.

If two triangles have two angles of the one equal to two angles of the other, each to each, and the sides adjacent to the equal angles in each also equal; then must the triangles be equal in all respects.

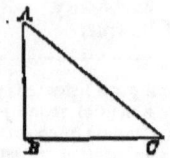
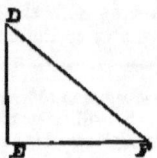

In △s *ABC, DEF*,
let ∠ *ABC*= ∠ *DEF*, and ∠ *ACB*= ∠ *DFE*, and *BC*= *EF*.
Then must *AB*=*DE*, and *AC*=*DF*, and ∠ *BAC*= ∠ *EDF*.

For if △ *DEF* be applied to △ *ABC*, so that *E* coincides with *B*, and *EF* falls on *BC*;
then ∵ *EF*=*BC*, ∴ *F* will coincide with *C*;
and ∵ ∠ *DEF*= ∠ *ABC*, ∴ *ED* will fall on *BA*;
∴ *D* will fall on *BA* or *BA* produced.
Again, ∵ ∠ *DFE*= ∠ *ACB*, ∴ *FD* will fall on *CA*;
∴ *D* will fall on *CA* or *CA* produced.
∴ *D* must coincide with *A*, the only pt. common to *BA* and *CA*.
∴ *DE* will coincide with and ∴ is equal to *AB*,
and *DF* .... *AC*,
and ∠ *EDF* .... ∠ *BAC*;
and ∴ the triangles are equal in all respects. Q. E. D.

Cor. Hence, by a process like that in Prop. A, we can prove the following theorem :

If two angles of a triangle be equal, the sides which subtend them are also equal. (Eucl. I. 6.)

ON THE MEASUREMENT OF ANGLES.

28. *To shew that the angle subtended at the centre of a circle by an arc equal to the radius of the circle is the same for all circles.*

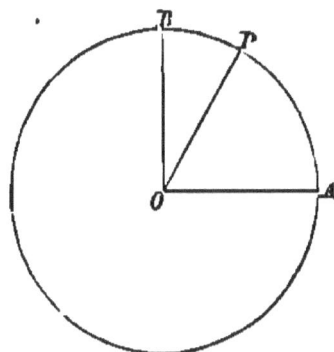

Let O be the centre of a circle, whose radius is r;

AB the arc of a quadrant, and therefore AOB a right angle;

AP an arc equal to the radius AO.

Then, $AP = r$ and $AB = \dfrac{\pi r}{2}$. (Art. 14.)

Now, by Euc. VI. 33,

$$\frac{\text{angle } AOP}{\text{angle } AOB} = \frac{\text{arc } AP}{\text{arc } AB},$$

or,

$$\frac{\text{angle } AOP}{\text{a right angle}} = \frac{r}{\dfrac{\pi r}{2}}$$

$$= \frac{2r}{\pi r}$$

$$= \frac{2}{\pi}.$$

Hence $\quad$ angle $AOP = \dfrac{2 \text{ right angles}}{\pi}$.

Thus the magnitude of the angle AOP is independent of r and is therefore the same for all circles.

[*Trigonometry. See page* 10.]

D. JUNII JUVENALIS

Praetexta et trabeae, fasces, lectica, tribunal. 35
Quid, si vidisset praetorem curribus altis
Exstantem et medio sublimem in pulvere Circi,
In tunica Jovis, et pictae Sarrana ferentem
Ex humeris aulaea togae, magnaeque coronae
Tantum orbem, quanto cervix non sufficit ulla? 40
Quippe tenet sudans hanc publicus, et, sibi Consul
Ne placeat, curru servus portatur eodem.
Da nunc et volucrem, sceptro quae surgit eburno,
Illinc cornicines, hinc praecedentia longi
Agminis officia et niveos ad fraena Quirites, 45
Defossa in loculis quos sportula fecit amicos.
Tum quoque materiam risus invenit ad omnes
Occursus hominum, cujus prudentia monstrat
Summos posse viros et magna exempla daturos
Vervecum in patria crassoque sub aere nasci. 50

35] These details are mentioned not as more ridiculous in themselves than anything Democritus had seen in Greece, but because Democritus regarded all human life as a farce, and at Rome the farce was more elaborate. *Lectica* refers to the procession of clients who accompanied it; *tribunal* to the display of empty eloquence before it.

36, sqq.] "What would he have said of the praetor's triumphal procession from the Capitol to the Circus?" The triumphal dress suggests the idea of triumph, and this *consul* (inf. 41).

38 **tunica Jovis**] Whom he personated, hence the eagle on his sceptre. The tunic was so costly that it was not till the third century that a private person possessed one of his own, even the emperors when they triumphed supplied themselves from the treasury of the Capitol or of the Palace.

— **Sarrana**] From the unhel-

39 **aulaea**] A whole stage-curtain of a toga.

41 **Quippe**] "No head could support it: why it makes the slave sweat to hold it up."

44 **longi agminis officia**] There is no more difference between this and longa agmina officiosorum, than between 'a high-spirited nobleman on a long-tailed horse,' and 'a long-tailed nobleman on a high-spirited horse.'

45 **niveos**] In bran new togas probably given for the occasion.

46 **Defossa**] To make sure that they've got it: also to make sure that they will not lose it, cf. Fallacem circum, Hor. *Sat.* 1. vi. 113.

47 **Tum**] Even between B.C. 460—357.

50] An Abderite would have hung himself. The cord giving way, he fell, and broke his head. He first went to the surgeon, and had his wound plastered, and then again hung himself.

[*Specimen Page, No.* 8.]

THE ELECTRA OF

ΗΛ. [*interrupting*] τί τῶν ἀπόντων ἢ τί τῶν ὄντων πέρι;
ΠΡ. [*solemnly*] λαβεῖν φίλον θησαυρόν, ὃν φαίνει θεός. 235
ΗΛ. ἰδού, καλῶ θεούς.
                [*clasping her hands*] ἢ τί δὴ λέγεις, γέρον;
ΠΡ. βλέψον νυν ἐς τόνδ', ὦ τέκνον, τὸν φίλτατον.
                                    [*turning her round to* ORESTES.]
ΗΛ. [*sadly*] πάλαι δέδοικα, μὴ σύ γ' οὐκέτ' εὖ φρονῇς.
ΠΡ. οὐκ εὖ φρονῶ 'γὼ σὸν κασίγνητον βλέπων;
ΗΛ. [*starting suddenly*]
    πῶς εἶπας, ὦ γεραί, ἀνέλπιστον λόγον;   240
ΠΡ. [*emphatically*] ὁρᾶν Ὀρέστην τόνδε τὸν Ἀγαμέμνονος.
ΗΛ. ποῖον χαρακτῆρ' εἰσιδών, ᾧ πείσομαι; [*incredulous*]
ΠΡ. [*pointing at a scar in* ORESTES' *forehead*]
    οὐλὴν παρ' ὀφρύν, ἥν ποτ' ἐν πατρὸς δόμοις
    νεβρὸν διώκων σοῦ μέθ' ᾑμάχθη πεσών.
ΗΛ. πῶς φῄς; ὁρῶ μὲν πτώματος τεκμήριον.   245
                            [*astounded, but still hesitating.*]
ΠΡ. ἔπειτα μέλλεις προσπίτνειν τοῖς φιλτάτοις;
ΗΛ. [*resolved*] ἀλλ' οὐκέτ', ὦ γεραιέ· συμβόλοισι γὰρ
    τοῖς σοῖς πέπεισμαι θυμόν. [*she rushes in a transport of
                   joy into her brother's arms.*] ὦ χρόνῳ φανείς,
    ἔχω σ' ἀέλπτως. ΟΡ. κἀξ ἐμοῦ γ' ἔχει χρόνῳ.
ΗΛ. οὐδέποτε δόξασ'. ΟΡ. οὐδ' ἐγὼ γὰρ ἤλπισα.   250
ΠΡ. ἐκεῖνος εἶ σύ;
ΟΡ.   σύμμαχός γέ σοι μόνος,
    ἢν ἐκσπάσωμαί γ' ὃν μετέρχομαι βόλον.
    πέποιθα δ'. ἢ χρὴ μηκέθ' ἡγεῖσθαι θεούς,
    εἰ τἄδικ' ἔσται τῆς δίκης ὑπέρτερα. [*with confidence.*]

[*Scenes from Greek Plays. See page* 18.]

[Specimen Page, No. 9.]

EXERCISE XXII.

HERCULES.

I was born a boy, stronger than brother Iphicles,
a new-born babe worthy of Zeus as father;
and I showed strength, released from swaddling clothes;
and I proved myself to all nobly bred.

5 Hêrâ sent on us two two snakes for murder;
and just before dawn flashed down a dreadful light on the bed.
Iphicles seeing monsters weeps in vain,
and silently crouches hidden in bed-clothes;
but I shouted aloud having conquered serpents:

10 and this is first of contests. And the neighbours asked, How is Ampītryon father of the boy?
for he prevails over hydra and savage lion;
running, not hunting, he catches a stag,

---

1. *I was born,* Ex. v. 8.
2. *New-born,* νεογνὸς.
3. *To release,* ἀπαλλάσσειν.
4. *Proved myself,* aor. pass. of φαίνω. *Bred,* perf. part. Anapæst in first foot, or tribrach in second.
5. *Two,* sign of the dual. *For,* πρὸς.
6. *Just before,* ὑπὸ with the accusative. *To flash down on,* κατασκήπτω.
7. *Monster,* δάϊκον. *In vain,* Ex. xvi. 6. Insert μὲν for the sake of contrast with the ninth line, as in Ex. xix. 1.
9. *To shout aloud,* ἀναλαλάζειν.
11. *To ask a question,* ἐρωτᾶν: aorist, ἠρόμην. The three last syllables of 'Αμφιτρύων make an anapæst.
12. *To prevail over,* κρατεῖν, with the genitive.
13. *Running,* δρομαῖος. *To hunt* = to be a hunter, static verb from κυνηγέτης. Tribrach in third foot.

Twenty-ninth Lesson.

CHANTING.

CHANTING is the arrangement of prose in a rhythmical form. The psalms, canticles, &c. are sung or chanted to melodies called CHANTS, which are either SINGLE or DOUBLE.

The melody of a single chant is, for convenience, written in phrases of seven bars of two minims each or their value.

The first half of a chant has three, the second four bars.

The first half is called the *mediation*, the second the *cadence*.

A double chant is simply a single chant form repeated.

A single chant is arranged to fit one verse of the psalms, a double chant two; for the long psalms quadruple chants, of which the phrase or melody is designed to include four verses, have been written.

A changeable chant is one whose key-chord may be either

INDEX

	PAGE		PAGE
HISTORY	1	LATIN	12
ENGLISH	3	GREEK	16
MATHEMATICS	6	DIVINITY	24
SCIENCE	11	MISCELLANEOUS	27
	CATENA CLASSICORUM	29	

	PAGE		PAGE
ABBOTT (Evelyn), Selections from Lucian	16	Bowen (E. E.), Campaigns of Napoleon	27
—— Greek Grammar	16	Bridge (Christiana), History of French Literature	3
Alford (Dean), Greek Testament	21	Bright (J. Franck), English History	1
Anson (W. R.), Reign of George III.	2	—— History of the French Revolution	2
Aristophanes, by W. C. Green	28, 32	Browning (Oscar), Great Rebellion	2
—— Scenes from, by Arthur Sidgwick	18	—— Historical Handbooks	2
Aristotle's Ethics, by Edward Moore	21		
—— J. E. T. Rogers	21		
Arnold (T. K.), Cicero	14	CICERO, by T. K. Arnold	14
—— Cornelius Nepos	13	Companion to the New Testament	24
—— Crusius' Homeric Lexicon	19	Companion to the Old Testament	24
—— Demosthenes	20	Cornelius Nepos, by T. K. Arnold	13
—— Eclogæ Ovidianæ	14	Crake (A. D.), History of the Church	1, 25
—— English-Greek Lexicon	17	Crusius' Homeric Lexicon, by T. K. Arnold	19
—— English Prose Composition	3	Curteis (A.M.), The Roman Empire	2
—— First French Book	27	DALLIN (T. F.) and Sargent (J. Y.), Materials and Models, &c.	14, 19
—— First German Book	27	Davys (George), History of England	1
—— First Greek Book	17	Demosthenes, by T. K. Arnold	20
—— First Hebrew Book	28	—— by G. H. Heslop	20, 31
—— First Verse Book	13	—— by Arthur Holmes	20, 32
—— Greek Accidence	17		
—— Greek Prose Composition	17	ENGLISH SCHOOL CLASSICS, edited by Francis Storr	3
—— Henry's First Latin Book	13	Euclid, by J. Hamblin Smith	9
—— Homer for Beginners	19	Euripides, Scenes from, by Arthur Sidgwick	18
—— Homer's Iliad	19		
—— Latin Prose Composition	13	FOSTER (George Carey), Electricity	11
—— Madvig's Greek Syntax	17	—— Sound	11
—— Sophocles	22	Fradersdorff (J. W.), English-Greek Lexicon	13
—— and Riddle (J. E.), English-Latin Lexicon	15	GANTILLON (P. G. F.), Classical Examination Papers	14, 20
BARRETT (W. A.), Chorister's Guide	28	Gedge (J. W.), Young Churchman's Companion to the Prayer Book	25
Beasley (R. D.), Arithmetic	10	Gepp (C. G.), Latin Elegiac Verse	13
Beesly (A. H.), Grecian and Roman History	1	Girdlestone (W. H.), Arithmetic	10
Bigg (Ch.), Exercises in Latin Prose	12		

INDEX.

	PAGE
Green (W. C.), Aristophanes	22, 12
Gross (E. J.), Algebra, Part II.	8
Handbook of Religious Instruction, by J. P. Norris	24
Herodotus (Extracts from), by J. Surtees Phillpotts	16
—— by H. G. Woods	22, 34
Heslop (G. H.), Demosthenes	20, 31
Historical Handbooks, edited by Oscar Browning	2
Holmes (Arthur), Demosthenes	20, 32
Homer for Beginners, by T. K. Arnold	19
Homer's Iliad, by T. K. Arnold	19
—— by S. H. Reynolds	19, 34
Iophon	17
Isocrates, by J. E. Sandys	20, 33
Jebb (R. C.), Sophocles	22, 29
—— Supremacy of Athens	2
Juvenal, by G. A. Simcox	15, 30
Keys to Christian Knowledge	26
Kitchener (F. E.), Botany for Class Teaching	11
—— (Frances Anna), a Year's Botany	11
Laun (Henri Van), French Selections	27
Lucian, by Evelyn Abbott	16
Madvig's Greek Syntax, by T. K. Arnold	17
Moberly (Charles E.), Shakspere	4
Moore (Edward), Aristotle's Ethics	21
Norris (J. P.), Key to the Four Gospels	26
—— to the Acts of the Apostles	26
—— Handbooks of Religious Instruction	24
Ovidianæ Eclogæ, by T. K. Arnold	14
Papillon (T. L.), Terence	15, 34
Pearson (Charles), English History in the XIV. Century	2
Pelham (H. F.), The Roman Revolution	2
Phillpotts (J. Surtees), Extracts from Herodotus	16
—— Shakspere	5
Pretor (A.), Persii Satiræ	15, 33

	PAGE
Reynolds (S. H.), Homer's Iliad	19, 34
Richardson (G.), Conic Sections	9
Riddle (J. E.) and Arnold's Eng. Lat. Lexicon	15
Rigg (Arthur), Introduction to Chemistry	11
—— Science Class-books	11
Rogers (J. E. T.), Aristotle's Ethics	21
Sandys (J. E.), Isocrates	20, 33
Sargeant (J. Y.) and Dallin (T. F.), Materials and Models, &c.	14, 19
—— Latin Version of (60) Selected Pieces	14
Shakspere's As You Like It and Macbeth, by C. E. Moberly	4
—— Much Ado and Tempest, by J. S. Phillpotts	5
—— Coriolanus, by R. Whitelaw	4
—— Hamlet, by C. E. Moberly	4
Sidgwick (Arthur), Scenes from Greek Plays	18
Simcox (G. A.), Juvenal	15, 30
Smith (J. H.), Arithmetic	9
—— Elementary Algebra	8
—— Key to Elementary Algebra	8
—— Exercises on Algebra	8
—— Hydrostatics	10
—— Geometry	9
—— Statics	10
—— Trigonometry	10
—— (Philip V.), History of English Institutions	2
—— (R. Prowde), Latin Prose Exercises	13
Sophocles, by T. K. Arnold	22
—— by R. C. Jebb	22, 29
Stainer (John), Theory of Harmony	28
Storr (Francis), English School Classics	3
—— Greek Verbs	16
Terence, by T. ... lon	15, 34
Thiers' Campaigns of Napoleon, by E. E. Bowen	27
Thucydides, by C. Bigg	21, 30
Way of Life	25
Whitelaw (Robert), Shakspere's Coriolanus	4
Willert (F.), Reign of Louis XIV.	2
Wilson (R. K.), History of English Law	2
Wilson's Lord's Supper	25
Woods (H. G.), Herodotus	22, 34
Wordsworth (Bp.), Greek Testament	21

www.ingramcontent.com/pod-product-compliance
Lightning Source LLC
Chambersburg PA
CBHW032050220426
43664CB00008B/941